THE POLICE

AND

RESOURCES CONTROL

IN

COUNTER INSURGENCY

BY

E. H. Adkins, Jr.
Public Safety Advisor
Public Safety Division
United States Operations Mission
to Viet Nam

A TRAINING MANUAL FOR POLICE

CONTENTS

INTRODUCTION 1
    Operations 3
    Personnel 3
    Public Relations 4
    The Budget 4

PART I

THE ROLE OF THE CIVIL POLICE IN COUNTER-INSURGENCY .. 4

CHAPTER I

NATURE OF THE PROBLEM 4

CHAPTER II

THE ENEMY AND HOW HE OPERATES 7
    The National Liberation Front 8
    Appeal of the Viet Cong 9
    Intelligence 11
    Logistics 11
    Recruiting Efforts of the Viet Cong 13
    Summary 15

CHAPTER III

THE STRATEGIC HAMLET 16
    Relocation and its Problems 18

CHAPTER IV

RURAL POLICE: FUNCTION AND ADMINISTRATION 20
    Organization 22
    Local Government Structure 24
    Police Administration 27

Budget 35

Supervision 37

PART II

RESOURCES CONTROL

REGULATION OF THE MOVEMENT OF PEOPLE AND GOODS .. 40

CHAPTER V

GAINING SUPPORT FOR THE PROGRAM 40

    Informing the People 41

    The Public Servant Image 42

    Methods of Notification 43

    Legal Rights of the Public and the Police 45

CHAPTER VI

PASSES AND MANIFESTS 49

    Restricted Goods — What Do We Want to Control 50

    Establishing a Control Center 52

    Preparation of Passes and Manifests 54

CHAPTER VII

IDENTITY CARDS AND FAMILY REGISTRATION 67

    The National Identity Card Program 67

    The Family Census Program 76

    Checking Identity Documents 82

CHAPTER VIII

CHECK POINTS AND SEARCHES 85

    Check Point Criteria 86

    Operation of a Check Point 92

    Waterways 99

    Search of Vehicles 100

    Search of Persons 105

CHAPTER IX

FIRE PREVENTION AND PROTECTION
FOR THE RURAL POLICEMAN 108

CHAPTER X

EVACUATION, ALARMS AND CURFEWS 112
    Organization 113
    Training 117
    Curfew 118

PART III

THE MALAYAN EXPERIENCE 119

CHAPTER XI

THE REPORT 119
    Purpose 119
    Historical Summary 120
    Organization of the Malaya Police — Introduction 121
    Resettlement of Population 129
    Movement Controls 133
    Marine Operations High Seas 139
    Family Census 140
    National Identity Card Program 140
    Coordination 140
    Incidental Intelligence 141

CHAPTER XII

WHAT THE AUTHORS SAY 142

CHAPTER XIII

THE STATUTES 145
    Suggested Statute Resources Control 145
    The Emergency Regulations Ordinance, 1948 (Malaya) 148

CHAPTER XIV

THE PLANNING PROCESS 179
    The Quang Ngai Plan 181

APPENDIX No. 1 194

THE REORGANIZATION OF THE NATIONAL POLICE 194

foreword

The adequate legal control of the movements of people and material — including such everyday items as food, medicines, and clothing as well as munitions — can be a vital factor in the war against subversion and guerrilla activities. We have only to look at the recent experience of the nearby Federation of Malaya where use of such controls was a major factor in starving out, tracing, locating and bringing to justice the insurgents.

We are indebted to a large degree for much of the philosophy expressed herein as well as for some the operational recommendations, to the British experience in Malaya. We have drawn from their excellent text «The Conduct of Anti-Terrorist Operations in Malaya».

The methods included in this text are emergency procedures not utilized in a normal, peace-time situation. They are stringent, *war-time* measures designed to assist in defeating the enemy and helping the people of Viet Nam. It is hoped that they will not be necessary for long.

It should be recognized that such controls are extremely bothersome and time-consuming to local citizens. Therefore, a sound public relations program explaining the need for such controls and how they will work must precede actual implementation of the program. This should be followed by training of the personnel concerned, in the courteous but firm, handling of the public.

The material contained in this text should be used both as a basis for establishing a control system and for giving training to the officers and men charged with the responsibility of placing it into effect. It is hoped it will meet these aims.

FRANK E. WALTON
Chief, Public Safety Division
United States Operations
Mission to Vietnam
Saigon, January 1964

INTRODUCTION

A vital and essential factor which allows the Communist guerrillas to continue their activities against ordered and legal government is their logistical support capability, that is, an ability to maintain lines of communication and supply. Necessary support ranges from the tangible — food, medicine, clothing, guns, ammunition, dynamite, people — to the intangible — dissemination of propaganda and threats and the establishment of intelligence nets and courier services. A major step forward in the isolation of the population from the enemy is the establishment of the strategic hamlets with all the attendant connotations stemming from the new economic and political stances. But building a fence around a group of families is just a beginning and by no means constitutes internal security, either within or without the villages and hamlets. Therefore, in addition to the political, sociological and military operations in and around the strategic hamlets, it is necessary to establish resources control and rural internal security. Rural internal security consists of the measures taken by a government through duly constituted civil law enforcement agencies to protect its society from subversion, lawlessness and insurgency with particular reference to rural areas. Resources control, with its more specialized meaning and well established fundamental concepts, needs further explanation.

Resources control may be defined as an effort to regulate the movement of selected resources, both human and material, in order to restrict the enemy's support or deprive him of it altogether, and to interrupt and destroy all enemy non-military communications. Such controls must be tailored to meet the needs of a given situation, but the fundamentals are known and may be uniformly applied in a guerrilla war anywhere in the world, whether it be Vietnam, Malaya, Colombia or Venezuela. A National policy is required prior to implementation of controls in order to avoid confusion and for the sake of uniformity and consistency, but this does not mean that the same degree of control should be applied in each locality. For example, a different approach is required in a state or province where the enemy has virtual control from that used in regions where loyal forces dominate the scene. How these matters are handled in specific instances will be developed in this text.

The need to apply resources controls and a determination of the political effects are usually determined at the policy or legislative level of government but the techniques and the coordination of application of these controls is strictly a job for the professional law enforcement officer. By his own experience and through research into the experience of professional colleagues, he is best qualified to organize, supervise and train men for a resources control program. Police are a necessary and desirable adjunct of any organized society. As each society modernizes and progresses it becomes more complex. Modern day law enforcement with its professional requirements meets these increasing complex demands. Control is historically a police function and there is nothing new or mysterious about it. In Vietnam the need of control is aggravated by a vicious, deadly guerrilla war. The need will continue even as the war is more and more successful in the overt sense; also continuing in the same way is the need for a rural internal security program. For both facets of police operations there is a long term and even after open hostilities cease. Only the most inexperienced or uninformed would argue that a communist is defeated just because the fighters lay down their arms in the public square.

Historically, long term control of the civil populace by the military generally has created more problems than it has solved. Likewise, the goal of the military is to complete a given mission where force is useful and return internal security and policing efforts to the civil administration. Police effort is best performed by local people with local alliances and intimate knowledge of local conditions. Therefore, regardless of the identity of the initial force implementing resources control, the ultimate aim is to return such activity to local civil authority without creating any new organization beyond the scope of the current police force. The level of the police force may have to be increased temporarily; the strength should decline as the situation returns to one of non-insurgency.

With this philosophy in mind, the specifics of resources control may be examined.

Prior to establishing any control program the authorities must be able to identify the people, something which can be accomplished through National Identity Card and the Family Census programs. In the first operation, all persons male and female, over certain ages are required to carry an identification card showing a photograph, fingerprints and personal description. In the second program, an initial registration is made of the occupants of every residential unit, roughly called the «family». A group photograph is taken and an effort made to tally the family's resources which might be of value to the enemy, as well as to gather facts bearing on its tendencies toward cooperation with the enemy. The Family Census data must constantly be reviewed and kept up to date (See Chapter VII).

The problem of restricting, depriving and denying of personnel, logistical and communications support to the enemy guerrillas is attacked on three broad fronts by interrupting flow in three ways (1) The establishment of static check-points along primary and secondary arteries; (2) The implementation of mobile or surprise checkpoints to catch the fellow trying to by-pass a static control in a vehicle, and the utilization of patrols to cover the footpaths and trails by which tons of material may be transported on the shoulders of volunteer or indentured coolies and (3) Establishing sound rural internal security along with appropriate controls in villages and strategic hamlets to obstruct the tremendous seepage of supplies and information from these population centers to the enemy.

At the outset, let it be said that a system of this nature is not a guarantee of absolute denial but is more in the order of diminishing returns to the enemy. Just as in conventional warfare one weapon is developed to defeat another, so here the pressure on the guerrilla to abandon his mission or to starve and die in the process increases as the ability to operate a resources control system improves. Conversely, the results will certainly be no better than the effort and thoughts applied to the operation. This presupposes adequate and informed planning so that objectives can be stated and the means to carry them out located and obtained.

The planning process may be divided into four main efforts which should be developed in the following order since one grows out of the other: [1]

1. OPERATIONS

Assuming that the objectives have been determined and spelled out, the first step is to lay out on paper just exactly what is proposed. The number of static checkpoints is determined by maps, surface and aerial reconnaissance, and investigation of local conditions including traffic counts. After this, the number of mobile checkpoints and patrols and a system of spot checks may be determined, as well as the amount of policing necessary to accomplish the goals of rural internal security.

Spot checking is simply a method developed to alleviate the impractical and undesirable situation which would arise if every vehicle on a busy highway were to be stopped and searched. It operates like this: as each vehicle stops at the checkpoint, the occupants' identity papers are examined and a brief search of the vehicle is conducted, such as looking into the glove compartment or the trunk. If nothing suspicious is observed, the vehicle proceeds on its way after a delay of not more than a minute. However, in order to conduct thorough searches, a certain number of cars are allowed to pass and perhaps every 9th or 12th or 13th car is searched completely. This varies from day to day to keep the enemy constantly off balance. Complete searches always are conducted if intelligence or suspicion indicates. Spot checks are covered in Chapter VII. The planning process also includes establishment of a system of passes and manifests, and control centers to issue and check on them.

2. PERSONNEL AND TRAINING

Once the operations requirements are determined, it is a matter of simple arithmetic to develop a manpower table. Usually this kind of a program will be new and will require substantial augmentation of existing police forces. Therefore, standards of personnel selection should be applied to recruit individuals who will make good police officers. An 18-year old lad might make a terrific fighting man but police

---

[1] Details of the planning process are dealt with in Chapter XIV.

must deal with the general public and the inexperienced youth is obviously unsuitable. Once the manpower table is filled, training in the specifics of the operation can begin.

3. *PUBLIC RELATIONS*

Most right thinking people agree that controls, while onerous, are necessary to the degree required by the situation. Wartime obviously requires more rigid controls than peacetime. Therefore, recognizing the problem of built-in resistance as part of human nature, a well planned public relations program is essential and should be implemented prior to the beginning of actual operations.

Such a program has four principal elements:

1. The public should be told what is expected of it and what the ground rules are. It is utterly unrealistic to expect people to comply with rules they do not understand.

2. The public should be told the reasons for the program on the basis that an informed public is a sympathetic public.

3. The blame for the program should be placed squarely on the shoulders of the Viet Cong, since without the guerrilla activity there would be no need for such restrictions. Properly done, this can be a very effective propaganda weapon.

4. The controls should be removed as soon as the need for them has passed; the public should be told of this in advance and the promise carried out. One technique, which serves as a very effective democratic brake, is to pass legislation requiring periodic renewal of controls so that the authorities will have to go through the motions of re-implementing the operations. (This is described in Chapter XIII).

4. *THE BUDGET*

An obvious, though often forgotten element in planning, is the thorough examination of financial capability. Having decided what is to be done in the way of operations, personnel and training and public relations, responsible authorities then must determine the amount of money required and the methods to be employed in obtaining and administering the funds.

PART I
THE ROLE OF THE CIVIL POLICE IN COUNTER-INSURGENCY

CHAPTER I

THE NATURE OF THE PROBLEM

Viet Nam is a country at war. There is no delineated front line; there is not a formally declared state of hostilities. But the tragic realities of war are obvious everywhere. Each day people die: soldiers and farmers, students and Government workers; women and children. There are no easily identified invading armies but thousands of citizens in rural areas are unable to live in peace. Around them is death, destruction, suffering, pillaging. Many live in sorrow over past tragedies, in fear of future ones.

The current term for the particular kind of war being fought in Viet Nam is *insurgency*, classically defined as an up-rising using force and illegalities against political or governmental authority; a state of rebelliousness. However, in Viet Nam the word has been imbued with a more specific meaning. An insurgent is described as an individual or group of individuals who enter or infiltrate an area for the purpose of overthrowing the governing authority of that area by subversive, guerrilla or other illegal activities. The actions of such an individual or group is here termed *insurgency*. It has many of the overtones and connotations of declared war; it involves attack by an enemy but is also characterized by much activity that is clandestine. This is the manner in which the Vietnamese Communists have chosen to conduct their illegal assault on the people of the Republic of Viet Nam and its legitimate Government. Although in actuality the war is to a large degree directed and supported from the outside, the Communists portray it to the citizens of Viet Nam, both in the North and South, as a «people's» uprising, a «justifiable rebellion», fought under the direction of the National Front for the Liberation of South Viet Nam. Herein lie the subversive, the clandestine aspects of this conflict, this insurgency.

To deal with it, the Government of Viet Nam has developed, with the advice, counsel and financial support of the United States, a *counter insurgency* plan to oppose, resist or counteract the action of the insurgents and to institute and maintain rural internal security. All elements in the nation, including the population in general who have any part in the organized effort to counteract the Viet Cong, are taking part in the counter insurgency program. The governmental agencies include the regular Armed Forces and local defense forces and cadres in all the Government services who find their regular duties changed or expanded by the exigencies of the emergency situation. They certainly include the National Police.

To specifically define the current role of the Police under the National Government's administrative policy, another word needs to be added to *counter insurgency* so that is becomes *defensive counter insurgency*. The mission of the military forces is both offensive and defensive; they must protect and defend on the one hand, and seek out and destroy on the other. The mission of the National Police is one of active defense only; attack by force is not their job and the tactics of the military offense are not used. Even the role of the Combat Police should not be considered one of offensive military action, but more akin to a raiding group seeking to arrest small numbers of gangsters or bandits holed up in a known location. The Combat Police will be discussed in Chapter IV. The usual police function in a peaceful society is that of investigating unlawful acts, locating and apprehending the offenders and maintaining law and order in the community. In Viet Nam, the Police must do all these things but they have the added responsibility of helping to institute and preserve peace and security in the nation. Expressed in terms of public safety, the Police enforce the laws protecting the state as well as laws protecting life and property.

Early last year a major development occurred in Viet Nam's counter insurgency effort. The National Government on Feb. 3, 1962, launched the strategic hamlet building program and since that time has devoted major attention and material support to it to try to establish rural internal security. As of Oct. 16, 1963, a GVN Department of Interior report said, 8,352 strategic hamlets had been built with 9,722,753 people living in them, or 77 per cent of the nation's population. The schedule then in effect called for 11,172 strategic hamlets to be built through the country. Some suggest the final figure will be even higher. But by any estimation, the program can be described as a nationwide movement of great proportions. The Government of Viet Nam has called the strategic hamlet program a «vast movement born in the heat of war», and referred to it as the Vietnamese people's «preemptory reply to the Communist challenge (bringing us), along with the certainty of victory, the pride to live as free men today and tomorrow». In this framework, the civil internal security of this many hamlets becomes a massive challenge and responsibility. It is a responsibility which lies principally with the local civil authorities who use civilian forces — the temporary and permanent members of the National Police.

There is nothing new in the concept of the strategic hamlets. They have been in existence in one form or another since man saw the advantages of grouping together for protection and eventually for the development of services which the community could provide but man alone could not. The old walled city of Hue was fundamentally a strategic town. The early American stockade was a place where pioneers who settled the virgin lands in the western United States gathered to protect themselves from raiding Indians. The American Indians themselves always lived and traveled in groups for defensive, economic and tribal reasons and they had highly skilled scouts and ingenious alarm systems. Almost every country has its examples of walled cities or villages built for defensive purposes. In more recent times, Malaya is the outstanding instance of a country which has developed a strategic hamlet program called «new villages» there. Her experience is particularly relevant to Vietnam because Malaya too, fortified her hamlets or « new villages » to counteract insurgency which also came in the form of Communist guerrilla activity.*

The strategic hamlet program has been established (1) to protect rural people; (2) to isolate the Viet Cong from the rural society by interrupting his communications and supply and to establish rural internal security, and (3) to help the villager build a better life in line with the political and economic development of Viet Nam. The third point, if accomplished, will help win the support of the populace in fighting the enemy on all fronts. The internal security or internal defense of a strategic hamlet is basically a civil police problem and it is this problem, combined with the control of

---
* Part III of this book: «The Malayan Experience».

the movement of people and goods throughout the countryside, with which this textbook in concerned.

In Viet Nam, the National Police is the principal law enforcement agency in the nation. It exercises general police functions, both rural and urban. Recently reorganized, it is responsible for internal security; highway and rural security; municipal, harbor and airport police, and immigration control, in addition to the general systems and operations for maintaining law and order. In normal times, the Vietnamese village police officer keeps order in the village area, conducts preliminary investigations of accidents and minor crimes and serves as a general representative of the government for the preservation of the peace. But in these days of national emergency much more is demanded of the individual Police officer, as it is demanded of all people in the society. He is called upon to be more resourceful, more courageous, more vigilant, more devoted to duty than ever before. As a member of one of the national security services, he must adopt a quasi-military function, at least in terms of hamlet, village, and chief town defense. He must exercise the added authority with which he is endowed by the emergency nature of the work under the strictest personal discipline so that his authority does not become authoritarian. If he allows that to happen, he undermines the cause for which he works and perhaps fights. He must have technical competence and know-how in his expanded responsibilities. He should know some military skills including how to handle weapons, set up a basic defense system, and develop an instinct for determining whether or not a man is what he says he is. He must be an amateur psychologist who can figure out a way to gain the cooperation, if not outright support, of people who bear resentments for having been moved against their will. It is the Police officer's job to try to show relocated citizens the necessity for their move, as well as it is to see that they stay in the new hamlet and fulfill their responsibilities to it.

CHAPTER II

THE ENEMY AND HOW HE OPERATES

The hard core Communist who leads the enemy in the Republic of Vietnam's war is foreign only in ideology. He is Vietnamese, but a Vietnamese who has pledged his allegiance to the Communist Party and who is directed in his broad general policies by the Communist dictatorships in Hanoi, Peking and Moscow. He is not particularly numerous but he is supported by many who, while not true Communists, also are the enemy, at least temporarily. The enemy forces may be categorized as fighters and members of the communist base in the people. All of these are people who ordinarily would be good Vietnamese citizens but through ignorance, fear, family ties, greed, ambition and for other reasons, have been persuaded, forced or coerced into the ranks of the Viet Cong as fighters or undergroud members. In this cruel guerrilla war, the enemy, largely directed from the outside, can operate as an insider, a native, because that is who he is.

Most of the hard core Communists who have been members of the party for a long time come from south of the 17th parallel. Nearly all of the hard core are either fighters or underground who have gone to North Viet Nam for varying periods of time for training and indoctrination, but in language and knowledge of local foods, habits, customs, terrain and resources, they are South Vietnamese; including members of various Montagnard tribes. They prepare themselves for Communist leadership in North Viet Nam, then infiltrate back into the South to become leaders in the villages or districts of their birth. With them lies the real leadership of the Communist movement in South Viet Nam.

It is extremely difficult to state categorically the number of hard core Viet Cong, or for that matter even the total number Viet Cong troops operating in the country. A cataloguing of the total effective support of the enemy by sympathizers, dupes and frightened peasants is even more difficult. However, some well educated estimates have been made for the figures are of necessity classified in order not to aid the enemy. Suffice it to say here that there are several thousand hard core Viet Cong operating in Viet Nam, and their effective strength including support of all kinds is many times this amount. In Malaya during the emergency there, lasting from 1948 to 1958, less than 20,000 Communist guerrillas occupied the full time of 41,000 temporary Special Police Forces, plus an even larger number of military troops. Even today, less than 100 communist «bandits» operating along the northern frontier are requiring the vigorous attention of many times that number of regular Police and military forces in a final effort to eradicate this menace.

A. THE NATIONAL LIBERATION FRONT

The Communist apparatus in the South is called the National Front for the Liberation of South Viet Nam.[1] The NLF is a bona fide Communist front system in that it consists of a number of member organizations, some of them nothing more than paper operations, such as the Liberation Front Youth Organization, the Women's Organization and others, all disclaiming loyalty to the Communist Party or any foreign ideology or government. All appeal to Vietnamese nationalism and the various discontentments found among people at lower economic levels; in areas of the country where the Communists are solidly entrenched, these organizations may operate openly and the rank and file members may not be true Communists but simply rural people living under the only government that presently exists in the region.

The Front portrays itself as a great nationalist revolutionary movement and, in its propaganda, rarely mentions North Viet Nam or any connection with the Hanoi regime. Nearly

---

[1] See «National Liberation Front Propaganda», a catalogue of such publications published by the United States Information Service, Saigon, February 1, 1963.

all of the anti-government propaganda which is distributed in the provinces comes from, or is inspired by the Front. Its lines are somewhat standard but often appealing and cleverly directed. It is important that Police officers who come across pieces of Viet Cong propaganda in their own areas, study them carefully rather than dismissing them as just more Communist lies. It is essential for the authorities to remember that many people believe what the propaganda says or are influenced by it. The basis for most of what the Front claims it stands for is contained in a 14-point «independence and neutrality» policy statement which Radio Hanoi, in an English language broadcast on August 10, 1962, said had been adopted by the NLF Central Committee.

According to the broadcast, the points are:

1. An end to military blocs and treaties.
2. Departure of all foreign troops from Viet Nam.
3. Complete internal sovereignty.
4. A neutralist foreign policy.
5. Maintenance of armed forces for defense only.
6. Political and religious freedom.
7. «No strings» aid welcomed.
8. An end to foreign economic domination.
9. Fair treatment for foreign businessmen.
10. Cultural exchanges with all nations.
11. Eventual reunification of the Vietnamese nation.
12. Neutral «federation» with Laos and Cambodia.
13. Support of world disarmament efforts.
14. Reaffirmation of the 1954 Geneva Agreements.

Most of these points cannot be disputed with much fervor at the local Vietnamese level without developing the history of Communist aggression and the resulting reasons for alliances and aid. But behind the fine words, lie the realities of Communist dictatorship.

Chairman of the NLF is Nguyen Huu Tho, a native of Vinh Long province, but the real force is Secretary General Nguyen Van Hieu, propaganda specialist and long time worker in Viet Minh and Viet Cong efforts.

B. APPEAL OF THE VIET CONG

What is the real basis for the appeal of the Vietnamese Communist to the people in the countryside? It is dangerous to generalize and try to reduce into a few principles an appeal which is complex, varied and emotional. However, there are three ideas or concepts which are known to be of great importance to the Vietnamese Communist in carrying out his mission; there certainly are more than three but to understand his appeal, it is essential to know at least these:

1. The Viet Cong says he is the rightful heir to Vietnam's revolutionary heritage. He sees himself, not as an insurgent trying to establish an alien form of government, but as the

Vietnamese nationalist who fought French colonialism and the old feudalistic system. He feels he belongs, that he is within his rights, that he is not the invader. Many Viet Cong sincerely and fanatically believe these things about themselves, but they are wrong. Whether they understand it or not, they are serving a foreign ideology, they are serving the Communist Party, they are serving Hanoi, Peking and Moscow.

2. The Viet Cong promises to solve all the people's problems, no matter what they are, and all people have problems. The promises do not have to be kept, the people only have to be made to believe. It is often said that the average farmer is not concerned about politics or political systems except perhaps on the village or hamlet level; he wants, for the most part, to be left alone to till his crops and live his life much as his ancestors have done for generations. But a closer look will indicate that while life seems to change slowly in the countryside, it does change. The country folk, like other members of the society, wants to make a better living, to have an easier, more productive life; he wants the advantages of modern medical treatment and to be able to send his children to school for more years than he has been able to do in the past. Many of the poorest people in Viet Nam live in rural areas; besides poverty, they must endure illness, natural disasters which can ruin a year's crop and cause mass starvation, and now the Viet Cong danger to life and limb. Unfortunately, there are many more poor than there are rich or even moderately well to do. To these desires for a better material life, equality and justice and, above all, peace, the Viet Cong responds with bright promises. And the only sure way to gain these ends, say the Viet Cong, is to join and support the violent overthrow of the government.

3. The Viet Cong works with the young. He knows that these are the people he can mold, the ones he can make loyal to the Communist cause; he needs their enthusiasm and their strength; he views them, correctly, as the future leaders of the society. Don't bother about the man 50 to 55 years old, the Viet Cong says, we may be able to use him for our purposes but we are not interested in making a Communist out of him. The enemy flatters the youth, appeals to his desire for attention and status, converts him; the Police must not forget this for a minute.

The Viet Cong uses different appeals in different parts of the country. In the Delta, it is land. He talks of nothing but land: land in the hands of landlords, the farmer's right to own land, the interests of the farmer all tied up in the land, and land as one of the achievements of the revolution and the people's struggle. In the Highlands, the enemy directs his argument to the tribesmen's desires for autonomy; he responds to their independence and pride. In the economically poorer Central Lowlands, the Communist simply promises a better standard of living — more work, more assistance, more of everything.

These appeals are clever and effective because they have been developed out of the true desires of the people. The Viet Cong's advantage is that he does not have to fulfill his promises as the Government of Viet Nam cadre does. The latter must gain permanent support of the people for a legally constituted democratic Government; the Communist needs voluntary support only temporarily — until a Communist government is installed or Communist power established.

C. INTELLIGENCE

The Viet Cong operates a very clever, thorough and capable intelligence system. Because he is with the people, he possesses a great intelligence advantage, a key factor in any guerrilla operation. He cannot exist without loyal help of or the non-interference from a large segment of the population. These are people who co-operate or stand neutral either because they are Communist sympathizers, or can see a personal advantage, or they have been threatened and are afraid not to cooperate. It would be a mistake to think that the enemy is not aware of the progress of the strategic hamlet program; whenever a new hamlet is established, he knows all about it. Anything known to the general public, and much that is not, is also known to the Viet Cong.

Information is furnished to him not by sinister, highly trained spies, but by the most ordinary people: a village merchant, a farmer, an old woman, a pretty girl, a child, a bus or a truck driver, even a civil servant. The Viet Cong knows how to appeal to each one of these individuals and make him do what the enemy wants. The merchant and farmer may be threatened economically; the old woman may have a son or grandson who fights for the Viet Cong and who will suffer if she does not cooperate; the young girl may be passing the information to her husband, brother or friend who in turn will give it to the enemy; the child may be thrilled by the adventure of carrying secrets; the driver may be a true sympathizer who has gotten his job for the specific purpose of gathering information; the civil servant may be discontent with his assignment and chances for promotion and irresponsibly decide to strike back at the Government, his employer.

The double hostage system also is used to good effect: the Viet Cong take a young man away from his family to serve in the guerrilla army. The boy and his family are physically separated so that there can be no direct contact between them. The Communists then begin their double threats. The boy is told that if tries to escape or does not cooperate and do his job, his family will suffer for it. The family is told that unless its members support the Viet Cong with supplies, information, shelter or whatever they can do to help the guerrillas, the boy will be made to suffer.

These are some of the reasons why many average rural citizens cooperate with the Viet Cong; perhaps the examples demonstrate the necessity, admittedly an unfortunate one, to be suspicious of everyone no matter how unlikely a suspect.

D. LOGISTICS

Viet Cong logistics must be understood if they are to be controlled.

Logistics means the supply, movement, quartering and hospitalization of military units; supply includes procurement and distribution of weapons, food, medicine and clothing. To fight, the Viet Cong guerrilla in the jungle needs weapons and ammunition. These he gets in three principal ways: (a) military action against armed Government military and civil positions, convoys and individual vehicles, (b) manufacture locally but secretly, (c) smuggling from North Viet Nam by sea, possibly by air, and across the land frontier. There also are occasional purchases from traitors, directly or through supporters. A number of the sources of supply come directly under military jurisdiction; however the civil police control action is involved to a greater or to a lesser degree in every government effort to lessen Viet Cong supply.

To live, the guerrilla requires a steady supply of food and the basic necessities of life and in this the police are deeply concerned. The Viet Cong fighters must have clothing, jungle boots and hats; he needs pieces of metal to attach to the bottom of his boots to keep steel barbs on traps from puncturing his feet; he requires flashlights for his nighttime activities which are more numerous and important than his daytime ones; he needs charcoal for cooking and medicine to treat the sick and wounded.

With the general exception of offensive weapons and their ammunition, nearly all the supplies he needs are readily available in local markets and can be purchased in quantity and with impunity. However, even guerrilla and defensive weapons such as «spring-guns» are made from locally obtained materials (see Ill. 1, below) and...

Ill. 1. *Spring powered and spike armed Vietcong flail made from locally obtained, possibly scrap, components which can be controlled by detection in transit of unusual and not justified material.*

and common bar stock and drill presses set him up as a manufacturer of rifle barrels (see Ill. 2, following). The Viet Cong production locally of military explosives (mines, booby traps and grenades) is highly important to the guerrillas; it too must be a target of police control operations.

The guerrilla establishes many supply lines: sympathizers or relatives in the hamlets aid him, the same categories of individuals who furnish him with intelligence information; in some remote areas, he cultivates crops; he steals food in raids on supply centers; sometimes he even arranges for friendly trucks to carry goods right down the main highways of the country and then off into the jungle for unloading. Without food and clothing and medicine the guerrilla cannot exist. By helping to cut his supply lines, the civil police in rural areas will make an invaluable contribution to the war effort and a big step toward winning the war will have been taken.

Besides the guerrilla and regular combat units, the Viet Cong have extensive base facilities scattered throughout the people and the country. Here food is collected and stored, these uniforms and military items are manufactured, again at this camp area training is accomplished, and perhaps over there is a command posts where planning is developed. All these bases need logistic support especially in the import of materials for fabrication into useable items. Also bases must have transport to move things in and to effect deliveries. A constant flow of messages via radio and runner is vital. All these lines are to be attacked.

Likewise police action is needed to counter directly, or in concert with intelligence, the activities of agitators, purchasing agents, propagandists, tax collectors, the terrorist teams and all others of the Viet Cong underground.

E. RECRUITING EFFORTS OF THE VIET CONG

The Communist uses other means besides philosophical pursuasion and long range promises to gather supports and recruits for combat. In English, there is a special saying to describe a way of trapping someone into doing what one wants him to do. It is called the «carrot and the stick» method and it is a good way to handle animals. A man feeds the animal, who remembers it and is held by the promise of more food supplied by his master; but if the creature does not obey or does not behave as his master wants, he is punished and the stick is applied. This is the way the Viet Cong approach human beings; they claim to offer more than any other government can (the carrot) and, at the same time, they threaten retribution against their enemies and those who do not cooperate (the stick). In Vietnam, the Communist claims to be able to give the villager protection where the government cannot, and in certain areas by exercising total control over the populace, this is true. The rural inhabitant is promised that if he will join the party, he will attain personal recognition, a status over and above his contemporaries. The enemy has conducted raids and

Ill. 2.a & b. *A hand made weapon, along with metal stock, hand tools and other materials for weapons manufacture confiscated from Vietcong smugglers through effective check point operation, a means of enforcement of resources control.*

Ill. 2.c & d. *Medicines, vitamins, dry cell batteries as well as miscellaneous materials needed for written propaganda also confiscated from Vietcong smugglers at National Police checkpoint.*

stolen often scarce supplies which he in turn distributes to loyal party members and sympathizers in the villages and hamlets. As an exercise in retribution, many heads have been cut off in the past two or three years. The Viet Cong has burned villages, stolen goods, weapons and materials, and he has killed children, often merely to inspire fear and insure future cooperation.

Some recruits are young men who have been kidnapped by the Viet Cong, treated well, politically indoctrinated and persuaded to accept the role of a Communist guerrilla fighter. This type comprises the largest group of guerrillas and the one most susceptible to re-indoctrination and intelligence interviews after capture. Its members are people who are easily influenced, who have been shown an opportunity to rise above their former status.

Another general category is the sympathizer, already described as a member of a guerrilla's family, a friendly neighbor in the village, or a person who has been politically indoctrinated to the extent that he believes the Viet Cong is right in his purposes. This is an extremely dangerous group because its members are hard to identify and may be anywhere. Recently, a number of sympathizers in the Youth Protective group sabotaged the alert system and opened the gates of a strategic hamlet, allowing the Viet Cong to capture it.

Still another type of recruit gaining in importance is the juvenile. The Viet Cong plays on the desire of all children and teen-agers to do what their elders do. He plays on the tendency of youngsters to want attention, to be important, to do exciting things. The Viet Cong has been successful in recruiting a substantial number of juveniles who, after training, generally make excellent guerrillas because of their youth, strength and endurance. Even the appealing little fellow of six, seven or eight, although not actually a recruit, is being used in many instances to purchase food, medicine, jungle boots, and other supplies and carry it back to Viet Cong concentrations. These youngsters also are being used as couriers and messengers and are very effective in their tasks.

SUMMARY

To counteract Communist political indoctrination is not the primary responsibility of the National Police but to defeat this assault on the minds of the people is the responsibility of all citizens, especially trained Government cadres and members of the security services. It is therefore up to Police officers to know as much as possible about the Viet Cong, particularly those operating in their own areas. They should know what the enemy is saying, whether it has an appeal to the people and, if so, why. It is not enough to say the enemy is bad if the person who says it knows nothing of the subject. It also is the responsibility of the police to create an image of themselves before the public which disproves Communist propaganda about authoritarian police tactics, corruption and cruelty.

This chapter has dealt with the

operations of the Communist fighters and guerrillas and their underground base and it may seem that he is invincible. He is not. True, the Viet Cong is smart, dedicated, tough and has excellent support; he is going to be around for long time. But the Government cadre, the soldier and the police are smart, dedicated and tough too and they are gaining more support and stature every day. And our big operational advantage is that we have only to lead one type of life. No hiding and starving in jungles, no lying and deception of family and friends. We do not need to be afraid of our speech uncovering our real purposes. Much is being done to resist and counteract the guerrilla's efforts and more can be done. This is the purpose of textbooks and training methods of establishing rural internal security. It is essential that the student know something of the nature of the enemy before he can begin to counter his efforts.

CHAPTER III

THE STRATEGIC HAMLET

In the strictest security sense, a strategic hamlet is nothing more than a collection of people and their homes located in a fenced off area to provide self - protection and to aid in the identification of the enemy, control his movements and interrupt his logistical support. (Commonly called «Resources Control».) A strategic hamlet is in a rural area but many urban communities have been organized into strategic subquarters or streets and the sectionalizing of cities and towns in a effort to apply some of the control methods used in strategic hamlets is continuing. This phenomenon is found in Dalat, Hue, Can Tho and all other large towns.

In Vietnamese terms, there are two major types of hamlets depending on the degree of security in a specific area. In relatively secure areas is the strategic hamlet (ap chien luoc), which is both socio-economic and military. It provides minimal security, certain economic opportunities and a degree of self-determination. It gives the Government an opportunity for population control. More heavily fortified and armed villages in less secure areas and in areas controlled by the Communists are called the combattant or tactical hamlets (ap chien dau). The latter, besides providing protection for people inside the walls, sometimes might be used as bases from which military and civic action operations can launched in an area. In the strategic hamlet, more effort is devoted to societal improvements — schools, sanitation and health stations, rural reconstruction — than in the combat hamlets. In both, of course, defense, both physical and mobile, is of paramount importance. Police responsibility remains much the same whether the hamlet is strategic or tactical. It is the job of the Police to maintain the internal security of the hamlet and keep a constant surveillance over the movements of people in and out of its limits. Therefore, to avoid confusion in definition, the term strategic hamlet (ap chien luoc) will be used throughout the remainder of their text to mean all types of hamlets which have been fortified to any degree at all in the

Governement's Strategic Hamlet Building Program.

A primary purpose of fencing in a town or a collection of dwellings obviously is protection. In strategic hamlets, this means self-protection as much as that coming from the outside. Naturally, police and military activities should be coordinated closely with the voluntary self-protection efforts of hamlet residents.

A second security reason for establishing strategic hamlets is identification of the enemy. Usually, in a situation where a communist insurgent is native to the area in which he operates, the problem of identification is extremely difficult. The enemy knows enough not to reveal himself through physical signs; more subtle and complex methods must be developed to identify him and this can be done better within a defined area. Once a strategic hamlet is established, with the population holding National Identification cards and registered under the Family Census program, the determination of Communist affiliations can begin in earnest. (Other methods of identifying the enemy are studied by Police in courses on loyalty investigations and the conduct of internal security matters — The subject of «Loyalty Investigations» is classified and not included in this text.)

Again, only by establishing defined areas, can a system of resources control be established. The control of resources, both material and human, is an essential factor in countering guerrilla warfare. To restrict the guerrilla's supplies, especially food, or deprive him of them completely will be a major factor in forcing him to abandon the war. In the course of control operations a great many of the underground will be surfaced and removed from society. This was true in Malaya and it will be true here. To control resources, one must control the movement of people; if a system for knowing who is moving from place to place, hamlet to hamlet, city to city, is operating effectively, the mobility of entire Viet Cong organization and communication among them will be inhibited.

The strategic hamlet also enables the Government to establish a comprehensive rural intelligence network. The villager, loyal or not, frequently knows what is going on in his area and is a prime source of information. It is possible that many villages who have been forced to cooperate with the Viet Cong or who have not before seen evidence of the Government's presence in their area, will find in the strategic hamlet both protection and economic help to the point where they are encouraged to work with Government cadres, the police and the military. It must always be remembered in this connection, that this kind of support must be freely given, it cannot be demanded. The Government cadre — police, agricultural, health, education — who gains the villager's trust and convinces him to turn from the Viet Cong has as great an effect in this kind of war as the military combatant because he is reducing the Viet Cong underground base.

In summary the two reasons for establishing strategic hamlets may be said to be (1) to establish rural internal security, and (2) to provide economic and social services to the farmer and villager so that the rural citizen moves forward with the city dweller in the development of the country and as such gives support to the Government against the common enemy. The two, of course, are closely related. The first reason may be divided further into the four principal ways in which strategic hamlets do establish rural internal security: (1) Physical protection of the people, (2) Identification of the enemy, (3) Control of resources, both human and material, and (4) Establishment of an intelligence network.

A. *Relocation and Its Problems*

Another distinction in the types of strategic hamlet, perhaps more pertinent to the Police responsibility, can be made between the «relocation center» and the «indigenous hamlet». The problems of security and loyalty are infinitely greater in a relocation center, a matter of which the Police must always be aware. It is in these centers that the people tend to be most discontented where the task of persuasion is the greatest and where surveillance must, of necessity, be strict.

The relocation center is an artificial creation — a designated area to which people from the surrounding region have brought to build homes and establish a new life for themselves with both Vietnamese and United States Government help. A relocation is a quasi-military operation and usually is by one of the following situations:

1. If the geography of a given hamlet together with Viet Cong military capabilities is such that the military decides it cannot defend it from the outside, then the hamlet will be relocated rather than fortified on its original location. Consider the difficulties of providing continuing protection to a village located in a mountain valley surrounded by uninhabited terrain where the Viet Cong forces can be based. The military requirements would be excessive and, unless there were some mitigating circumstances, a decision would be made to relocate the village.

2. If the dwellings of farmers are scattered sparsely over an area too wide to permit proper defense, those farmers are likely to be moved and resettled into a new strategic hamlet. If houses are widely dispersed, perhaps one or two kilometers apart, it is impractical to build a fence around them and impossible to set up an effective mobile defense and alarm system.

3. If a group of people living in an area dominated by the Viet Cong are loyal to the Government and wish to be protected from the pressures of the enemy, they may request relocation. A specific example of this occurred in a province where some 50,000 Montagnards live in a remote area largely under the control of the Viet Cong. About 12,000 of them asked to be moved to a safer location; the Government's response was to set up a number of strategic hamlets in a controlled

area and move the people into them.

The decision to relocate a village or a group of people is made by the military. Once a successful relocation has taken place, Government troops are reasonably sure that the only people remaining in the area are the enemy. In an ideal situation, the military forces move in, conduct a «clear and hold» operation to secure the region and ultimately turn the governing authority back to civilian officials, an effort which is extremely complex and lengthy.

It can be seen that relocation is essentially a military operation in which Police authorities have very little part initially except to be aware of the situation and make plans to handle the internal security problems at some future time. The relocation procedure works something like this: After the Army makes its decision, it is referred to the province chief or higher authority for the necessary approvals. When these have been obtained, the Army informs the residents of a given area of the impending move and explains the reasons for it. The people are given a certain time in which to gather their belongings and prepare to evacuate. Sometimes advance notice cannot be given because too many people would flee beforehand or would inform the Viet Cong of the forthcoming relocation. However, if at all possible, both notice and explanation are essential.

Most of the people who will undergo relocation are peasants who will not have many more belongings than their farming tools, simple furniture, clothing, food supplies, animals and simple means of transportation such as carts and wagons. Piling their belongings into what transport they themelves have or into Army trucks, the villagers move their goods to the area designated for the new hamlet along a route indicated by the military. If absolutely necessary, the troops will burn the old village and even excess food supplies to prevent them from falling into the hands of the Viet Cong. This move is desirable only in situations of proven military necessity, mainly because of the psychological effect on the people whose homes are being destroyed.

There are sure to be certain unfavorable reactions when a large number of families are ordered to move from areas in which they have lived for many years and where their ancestors lived before them. Imagine the feelings of a peasant or a tribesman when men in uniform suddenly appear and announce that he is to move away from his home, immediately and with all belongings, that he may not return to the area for an indefinite period and that there will be nothing to return to anyway because his house is to be burned. Compound this admittedly unpleasant situation with the fact that the peasant or tribesman, because of ignorance and provincialism, will not readily understand the necessity for the move. It must be remembered that rural Vietnamese people are not accustomed to moving around the country, but either have lived all their lives in one spot or moved about in an area encompassing only a few square kilometers. Tribal peoples, while they may be nomadic, are used to selecting their own new settlement sites in remote Highland areas and are highly independent individuals with the customary superstitions and suspicions of the aborigine.

Among the reactions likely to take place are resentment, fear of what is ahead and perhaps even panic leading to flight. Resentment occurs because the people are forced to do something against their will before an understanding of the necessity for the move can be established. Fear is of the unknown. Many people have been subjected to Viet Cong propaganda, some of it dealing directly with the subject of forced relocation. When the soldiers actually do appear and announce that a move is required, the people are afraid they will be imprisoned. Flight is the greatest danger, both because all possible manower is needed to build the new hamlet and because the fleeing villager most likely will fall right into the arms of the Viet Cong.

Relocation is one of many situations which point to the conclusion that the ability to implement decisions based on military necessity is not enough to win this war. It also must be won on the political level; the people must be made not only to accept decisions and actions of military and civilian authorities, but also to actively cooperate with them. Our democratic form of government has certain things to offer to the people and they must be led to understand this; they must be convinced of ideas rather than have ideas forced upon them. Everything must be done by the Police to help their fellow citizens understand what the authorities are trying to do and why. Feelings must be considered, reactions predicted and solutions, based on knowledge and understanding, developed. The idea of communicating ideas to the people and going support for the program will be emphasized throughout this text. While good communication alone will not insure success, lack of it can ultimately invalidate the accomplishments of the strategic hamlet program.

CHAPTER IV
RURAL POLICE:
FUNCTION AND ADMINISTRATION

The functions of a rural police organization are fundamentally the same as those of police in urban areas, but there are many differences in the problems confronting the two groups and the methods used to solve them.

One of the major differences is geography. A specified rural area making up one rural police precinct or administrative division might cover a wide, sparsely inhabited region; it might include mountains, desert land, marsh or swamp, jungle or a combination of geographical characteristics. A city or town precinct is small, compact and crowded with people. Inhabitants of the Vietnam countryside usually are gathered in small hamlets or villages of from a few families to several hundred, often lacking of the customary municipal or urban facilities such as public transport for local movement, electricity, telephones, running water and limited fire and police services.[1] The principal occupation of a rural area is farming, with mineral and forest exploitation important in some areas. This compares with the manufacturing, trade and financial activity of the urban community.

Systems of communication differ in the country and the city. Few villages have telephone service and radio transmitters, if they are found at all, usually have been installed to handle emergencies such as summoning help from the closest military unit or the district headquarters in the event of guerilla attack. The paved streets and alleys of the city are replaced in the country by rough lanes, often impassable in the rainy season. Although paved highways connect the cities with major province towns, hundreds of hamlets and villages which are not located along principal arteries can be reached only by poor roads or trails and sometime by canal. Thus, traffic in the countryside is much lighter than in the city and different in character as well. More of the vehicles are trucks of one type or another and animal-drawn carts also are common.

Obviously, geographic characteristics and lack of communication facilities directly affect the operations of a rural police unit. Patrol duties cannot be carried out over rough and sometimes impassable terrain in the same manner or with the frequency that they can on city streets. A patrolling policeman usually is not able to call headquarters for assistance or instructions by telephone, a facility accepted without question in the city. Most likely, there are no street lights to aid patrol inspections, no electricity — except as specially generated — to re-charge radio batteries or power fire pumps. In fact, there usually are no fire pumps and no street water mains to furnish an immediate supply of water.

Statistics reveal that large urban areas, with their ever present, crowded slums, are breeding grounds for crimes against property and person, while rural areas are more free of such activity. Unfortunatly, there is an unusual situation in rural Vietnam today with crimes against the state, that is, subversion and its related offenses, occupying a far larger portion of the crime picture than the so-called conventional crimes. The most violent offenses of the Viet Cong guerrilla are assassination of officials and sabotage of public facilities, but no less subversive are propaganda activities, stealing of property and «recruiting» of young people. Further, it is important to note that the bulk of Communist criminal activity is in rural areas. There is, of course, a certain number of the usual crimes being committed in the countryside but they are relatively few when compared with the crimes of subver-

---

(1) The terms hamlet and village are used here to apply generally to small to medium-size population centers rather than to the administrative or specialized «village» and «strategic hamlet» used elsewhere in this text.

sion. Therefore, the situation facing rural police in Viet Nam today cannot be viewed in the same frame of reference as that of a peaceful farming county in the United States, a departement in France, or similar administrative sub-divisions in Japan, Malaya or any other country which is not seriously threatened by insurgents.

Accordingly, the principal rural policing effort in Viet Nam, or any other place with a like problem, should be directed toward the identification, apprehension and conviction in a court of law of the subversive enemy, and to control all resources, human and material, which might help him to exist. From a police standpoint, there has not yet been in Viet Nam any group specifically designated to accomplish this objective on a national basis. However, legislation does exist in the form of National Decree No. 146/PTT/NV, signed by the President of Viet Nam on June 27, 1962, which completely reorganized and consolidated the principal police units in the nation into one cohesive force.[2] The legislation is quite broad and could well be utilized to organize effective resources control and attain the goal of rural internal security. Undoubtedly, administrative regulations will be required to define the activities to be carried out.

A. ORGANIZATION

To have a sound grasp of law enforcement requirements in the context of the situation in which he will work, a policeman must understand the structure of his organization. The pertinent parts of Decree 146/PTT/NV, therefore, are mentioned below with direct quotation as required. Article 1 states:

«There are hereby integrated all the (present) National Police and Surete services, Municipal Police of Saigon, the Municipal Police of the provincial chief towns, and the Rural Police of Southern Viet Nam, into one single organization called the «National Police» having jurisdiction all over the territory of the Republic of Viet Nam. Wages, allowances, uniforms and badges of the National Police shall be standardized».

The duties of the National Police are spelled out clearly in Article 2 of the decree and graphically outlined in the organization chart (Appendix No. I) Article 2 says in part:

«The National Police shall have the following responsibilities:

1. *The Special Police*

Responsible for prevention and detection of all activities prejudicial to national security and for bringing the offenders before competent authorities for action.

2. *The Judicial Police*

Responsible for assisting the judiciary in searching, ascertaining and investigating all high, serious and petty offenses, and for bringing subjects, evidence and records to the appropriate public prosecutor charged with prosecuting such offenses. The Judicial Police also carry out all operations as may be assigned by the

---

(2) See Appendix No. I for full text of the decree.

Courts of Justice according to laws in force.

3. *Uniform and Traffic Police*

Responsible for maintaining order and regulating daily traffic in public places; carrying out local police and administrative regulations.

4. *Administrative Police*

Responsible for controlling organizations, activities, events and goods which might affect public peace and order, such as civilian associations and missions; use and storage of weapons and ammunition, radio receivers and transmitters; entry and exit activities of Vietnamese, and for making administrative investigations of legal entities.

5. *Combat Police*

Responsible for supporting intelligence activities and police operations and for destruction of armed terrorist activities or isolated cases of sabotage by the enemy. It is also responsible for supporting local police units.

6. *Scientific Police*

Responsible for making analysis, comparison, and examinations of physical evidence or traces and marks collected at the scenes upon request of responsible authorities.

7. *Immigration Control*

Responsible for controlling the number of foreign nationals residing on the territory of the Republic of Viet Nam, their backgrounds and their movements; for issuing entry and exit visas and making administrative investigations concerning these foreign residents.

8. *In Service and Technical Training*

Responsible for giving technical and special training to police personnel.

The above description of responsibilities is very broad; it would be difficult to think of a police activity not covered in the legislation. Therefore, the National Police would be legally sound in embarking on an intensified program of resources control and rural internal security, with only administrative action to define the scope and limits of the activity required.

Article 3 describes the general organization of the National Police as follows:

At the central (seat of government) level: *Directorate General of Police*

At the regional and municipal levels: *Regional and Municipal Directorates*

At the province, city and precinct level: *Provincial, City and Precinct Police*

At Provincial, District, and Sector in Saigon: *District Police*

At village level: *Village Police*

Thus, rural police would operate in the province at various levels, including the provincial, district and village, all of which now have some police operating and resident. At this writing, no members of the National Police are resident in strategic hamlets (unless a hamlet is coincidentally a «village» in the administrative hierarchy) so that all police effort or assistance concurrently must come from the village, district or province level.

LOCAL GOVERNMENT STRUCTURE

It is necessary for the rural policeman to understand the workings of provincial government to properly understand his own group's place in the local picture. For administration, Viet Nam is divided into 40 provinces which, in turn, are made up of districts, cantons, villages and hamlets.[3] In many districts, particularly in central Viet Nam, the canton does not exist. There also are the municipalities of Hue, Da Nang, Dalat, and Saigon which have their own National Police units, as well as the hydroelectric project in Da Nhim, Tuyen Duc province, and the demilitarized zone at the 17th parallel.

(a) *The Province*

Each province is headed by a province chief, appointed by and representing the authority of the central government in Saigon to the isolated villages and hamlets in the countryside. Under his general administrative direction and supervision, subordinate provincial and district official and local services of national departments and agencies provide medical facilities, assist in rural development projects, and maintain police and security forces. Viet Nam is a highly diversified country whose transportation and communication difficulties, as well as the presence of different ethnic groups such as the Montagnards, make too centralized administration from the Saigon government a practical impossibility. Recognizing this, the province chief has been relied upon to assume great responsibility in carrying out national policy at the local level.

Decree No. 57-A, of Oct 24, 1956, states that the province chief is charged with the enforcement of laws and the general management of all provincial services; he may propose transfers of technical officials assigned to his locality; he is responsible for order and security and shall coordinate all local security and police forces.

By Decree No. 3NV, of March, 1959, the post of deputy chief of province for internal security was established by the President of Viet Nam. Among other things, the responsibilities of the deputy for security include: «B. With regard to security matters (he) must develop the pacification plan... coordinate reports and develop information. He has at his disposal the use of police, surete,[4] civil guard, and the village self-defense forces». In practice, it will be found that the chief of the National Police organization in each province reports to the province chief through the deputy for security.

In general terms, the provincial police chief looks to the Director General of National Police in Saigon for technical and policy guidance, general programs and budgetary support. He looks to the province chief for managerial direction within the scope of the above national plans and policies.

There is another law enforcement

---

[3] Jason L. Finkle and Tran Van Dinh «Provincial Government in Viet Nam» National Institute of Administration, Saigon, August, 1961.

[4] The police and surete were combined into the National Police by the 1963 decree.

agency in Viet Nam known as the Gendarmerie. This relatively small group of policemen concern themselves with general law enforcement, highway patrol and crimes involving military personnel. The Gendarmerie is responsible to the Ministry of Defense.

(b) *The District*

Headed by a district chief appointed by the president of Viet Nam on recommendation of the province chief, the district is intermediary between province and village. Some sections of a National Institute of Administration study by Professor Bui Quang Khanh are quoted below to describe the position of the district in the government hierarchy.[5]

«Unlike the villages and provinces, the districts are the only administrative areas having no legal entity, no property nor budget.

«They serve as an intermediary agency between the province and the village and the district chief is the liaison man between the province chief and the village chief...

«Since 1954, a concentration of power has been applied at district level. District chiefs are appointed by the President of the Republic upon recommendation of the province chief (Ordinance 57a, Article 15)...

«The current powers and duties of the district chiefs are still fixed by decrees left from the French regime, the basic one being Arrete dated December 6, 1941.

The district chief is the representative of the province chief at the district and must carry out responsibilities under control and command of the province chief. His responsibilities fall into three categories:

(1) Administrative and political

(2) Financial

(3) Judicial

1. Administrative and political

The district chief enforces laws and regulations, but has no legislative authority. He can take police action for security purposes either upon instructions of the province chief or on his own initiative...

The district chief controls and coordinates activities of the villages. He can make recommendations to the province chief for disciplinary measures against the officials under his jurisdiction.

He maintains public buildings and roads in the district... inspects the schools, the medical installations and police posts, but the job is purely administrative in nature and he is not allowed to interfere in the technical activities of these organizations.

He controls the village councils from the standpoint of administrative, financial and taxation activities...

At present, due to the state of emergency, the district chief is responsible for maintaining security against communist subversive activities. Therefore, he is entitled to

---

(5) Bui Quang Khanh, **Political and Administrative Organizations of Viet Nam**, National Institute of Administration, Saigon, 1963.

command and move paramilitary forces such as the Police, the Civil Guard, the Self Défense Corps and the Gendarmerie...

2. Financial

(He is the chief financial officer of the district and his responsibilities include tax collection.)

3. Judicial officer, the district chief has the responsibility for investigating major and minor offenses, collecting evidence and transporting criminals to court.

He reports to the public prosecutor or the Court of Peace with Extended Jurisdiction and to the province chief concerning these offenses.

In case of a crime *in flagrante delicto,* the district chief has a right to detain the criminal, make a report of his search and seizure, take the statement of the criminal and remand him to court...

The district chief may be assigned by the public prosecutor, the examining judge or the chairman of the Criminal Court to conduct an investigation in his district...

He certifies signatures of officials who issue official documents. In the present anti-communist fight, the district chief unquestionably plays an important role and the participation of the district chief in the maintenance of security is considered necessary by the Government. A number of the more important districts are currently commanded by a military officer».

(c) *The Village and Hamlet*

With the promulgation last May of Decree No. 45-NV,[6] the Government of Viet Nam established the composition, administrative responsibilities and election procedures of village councils and hamlet administrative committees. It left the village as the lowest echelon of government with a legal personality and the hamlet as an administrative sub-division of the villages are legally constituted in the government hierarchy and given a certain amount of autonomy, their government authority is limited by the requirement for higher approval of routine matters, usually by the province or district chief. The village governing council, headed by the village representative, consists of an economic and finance member, a police member, a youth member and a civil status and health member. They are not elected to specific positions but rather decide among themselves who is most qualified for which job. This does not apply to the village representative who is the one receiving the most number of votes in the election. Thus, even though the police member is selected as most qualified for this position, it does not mean he has had any police training or experience whatsoever. The police member is an elected official and there is no direct relationship between him and a member of the National Police. It is the duty of the police member, according to Article 10 of the Decree, to «Take charge of administrative and judiciary police action in the village, deliver summons and notifications of the court and maintain order and safety in the

---

(6) Chapter III, this manual, «The Strategic Hamlet».

village». A village may or may not have a representative of the National Police in residence, depending on its size, location and needs.

The hamlet administrative council, also elected and consisting of three or five people, depending on size of the hamlet, has either a single security member or a combination security and youth member. The Decree states that «the Security Member assist the (village) Police Member and maintains safety and order in the hamlet».

The organization and operations of the Royal Federation of Malaya Police Force should be studied by all police organizations facing a counter-insurgency problem. It successfully countered a major communist guerrilla operation and its accomplishment was due in large part to resources control and the establishment of rural internal security. (See Part III of this manual, «The Malaya Experience»).

B. POLICE ADMINISTRATION[7]

Except for the added complexities of a big city operation, police organization and administration are about the same in rural as in urban areas, regardless of the country involved. In his basic text, *Police Administration,* O. W. Wilson says:

«An understanding of the processes involved in the accomplishment of police tasks is essential to the development and operation of a suitable organization of the force. Three processes — planning the operation, doing the job, and controlling the results — are vital to the attainment of any objective of the performance of any task. A sound organization facilitates these processes.

The police force must be organized in a manner to assure the most effective direction, coordination and control of its members in the accomplishment of the police purpose. The best results are achieved when all members work to the best of their ability, consciously conforming to the structure of the organization but not so conscious of it as to retard the free movement of ideas and efforts up and down and sideways.

For the attainment of police objectives, the police chief has the help of a number of men. In order that objectives may be achieved, it is essential that all tasks should be specifically assigned and that each officer should know his particular duties and responsibilities. The regular assignment of similar or related duties to one man or the same group of men is advantageous and police tasks should be arranged so that similar or related ones may be regularly assigned to the same personnel group.

«Duties may be considered similar or related on the basis of (1) their purpose (to control traffic, vice, and juvenile crime are examples. (In Viet Nam today, to control vital resources of value to the enemy), (2) their method (for example, patrol, investigation, clerical, laboratory, and maintenance duties employ distinctly different

---

[7] This section is of necessity a very brief summary of the subject of police administration. A number of basic and valuable texts exist in English on this subject, some of which are referred to in this chapter.

methods), and (3) their clientele i.e., the people served or worked with (the juvenile division works primarily with children, the traffic division with motorists and pedestrians; the vice division is concerned with gamblers, prostitutes, and narcotics peddlers. (In Viet Nam, checkpoint personnel work with drivers of vehicles and their passengers; hamlet police work with the residents of strategic hamlets). Each of these bases is used in police organization and this division of work is called specialization. Police tasks also are classified according to the time of the day when they are performed and according to the place where they are located. They are also divided according to the level of authority needed in their accomplishment».[8]

A simple type of organization, suitable for carrying out the requirements of resources control and rural internal security, is charted in Ill. 3, opposite.

«Police duties must be analyzed so that similar or related tasks may be grouped together and the force divided into corresponding units for assignment purposes. The tasks may be classified as line, auxiliary, and administrative.

«Operations that a police department is primarily created to perform are called primary, line or operational duties. By their accomplishment the fundamental police purpose is fulfilled. These tasks may be grouped according to their immediate purpose».[9]

In rural Viet Nam, the following operations or tasks bear special study:

Patrol — to repress criminal activity; regulate conduct; detect resources violations and seepages; report suspicious activities which might indicate Viet Cong attack, infiltration or subversion; observe incipient fires, and perform certain of services to the population.

Enforcement of Resources Control — to check food parcels, observe and report unusual stocks of vital commodities, search vehicles, inspect Identity cards and make the family census head counts.

Crime Investigation — to apprehend criminals, recover stolen and contraband property and detect violators of control regulations.

There are also special operating units, such as the checkpoints listed in the organization chart (Ill. 3), which consist of highly trained personnel performing a specialized function. But, as Wilson points out, a special unit, in this case a checkpoint, «does not have exclusive jurisdiction in the performance of its principal function»;[10] all police are responsible for the controlling of resources and checking vehicles when the need arises. In the same way, the checkpoints are not relieved of the responsibility for detecting all kinds of law violators, not only those who are transporting materials for the benefit of the Viet Cong.

The auxiliary or support functions of a police department are an essential

---

(8) O. W. Wilson, **Police Administration**, McGraw-Hill Book Company, Inc., 1950 pp. 19 - 20.
(9) Ibid., p. 22.
(10) op. cit., p. 23.

A COMMAND ORGANIZATION FOR THE FUNCTION OF CONTROL OF POPULATION AND MATERIAL MOVEMENT

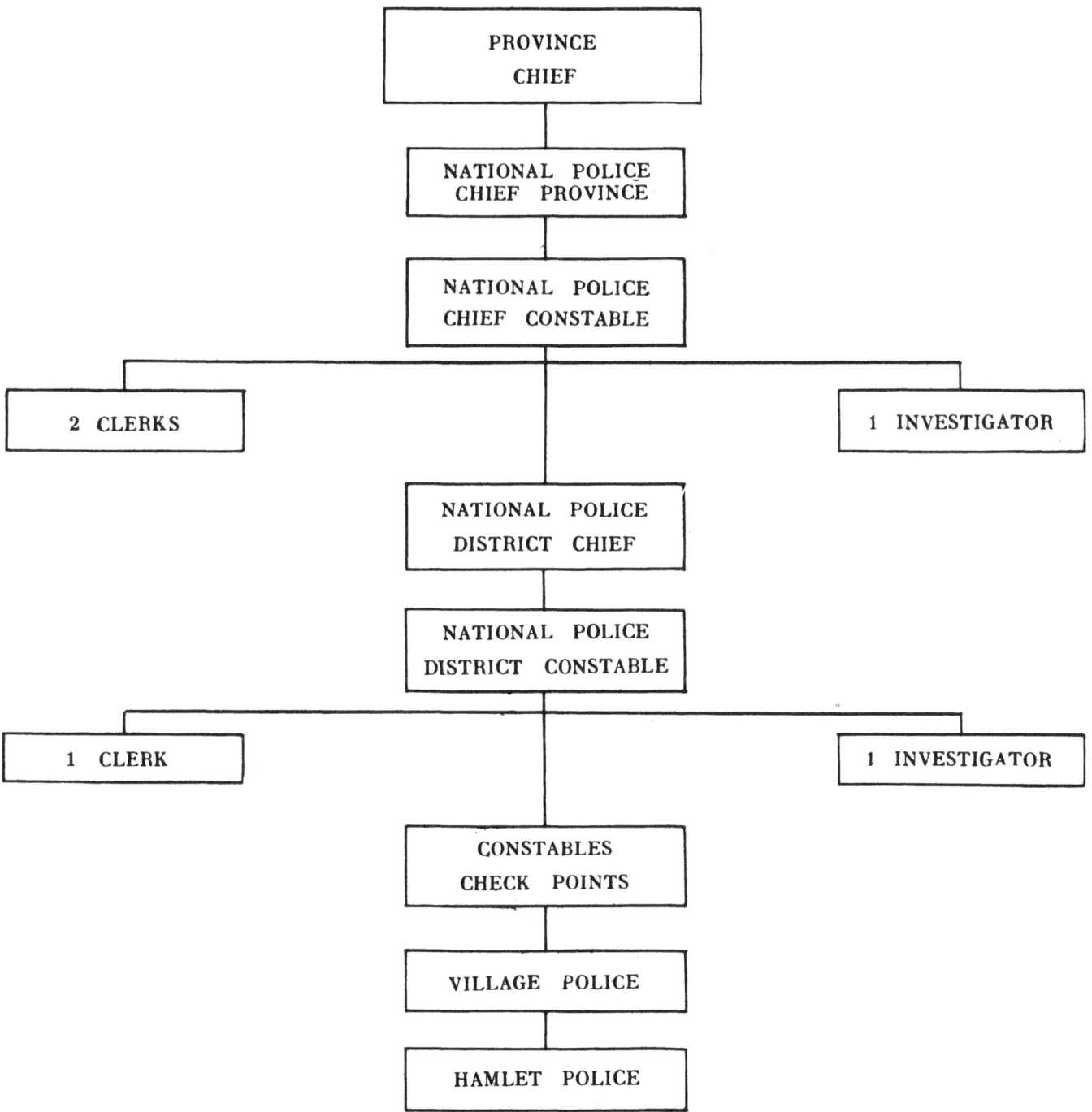

Ill. 3. *A typical command organization for the function of control of population and material movement.*

part of its organization and important to the accomplishment of the police purpose. Among them are records and identification bureaus, communication facilities, technical laboratories, jail or custodial services, property management and maintenance.

Finally, a police department must have administration. This function, Wilson says, «includes the tasks of management, which facilitate and make possible the effective accomplishment of the other two, i.e., operations (primary functions) and services (auxiliary functions).» Management is represented by the chief or director, who, with his staff, runs the organization and directs the department or force. Administrative duties consist of directing «the resources of the department toward the accomplishment of the primary police objectives» and «staffing the organization with qualified personnel and equipping it to do the job».[11]

1. *Orders*

It is sound administration to issue most orders in writing. Operating policemen are entitled to be told explicitly what they are supposed to do and they are entitled to have these orders clearly stated in writing, both for their own protection and as an aid to efficiency. If a policeman's action is questioned by his superiors or by the public, written orders should be in existence as evidence that he acted properly or improperly; individual police officers also need written orders to refer to in order to refresh their memories and thus improve operating efficiency.

Orders usually are classified into three types: general orders, post orders and special orders.

A General Order is a policy statement by the department and applies to most related units of the organization. For example, a memorandum to all checkpoints in a province might state that vehicles will be spot checked at intervals to be established by the district police supervisor according to the needs of each post.

A post order is a document which provides specific instructions on the operations of a single post because of conditions surrounding that particular unit of operation. For example, the static checkpoint at km.7 on the Saigon-Bien Hoa highway might receive a post order that, due to heavy traffic, spot checks shall not be made with greater frequency than every 15 vehicles between the hours of 0700 and 1800, except in special circumstances.

A special Order is one issued to cover a specific circumstance or set of circumstances for a limited period of time and usually for a limited number of posts. For example, Ho Chi Minh's birthday is sometimes used by the communists as a day to cause riots or terrorize cities. Therefore, a special order might be issued to all checkpoints on highways leading into Saigon to spot check not more often than every five vehicles nor less than every 10, for a period of 24 hours before and after the date in question.

Orders should be kept at each post until they are no longer in effect or until

_____
(11) op. cit., p. 24.

they have modified or replaced. Usually they are maintained on a clipboard of some kind; they should be reviewed periodically so that out of date orders are regularly eliminated.

2. *Records*

In a modern law enforcement agency, the records and communications facilities form the hub of the administrative wheel. Authorities generally agree that the quality of records maintained is directly related to the quality of police administration.[12]

The modern police administrator or supervisor relies heavily on sound records practices and an efficient communications system in the direction of his force. The centralization of records in a police department brings together at one point all information concerning police activities and it is through such centralization that the various line functions of a police department are coordinated. For example, the uniformed police at a check point might handle the preliminary search and detention in a case, while the investigating unit or judicial police would follow and report the results of subsequent investigation. Without this centralization there would be a tendency for each unit to operate as a small, independent police department, obviously an undesireable situation.

Records need not be complex and rural policing operations are generally recorded by way of a simple reporting system. The suggested report forms described below have been specifically designed with resources control and rural internal security in mind, but there is nothing particularly original in them. What the rural police organization should try to do is establish a simple system of reports which will efficiently provide for accurate written communication of sufficient permanence to fulfill the requirement of its job but without creating a complex «paper factory».

The purposes of written reports have been well stated in a book by John C. Hazelet.[13] He lists four principal ones: (1) to preserve knowledge; (2) to provide accurate details; (3) to aid other personnel and other agencies, and (4) to coordinate the activities of a police organization. A fifth purpose could well be added: to protect the interests of the individual policeman who tries to do a good job.

Two resources control reports, the Incident Report (Ill. 4, page 32) and the Shift Log (Ill. 5, page 33), are presented here for study.

The purpose of the Incident Report is to explain in an organized fashion exactly what happened at a particular checkpoint — mobile or static, on a main highway or at a hamlet gate — in a case involving the efforts of one or more persons to violate the law by illegally transporting themselves or property. Three copies are distributed in order of supervisory responsibility, beginning at the post, the level of actual operation which could be a road checkpoint or hamlet gate, and going

---

(12) Federal Bureau of Investigation, «Manual of Police Records», U.S. Dept. of Justice, Washington D.C., Rev. October 1953.

(13) John C. Hazelet, **Police Report Writing**, Charles C. Thomas, Springfield, Ill., 1960.

Copies :
1 Post File
1 District Police
1 Province Police

INCIDENT REPORT
RESOURCES CONTROL
THE NATIONAL POLICE

1. Province _____ Village or hamlet _____ District _____

2. Place incident happened _____ Date of incident _____ Time _____

3. Reported to or observed by (if. diff. frm. 1) _____ Date _____ Time _____

4. Vehicle Used : Type _____ Make _____ License No. _____ Motor or Serial No. _____

        5. Persons detained or questioned
        (Use another sheet if required)

  a) Name _____ ID No. _____ Address _____

  b) Name _____ ditto

  c) Name _____ ditto

6. Signature of person receiving prisoner (Name, Rank, Address) _____

        7. Property confiscated
        (Use another sheet if required)

  a) Kind _____ Weight _____ Serial No _____

  b) Kind _____ ditto

  c) Kind _____ ditto

  d) Kind _____ ditto

8. Signature of person receiving prisoner (Name, Rank, Address) _____

9. What happened (Use another sheet if required) _____

        Policeman's Signature   Date

        Supervisor's Signature   Date

(Destroy one year from date)

Ill. 4. Suggested Incident Report form for local production.

Copies:
1 Post File
1 District Police
1 Province Police

SHIFT LOG
RESOURCES CONTROL
NATIONAL POLICE

Date _____ Time: From _____ to _____ Post Name or No _____

VEHICLES SEARCHED

1. Type _____ Make _____ License No _____ Motor or Serial No _____
   Driver's Name _____ Address _____ Id No _____
   Time: From _____ to _____ Incident Report: Yes ___ No ___ Driver's Initials _____

2. Type _____ Make _____ License No _____ Motor or Serial No _____
   Driver's Name _____ Address _____ Id No _____
   Time: From _____ to _____ Incident Report: Yes ___ No ___ Driver's Initials _____

3. Type _____ Make _____ License No _____ Motor or Serial No _____
   Driver's Name _____ Address _____ Id No _____
   Time: From _____ to _____ Incident Report: Yes ___ No ___ Driver's Initials _____

4. Type _____ Make _____ License No _____ Motor or Serial No _____
   Driver's Name _____ Address _____ Id No _____
   Time: From _____ to _____ Incident Report: Yes ___ No ___ Driver's Initials _____

Policeman's Signature
Date   Time

(Destroy one year from date)

Ill. 5. *Suggested Shift Log form for local production.*

up to the district and province police. Following are explanations of the numbered items in the Incident Report:

1. Refers to the province, district and village or hamlet in which the incident took place, not where it was reported, should there be differences.

2. Refers to exact spot at which the incident occurred, such as Checkpoint Hai Yen. Date and time are recorded as accurately as possible and in a consistent manner. Preferred as least likely to cause confusion is this form: 1705 hours, 29 August 1963.

3. Occasionally a citizen, not a policeman, observes something out of order and reports it to one of the rural police officers or small operations units. This would be in the nature of a complaint and his name, together with the date and time of the actual reporting, should be recorded. The details concerning the identity of the complainant should be included under items no. 9 «What happened?».

4. A large number of the incidents in resources control policing will involve vehicles. Therefore, it is necessary to properly identify the truck, auto or motor scooter.

5. People are always involved and descriptive information as outlined in this section. If such information is not readily available, if, for instance, the subject has escaped, the spaces should be marked «Unknown» and a physical description should be included in item no. 9 and a follow up investigation should be conducted to identify and locate the individual.

6. This item is one which, in addition to serving good administration, helps to protect the individual police officer. It is used if a person is detained. Obviously the prisoner would be removed from the check point or hamlet gate as soon as possible and turned over to another police officer for interrogation, jailing, etc. Therefore, the person receiving the subject from the arresting officer should sign for the prisoner. Any unusual conditions concerning the prisoner's physical self, such as wounds or drunkeness, should be shown in item no. 9.

7. Often contraband or suspected goods will be confiscated. These goods will either be evidence for some court, or are the rightful property of an owner and must be returned to him in good condition after the investigation. Therefore, it is essential in order to identify the goods and to prove the chain of possession,[14] or to account for them to the owner, that this item should be carefully completed. The form is designed to be universal, so that a 100 kilo sack of rice or a generator could be listed. Obviously, the rice would have no serial number as would a generator, but would be shown by weight.

8. This item is another policeman's protective device, to make an official receipt to show who actually got the property, and also to help prove chain of possession.

9. «What happened?» is intended

---
(14) «Chain of possession» is a legal expression meaning, in criminal law, the proof necessary to establish, in court, exactly where the goods were from the time of their seizere to their introduction as trial evidence.

to be that part of the report which is an account of «what happened?» in essay form and should include the six usual elements, Who? What? Why? When? Where? and How? This is developed thoroughly in other texts under «report writing».

The report is signed and dated by the preparing policeman and signed by his supervisor to show that he has read and approved it. The form is to be destroyed after one year unless there is a good, individual reason to keep it.

The purpose of the «Shift Log» is to provide an itemized report of the activity of a check point, mobile or static, or of a village or hamlet entrance gate.

It reports to supervising officers what has happened and serves as the policemans' defender in case of complaint against him. Copies are designated for the originator and for supervisory levels.

The space for date and time refers to the shift worked, usually on an eight hour basis. In other words it would show 23 August 1963, from 1600 hours to 2400 hours, as well as the post name or designation.

Referring to Chapter VIII, «Checkpoints and Searches», it can be seen that spot checks, or random searches of vehicles on an organized basis are part of the control techniques utilized. The «Vehicles Searched» items are intended to record identifying data relative to all vehicles searched, either by spot checks or on suspicion. The first two lines are self explanatory.

The «time» should show the exact number of minutes required to complete the search. If anything unusual is discovered, a person is detained or property confiscated, an Incident Report should be prepared and its existance should be indicated as Yes or No. The driver of the vehicle should be requested to initial the log for the policeman's protection so that if he complains that the search was unreasonably long, reference to the log and his initials will show the true and agreed to facts.

The policeman in charge of the post should sign the log, date it and forward it immediately to his supervisor. Logs should be destroyed after one year.

BUDGET

A police organization cannot operate without three fundamental things, men, materials and money. Probably «money» should be mentioned first because until the organization has some financing the other two items are not procurable. Therefore, it is essential for the policeman, as well as the supervisor, to know some of the basic things about money and finance which will be presented in this brief study of budgets.

A budget is, in effect, a comprehensive plan expressed in financial terms by which an operating program becomes effective for a given period of time. Budgeting is primarily an instrument of planning in the sense that it enables the administrator to foresee his resource needs and to express his plan in terms of these needs.[15]

No governmental organization, whether it be the United States AID program or the Vietnamese national treasury, is a bottomless bank constantly replenished with currency to finance the many worthwhile projects that are presented. Therefore, since there are more worthwhile projects than there is money to go around, the police organization is in competition with others for the available financing. Accordingly, it is essential to present the budget in a form which will clearly express the need for people or things and adequately justify this with logical reasoning based on as many facts as possible.

So the supervisor must prepare his budget to acquire the people and things, or men and materials, that are needed to do the job. Since in all probability most readers of this manual will be dealing with the initial establishing of counter-insurgency police forces, justification must take the form of established facts rather than collected facts. For example, in establishing a new operation of resources control some of the established facts available are: the geography and terrain to show the need for vehicles, including boats; proven police administration to justify the manpower needs, post by post. As the organization progresses, the needs may be justified by collected facts which the supervisor gathers during each year. Some of these facts are the man-hours worked, cases handled to justify manpower, the kilometers driven to justify gasoline and vehicle maintenance.

Referring forward to Chapter VIII, «Check-points and Searches», under the «Operation of a Check-point» is a discussion of personnel requirements for the post. Study of this will show the logical justification used to support a budget request, including such things as size and importance of the highway, traffic counts, man-hours of operation and supervision.

In a budget request for materials, justification for the purchase of motor vehicles might be used as an example. A good starting point would be that each District supervisor needs transportation to get around his District. In marshalling the facts, it would be necessary to show such things as the number of kilometers of road in the district, the number of policemen and posts to be supervised, the number of hamlets, villages and towns in the district. If a Jeep is desired four-wheel drive, the number of kilometers of unpaved road versus that of all-weather bad should be stated. Since this is considered to be a new operation there would be no need to show how the supervisor inspected his operation before, but alternate possibilities should be considered and rejected.

An alternate might be a bicycle or a motor scooter since they are cheaper to buy and operate. Such would not be practical for the supervisor since he must be able to transport personnel and prisoners and operate in all kinds of weather as well as daylight and darkness.

---
(15) «Police Management Planning» by John P. Kenney, published by Charles C. Thomas, Springfield, Ill. 1959.

But the acquisition of the vehicle is not the end of the story. Provisions must be made for spare parts, maintenance and gasoline and oil which must be justified in the budget as well.

The initial request for men and materials has been mentioned, so planning for the ensuing years becomes necessary. Here the duty for planning and budgeting falls not only on the supervisor but the men as well. The patrolman or checkpoint constable works with the facts every day; i.e., how many vehicles were checked, how often does it rain (if he has no shelter to work in), how many prisoners were transported, how many patrols were made over what distance, and a host of other workaday facts. The patrolman, then, should be ever on the alert to collect these facts as he goes about his daily duties and report them so that supervision will have the information to make up a budget request at the end of each year.

A good summary of just what is needed in substantiation of a budget request is contained in U.S. Operations Mission (AID) to Viet Nam in General Order No. 100-1-1 of August 16, 1963, as follows:

«In order to justify procurement of commodities the following information must be furnished together with the commodity request:

1. Consumption rate and quantity of commodities now on hand;
2. Quantity of similar capital items previously made available and their present distribution;
3. The manner in which the commodity itself supports a particular program;
4. The location at which the commodity will be used;
5. The reasoning supporting the determination of the quantity of each commodity requested;
6. Any other pertinent data which would enhance the overall justification for the procurement».

SUPERVISION

Supervision is the overseeing and directing the work of others. However, its execution is far from this simple statement as it involves many things including leadership, knowledge, understanding, integrity, fairness, impartiality and a host of similar personality traits and techniques. It is hoped, however, that a few of the basic fundamentals can be learned and applied by those who are now, or expect to be, in supervisory positions.

There is a distinct difference between supervision and management.

Perhaps the most significant difference between supervision and management[16] is that the first inevitably involves a relationship with people, for there comes a point in every organization where face-to-face leadership and direction must be established. The supervisor is the man who translates the directives into action at the check-point or on the patrol. While he too is concerned with

---
(16) Frank P. Sherwood & Wallace H. Best, «Supervisory Methods in Municipal Administration», The International City Managers' Assn., Chicago, 1958.

the use of other resources, his major concern is with people. Supervision, by its very nature, cannot exist without people. The man who oversees the operations of twenty-five machines is not a supervisor. He is a specialist, a technician. The man who oversees the work of twenty-five operators at their machines is a supervisor. He is a supervisor because people have been added to the situation. Supervision exists where there is immediate contact with people in the direction of work.

The above are some of the generalities. However, the supervising policeman is interested in the specifics of how to get the job done. The following is an outline which the supervisor can use not only as a guide, but to test himself in his daily operations.[17]

1. UNDERSTANDING MY ORGANIZATION
    a. Know the functions of my unit and how they contribute to the total task.
    b. Show each policeman how his job fits into the overall picture.
    c. Determine lines of authority and responsibility.
    d. Determine number and type of policeman required in my unit.
    e. Make logical duty assignments based on clear outline of responsibility and authority.

2. GETTING THE WORK OUT
    a. Give directions that are clear, understandable and specific.
    b. Review work for progress in meeting schedules.
    c. Coordinate the work of my unit and take action as necessary.
    d. See that my men do what is rightfully expected of them.

3. PLANNING AND SCHEDULING WORK
    a. Keep up with the work capability of my unit.
    b. Keep up with the workload of my unit.
    c. Plan priorities of work and schedule accordingly.
    d. Plan for the best use of manpower, space and equipment.
    e. Establish realistic goals for the group.
    f. Have my group participate in setting its own goals.
    g. Plan to meet deadline and emergencies.

4. IMPROVING WORK METHODS
    a. Analyse operations of my unit as a whole.
    b. Develop and apply improved methods.
    c. Encourage and assist workers in submitting their ideas.

5. DETERMINING PERFORMANCE REQUIREMENTS
    a. Determine what is required of each policeman.

---
[17] «Responsibilities of a Supervisor», Management Course for Air Force Supervisors, AFP 50-2-1, Government Printing Office, Washington, D.C., 1958.

b. Discuss tentative requirements with each policeman concerned.

c. Make final determination of requirements based on needs of management, supervisory experience and policemans' suggestions.

d. Evaluate objectively each policeman's performance based on requirements.

6. DEVELOPMENT WORKERS

   a. Select right person for the job.

   b. Help the policeman make adjustment on a new job.

   c. Determine training needs of workers and provide training.

   d. Let workers know how they are doing.

   e. Discuss career opportunities with workers.

   f. Develop an understudy to replace me.

7. MAINTAINING A COOPERATIVE POLICE FORCE

   a. See that workers are rewarded for jobs well done.

   b. Commend entire group on performance when deserved.

   c. Transfer and reasign policemen for the best use of their abilities.

   d. Earn policeman's confidence and loyalty.

   e. Encourage workers to discuss their problems with me.

   f. Adjust differences fairly and objectively.

   g. Keep workers informed.

   h. Develop and maintain effective discipline within the work group.

   i. Initiate corrective and penalty actions as needed.

   j. Insure safety and welfare of policemen.

8. SELF-IMPROVEMENT

   a. Recognize my shortcomings.

   b. Improve my technical knowledge and skills.

   c. Improve my ability to get along with people.

   d. Develop a cooperative relationship with my workers, my superiors and other personnel.

   e. Develop a good attitude toward my job and the organization.

* * *

From the above it should be obvious that supervision and leadership is far more than shouting a series of unilateral, uncoordinated orders at the top of the voice and berating the employee if he steps out of line. Supervisory skill is not born in a person, although some have certain natural aptitudes for it, but it can and must be developed if one is to succeed in the directing the efforts of others. Therefore a practical man-to-man relationship between the leader and his group must be developed.

Essentially, the treatment of the subordinate justly and as an individual is required. Some practical self-examination questions to insure such treatment are:

1. Do I? Lead the way into a dangerous or difficult situation?

2. Write my reports properly and promptly?

3. Report to work on time and regularly?

4. Give the same respect to my superior, behind his back, as I expect from those I supervise?

5. Perform my job as a public service instead of building my individual records toward advancement?

These then, are some — not all — of the specifics involved in leadership. It is almost trite to say that the supervisor who does not exercise leadership is not a good supervisor, but trite or not, it is true.

PART II
*RESOURCES CONTROL
REGULATION OF THE MOVEMENT
OF PEOPLE AND GOODS*
CHAPTER V

GAINING SUPPORT FOR THE PROGRAM

A program of resources control involving passes for individuals, manifests for goods, checkpoints and searches is a defensive security measure with the purpose of restricting intelligence information and the movement of all kinds of supplies to the Viet Cong. It is no guarantee that the enemy's supply line will be cut completely, but history tells us, and this includes the recent experience in Malaya, where a guerrilla force was strangled out of existence. Many people who are now fighting with the Viet Cong would surrender if they knew their supplies of food, medicine and other necessities were being slowly but surely cut off. Obviously, to control the movement of supplies, the authorities must regulate the movement of people. Further, it has been well established that the Viet Cong has a courier service operating with messengers and intelligence agents traveling somewhat freely around the country. It is known, for example, that when the pressure on a Communist agent gets too heavy in an area, he will leave it and go to Saigon to hide. Hoodlums, gangsters, and subversive individuals for years have followed the patterns of hiding out for varying periods of time in big cities where they easily can be absorbed among the inhabitants of crowded sections. Thus, restriction of the movement of goods and the movement of persons is a simultaneous effort which can be carried out effectively under the same program using some of the same methods and procedures.

The resources control program should be administered through regular National Police channels, through the province down to the district level. The office of the district Police chief, in most cases, should be the lowest level of authority. Checkpoints should be operated directly out of this office. Centers for issuing passes, permission for change of residence, and manifests for travel in and out of restricted areas should be set up in district headquarters and police stationed in villages and hamlets should report directly to the district police chief, as they do even now. Delegation of authority to issue passes for travel should exist at the village and hamlet.

The remainder of this text will be devoted to an explanation of resources control methods which have been applied succesfully elsewhere and can be tailored to fit the specific needs of any revolutionary guerrilla warfare situation. This text, used as the basis for training courses for rural police throughout the country, will complement the strategic hamlet program and will contribute toward the goal of the Vietnamese and all free peoples who help her in her struggle against aggression: to establish and maintain security and a better life for all citizens.

A. INFORMING THE PEOPLE

Together with the training of police in the conduct of a resources and population control program should come a simultaneous effort to bring the program to the attention of the general public. Just as it is important for villagers and farmers to know what to expect in the building of a strategic hamlet or in a relocation program, so it is important that they be fully informed about any system to regulate their movement. It should be emphasized at all levels that there is nothing secret about this program; unlike a military operation, the element of surprise is not important, except for mobile checkpoints and patrols. The existence of a nationwide system of resources control, therefore, should not be regarded as security information. Instead, a real effort should be made to inform the population of what is going to be done and how.

No one who drives on the highway, whether he is a truck driver following his regular route or a father driving his family to the city, likes to be stopped at checkpoints. No driver likes to have his vehicle searched and to have his person searched is an even greater indignity. Such inspections are frightening experiences to persons who do not understand the system. They feel suspicion is centering on them for some reason, that they have been singled out as suspects. People do not want to be bothered with getting passes whenever they leave their hamlet, their village or their district; truck and bus drivers are not pleased at being burdened with the extra duties involved in preparing manifests of goods and passengers. These methods — checks, searches, passes — are tolerated only in situations of national emergency in which they are necessary to combat the enemy. Viet Nam today is in the midst of such an emergency. Experienced individuals believe that a system of resources and population control can cut supply routes to the enemy and that this, along with other internal security measures conducted by military and civilian security forces, will curtail the enemy's effort and lead to the downfall of the Communists in South Viet Nam.

The fact remains, however, that a system of checkpoints and passes is highly objectionable to the average citizen, even under the best of circumstances. Recognizing this problem, the program must be administered with scrupulous regard for the rights of the people and for their dignity, or it will become an intolerable expansion of authority and defeat its own purpose. Certain rights, jealously guarded in ordinary times, are abrogated in a national emergency. Police are given extended authority to restrict travel and make searches. Only if the need for a system of controlling the movement of human and material resources is understood and if a full statement of the extent and method of regulation is widely disseminated, can the Police expect support and cooperation from the general public. Thus, the Police should seek the assistance of provincial, district and village Information Service cadres in developing a plan to inform the people.

B. THE PUBLIC SERVANT IMAGE

The conception of himself as a servant of the people and not their director or overseer should be instilled in every Government employee, and most certainly in each member of the National Police. True, the Police officer issues orders to the people but he does it because the people have, in effect, hired him to help administer the laws of the Republic and to aid in the protection of their persons, property and nation. When an unpopular operation, such as resources control, is being instituted, the Police at all levels should be given some special instruction in public relations and the continuing necessity for simple courtesy in contacts with the public.

The vast majority of people who will pass through checkpoints will be good, honest citizens who have nothing to hide. Their impression of the Police is particularly important when one remembers that large numbers will be stopped and checked and the Police, therefore, will be in direct daily contact with a substantial portion of the population on not entirely pleasant matters.

Officers who are assigned the duty of manning checkpoints and conducting searches sometimes undergo personality changes. They often become domineering, surly or just plain mean. It is essential to impress upon all officers that they must be firm but polite at all times. The same thing is true of the individuals who operate control centers issuing passes or permits for the transportation of goods. A control center must be operated just as any other public service. If a man wants to send a telegram and it violates no law, such as that forbidding the transmission of obscene material, he has a right to send it and no postal employee has a right to stop him. So, an employee in a control center must issue a pass without delay to an individual who wants to go from Qui Nhon to Hue, for example, unless he has good reason for not issuing it, mainly the knowledge or suspicion that the person is not who or what he pretends to be or that he is going to violate regulations. The Police officer is paid by the public to issue passes and manifests for goods to all citizens who apply for them and who are entitled to receive them. He is required to do so and must not act as though he is granting a man a personal favor by giving him movement authorization.

Bribery or corruption on the part of individual policemen working in a resources control program must be dealt with immediately and severely. There have been instances, for example, of Police selling lottery tickets at certain already existing checkpoints; the people passing through have felt pressure to buy them. Checkpoint officers, of course, should not be allowed to sell these tickets in the first place but, to make matters worse, they often sold worthless ones from the previous week's lottery. This sort of behavior, along with acceptance of bribes and intimidation of the public, must not be tolerated.

With the institution of a system of resources and population control, many people will be in direct contact with public servants for the first time because the control measures will affect the general public as the work of the police and the office of the district chief never have before. The average citizen is not accustomed to dealing with police officials unless he is in trouble or is the victim of a crime; under this system millions of people will come into direct and intimate contact with law enforcement officials for the first time. They will include airline pilots, railroad engineers and conductors, boat captains, truck and bus drivers and the passengers and workmen associated with all of these forms of transportation. They will include all bicyclists and vehicle drivers and the passengers in every automobile driving on every highway in Viet Nam. Kind, courteous treatment will make friends for the Government; high handed, arbitrary and discourteous treatment not only will not make friends but will lose those it already has.

C. METHODS OF NOTIFICATION

In a country where there is no well established mass media communications system, various methods have to be devised to get information out to people at all levels. In a resources control program, it is necessary to see that the people are told what is expected of them, what the program will do for them and what their rights, privileges or loss of privileges will be under it. From their work in the National Identification Card program, many members of the National Police already are familiar with notification measures.

The past year, however, has seen a great increase in local information facilities in Viet Nam and more are being installed now or planned for the near future. Three principal local information systems, operating out of provincial and district information services, are in operation. They are:

1. The mobile information unit. In the past, these units have been jeep station wagons equipped with projection equipment and loudspeakers which have operated out of provincial capitals. Some 50 of them are currently in use. But within the past year, 124 tri-Lambretta's with generators, film projection equipment, a public address system, tape recorders and transistor radios — all the equipment

contained in the bigger provincial unit — have been distributed to district information offices and 130 more are expected to be made available this year. This will be enough to serve all areas where security permits. These units can distribute informational leaflets and posters as well as perform their usual function of showing films and setting up listening centers for special radio broadcasts or tape recorded programs.

2. The district newspaper. Two hundred district information services now have equipment and cadres trained to produce local newspapers. These papers, usually four-page mimeographed sheets, reprint news programs carried over the radio but their main function is intended to be one of gathering and publishing local news. The papers are distributed to civic groups such as Cong Hoa Youth and the Women's Solidarity Movement, to inter-family groups in strategic hamlets (lien gia) whose members are supposed to form into reading groups and, of course, are available in all Vietnamese Information Service (VIS) reading rooms. The information cadre who runs the operation, from gathering the news to delivering the papers, has received training in Saigon for his job and has been equipped with a radio (on which he listens to news broadcasts), a typewriter, a mimeograph machine and a motorbike. Some publish nearly every day, others may be able to print a paper only three times a week.

3. Community Listening Centers. Some 1,700 strategic hamlets now have battery operated, transistorized radio receiving sets with loud speakers. They also have tape recorders. In addition, 10,000 small, table model transistor radios are being supplied to hamlet councils intended for the use of small groups, perhaps 15 or 20 people. The first type is set up in market places, or some central spot in a hamlet where people can gather and listen. In some compact hamlets the radio or tape recorder can be heard from any point in town. In the Delta, where dwellings are widely dispersed or follow along a canal for a long distance, the table model set is more useful. Here people are brought together in small groups to listen to news and other programs.

These local news services provide the ideal means of disseminating information on the resources control program. General stories can be broadcast over Radio Viet Nam in Saigon. Regional stations can carry the same items but with additional information pertaining to the station's listening centers and on the tri-Lambretta units. A documentary film should be made and shown throughout the country. The sign boards on the sides of the tri-Lambretta's and Jeep mobile units can be made up with posters on resources control — a good way of depicting graphically what the public can expect from the program. Leaflets can be distributed by the mobile units and posted on community bulletin boards set up in strategic hamlets and villages.

The Montagnard peoples present a more difficult problem in communication. There are a multitude of tribal languages in South Viet Nam and even if written information could be prepared in all the dialects, the majority of the tribesmen would not be able to read it. Two methods seem to stand out as the best way of disseminating information to Highland peoples : (a) through administrative channels from the province chief's office through the district, to the village, to the hamlet, and finally to the individual tribes and family groups, and (b) through mass meetings at which all the inhabitants of a hamlet will gather to hear the program explained to them in their own language. Special efforts must be made to see that these people understand the major points in a resources control system, principally how it will help them and what they must do to make it work.

Different problems and facilities exist in different areas; a much better information job will be done if the Police and the Information Directorate cooperate closely and its provincial and district employees.

D. LEGAL RIGHTS OF THE PUBLIC AND THE POLICE

«The principle set forth in article 9 of the Universal Declaration of Human Rights — «No one shall be subjected to arbitrary arrest, detention or exile» — is no novelty in Viet Nam.[1] The laws embodying this principle are constantly and strictly enforced. This goes to show the evolution of Viet Nam society, the respect paid to the human person, and the sovereignty of the law in Viet Nam.

Arbitrary Arrest

Article 341 et seq of the Viet Nam Penal Code lay down correctional penalties for any private individual arresting any other person without orders from the lawful authorities, except in such cases as are authorized by law.

(a) If the person arrested, placed under illegal restraint or detained is set free before ten full days have elapsed since the day of such arrest, illegal restraint or detention, the guilty party is liable to imprisonment for six months to two years, with a fine of 50 to 1,000 piasters, and in certain cases from five to ten years local banishment.

(b) If the loss of liberty has lasted not more than one month, the guilty party is liable to imprisonment for one to three years with a fine of 100 to 1,500 piasters.

(c) If the detention or illegal restraint has lasted more than a month, the guilty party is liable to imprisonment for one to five years and a fine of 500 to 3,000 piasters.

(d) If the arrest was made in a false uniform or under a false name or on a spurious order from the public authorities, or if it was accompanied by the threat to kill, the penalty may be raised to twice the penalty laid down for the cases mentioned above.

(e) If the persons arrested, detained or held under illegal restraint were subjected to physical torture, the guilty party is liable to hard labor for life.

---
[1] «Note on Protection against Arbitrary Arrest, Detention or Exile», forwarded on 11 May 1956. Freedom from Arbitrary Arrest and Exile. Yearbook on Human Rights, United Nations, New York, 1959.

(f) Anyone providing a place where a person may be held under illegal restraint is liable to imprisonment for one to three years and a fine of 100 to 1,500 piasters.

Arbitrary Arrest or Detention by Officials or Agents of the Administration

An official or agent guilty of arbitrary arrest or detention is liable to forfeiture of civil rights. The injured party may claim damages either during the criminal proceedings or by a civil action, the amount of such damages not to be less than twenty-five piasters for each day of detention.

Arbitrary Detention by Prison Warders

Prison warders who take a prisoner into custody without a warrant or judgement or government order (in cases of expulsion or extradition) are liable to imprisonment for six months to two years and a fine of 16 to 200 piasters (article 120 of the Penal Code).

The same penalty applies to prison warders who keep a person illegally in prison or refuse to hand him over to the police officer or to the bearer of a court or Government order.

Detention of Persons In Places Other Than Those Specified in the Regulations

Magistrates or public officials who detain or cause to be detained any person in a place not intended by the Government or the Administration for that purpose, are liable to forfeiture of civil rights.»

Viet Nam Penal Code Provisions

Such duties as required by judicial police investigation also have individual rights protected. The following are pertinent excerpts from the Penal Code.[2]

Duties of The Judiciary Police.

439. — They may generally consist of three following kinds:

1. Receive reports, denunciation, complaints relative to offenses whether petty, minor or criminal.

2. Make investigations and entries concerning offenses: find and record all details to reveal the truth, centered generally around the following points:

— Who is the offender? (QUIS)
— What offense? (QUID)
— Where is it committed? (UBI)
— When? (QUANDO)
— How? (QUOMODO)
— With what means? (QUIBUS AUXILIIS)
— For what reason? (CUR)

In other words, discover all the circumstances relative to space, time, manner, origin... of the offense.

440. — 3. Transmit those documents and witnesses to the competent Public Prosecutor (he may take action or not).

Whenever they receive complaints or denunciations, the judiciary police officers should transmit them to the competent Public Prosecutor who examines the complaint and requests them to conduct investigations. But in

---

(2) «Handbook of Criminal Law» by Dam Trung Moc, lecturer, National Police Training Center, Saigon, 1961; Title II, Sec. 4, Pars. 439-448.

practice, to speed up the repression of malefactors, and avoid losing time, the police judiciary officers immediately start investigation, and once this has been done, transmit at the same time the entries and complaints and denunciations to the Public Prosecutor.

It is on this account (gain of time) that entries must be made 24 hours after recognizing the offense. In practice, however, the Public Prosecutor would give more time to the Judiciary Police, provided there are good reasons.

441. — All those activities make up what is named semi-official investigation, which aims at assisting the Public Prosecutor by giving him an idea of the offence in order to decide whether to bring action or not. Because of the semi-official character of the investigation, the judiciary police officials may not force the parties or the witnesses, may not apprehend people or take them into custody (except in case of flagrant delicto); search of houses, seizure... must be agreed upon by the owner.

442. — Investigation is official only when it is conducted by the examining magistrate, but if the judiciary police official is handed over to the magistrate's competence, his investigation will then become official, since he has almost the same powers as the other magistrate; so whenever the judiciary police official foresees hindrances, he reports to the Public Prosecutor who then brings the action before the Examining Magistrate. The latter then hands his powers to the Judiciary Police official who has from then on all the authority required and means for action.

Addendum. — House search. Arrest.

1. House search.

443. — Who has the right to search a house? In principle, only the examining magistrate has the right to search a house and seize pieces of evidence, whether the house belongs to the offender, a third person or a public office.

The public prosecutor and the judiciary police officers may only search someone's premises in special cases, as in the following:

— flagrant delicto in crimes,

— requested by someone, whether for minor or criminal offenses,

— delegation of powers by the examining magistrate. The owner must witness the search. If he is out, two neighbors must witness and sign the entry with the official.

444. — Time for search.

House search may be done during the day (from 6:00 a.m. to 6:00 p.m.). By night, no officer of the judiciary police may enter a private house, except in the following cases:

— flagrant delicto,

— the owner assents to it,

— the search began at the lawful time, but it must go beyond the time fixed,

— at places open to the public (tea-shop, inns, theatres...) as long as they remain open, search may be carried out,

— gambling-dens, bawdy-houses.

(Order 115, B. SG 1949.)

2. Arrests.

445. — Principle: only the examining magistrate may order arrest. Assistants (judiciary police) of the Public Prosecutor may only make arrests:

— if ordered by the examining magistrate,

— in case of flagrant delicto.

In practice, arrest must sometimes be made immediately, without waiting for the order of the examining magistrate. In case of an offense which has just been denounced to the judiciary police and the offender is about to escape. If he is not apprehended immediately, punishment will lose its effect (no flagrant delicto here).

In such cases, justified by lawful reasons, the judiciary police are generally authorized to make arrests and bring the guilty party to the magistrate, or report to him after the arrest.

446. — What is flagrant delicto?

The offense is being committed, or has just been: a pickpocket is caught red-handed, with his hand thrust into the pocket of someone, a murderer has just killed someone, and is still on the spot...

The offender is being pursued by people shouting his arrest, the place of offense is not yet known, but people are pursuing the offender and shouting «stop».

The offender is still holding the piece of evidence-a fire-arm is still hidden about him.

447. — In a flagrant delicto case, the Judiciary police have all the required powers to take all necessary steps for investigation:

— Record statement of denouncer;

— Search the premises;

— Seize pieces of evidence (or have them watched over);

— Question witnesses;

— Summon experts (doctors, finger-print);

— Order search for co-offenders, accomplices...

They make entries for each item, gather them in a file to be transmitted to the Prosecuting Department. The affair must immediately be reported to the Public Prosecutor, especially if it is a crime, or if it comprises some interesting points.

448. — All the principles concerning house search or detainment are dealt with by a joint communique of the Ministries of Interior and of Justice; # 3845 BNV/VPTC/M, 13-5-1959 reminding the main points. The communique also deals with the question of «exhibit»:

1. Precious pieces (diamond, silver or gold...) must be carefully kept. When handed in by the Police, they must be checked by the Clerk, entry must be made and signed by both Police officers and the Clerk.

2. Perishable pieces (food, cement...) are put in the care of offenders (if they are reliable), if not, they are sold by auction, proceeds of the sale are deposited in Clerical Department.

3. Cumbersome pieces, liable to deterioration (cars, etc...) are sold if owners agree, the sale price is deposited in the Clerical Office — if owners protest, the Security Service will look for a place to park it (inexpensive cost).

Chapter VI
PASSES AND MANIFESTS

Although a portion of the Viet Cong's food requirements is obtained by cultivation of crops in the jungle or in areas under his control, much of his food and other needs — clothing, medicine, munitions, intelligence, propaganda materials, and money — must come from his supporters in towns, villages and other centers of population. Communication among individual Viet Cong and constant contact with town and country people are enemy capabilities which must be controlled. One way to deprive the communists of logistical and communication support is to establish controls over the movement of certain *restricted goods* and spread a network of *restricted areas,* characterized by strategic hamlet gate checks, travel passes for vehicles and persons, manifests for goods, check points, searches, curfews and other means, across the country as needed to fulfill province and area requirements. These restrictions are for use in times of emergency and are not meant to be normal peacetime operations. They are burdensome in nature and the quicker the situation can be restored to normal the better for everyone.

To prevent the emergency restrictions from developing into a permanent control system which would oppress the population more than protect it, it is desireable that national legislation be put into effect which would authorize province chiefs to establish restrictions for specific periods of time but not longer than 90 calendar days. At the end of the 90-day period, each chief would review and, if necessary, renew the controls. If the situation had changed, the system of restrictions could be eliminated from some or all areas of a province, or modified in some or all areas. A restricted area might cover an entire province or only designated portions of it.

The legislation also should provide competent officials — the Police and the Military — with the legal authority to implement a resources control system. The appropriate official, for example, should have specific authority to stop vehicles and, upon suspicion, search them. He should be able to search any premises where he has reason to believe contraband is hidden. He should have the authority to detain persons who are suspected of carrying contraband and to detain restricted goods which he believes are being illegally transported. The law also should place certain responsibilities on the drivers of vehicles so that they do not deviate from their stated route or unload goods at any spot except the destination designated on their travel manifest. In addition, a province chief should be given fairly broad authority to determine what crops may be grown in certain areas and to prohibit itinerant vendors from setting up shop outside legally constituted villages or hamlets. He also should be authorized to set a curfew in restricted areas for any or all of the travel over which he has control.

The temporary nature of the emergency restrictions would serve as a democratic restraint on a control system which must not be allowed to develop beyond the purposes for which it is created. A sample statute, which appears at the end of this book as Appendix B, suggests what points must be covered in any national legislation governing resources control.

A. RESTRICTED GOODS — WHAT DO WE WANT TO CONTROL?

A restricted article is difficult to define because it can be almost anything that the enemy can eat, wear, sleep in or put to good use for any purpose whatsoever. However, the government has authority to list, and prohibit in entirety or in certain quantity, critical items as contraband. In order to arrest and prosecute persons for carrying contraband, the statute should be drawn so that a Police officer only has to have evidence that the goods in question could be useful to an enemy guerrilla outfit and that the person in whose possession the goods are found has no legitimate reason to have them or the goods themselves, or certain quantities thereof are illegal in themselves. The emergency legislation should provide a legal framework within which persons found carrying contraband can be tried before a legally constituted court with due consideration for their rights. The National Police, along with all the other agencies of the Vietnamese Government, is fighting for a system of free democracy and officers must not treat their prisoners as totalitarian dictators do, sending them to prison without trial or executing them as the result of a kangaroo court decision. Some time was devoted in Chapter IV of this text to the idea of winning the political battle as well as the military one, winning the minds of the people and convincing them that the Government's policies are dictated by the needs and desires of all the people. All efforts in that direction will be undermined and destroyed if illegal methods are used in arrests and imprisonment.

The legislation must have provisions within it for the transportation of normal amounts and kinds of goods with minimum interference. The controls are in no wise intended to stop the legitimate movement of people and materials.

Heading the categories of restricted goods are food items. The movement of animals, alive or dead, which are used for food must be strictly controlled. The same applies to feed for animals and to all other food products which are fit for human consumption.

The Viet Cong has a desperate need for drugs and medicines of all types. The relatively isolated Ben San leprosarium in the Phuoc Thanh province has been attacked and looted of drugs several times in the past two or three years. The last time, a priest and three nuns were kidnapped and when the Viet Cong agreed to give the priest an injection of the drug he needs, the nuns saw that their captors were using syringes which had been stolen from the leprosarium in an earlier raid. The drug too, may have come from Ben San but there were no identifying marks. Mobile health units often are attacked for their drugs, health workers are kidnapped and any isolated hospital is subject to raids. Drug shipments and storage are subject to tampering. When men are being wounded every day in a guerrilla war, and where jungle bases are operated under fatiguing and unhealthy conditions leading to sickness, medicine becomes as important a commodity as food.

Nearly every time a guerrilla headquarters or hideout of any size is captured, mimeograph or hand printing materials are found. The Viet Cong regards his propaganda output as one of his most effective weapons and this means he must have at least rudimentary reproduction equipment, if not an actual printing press, as well as paper and ink. Printing materials of all types are included on the list of restricted goods.

The flashlight is an important item to the Viet Cong. While it is perfectly normal for a person to carry a flashlight in his car or truck, a dozen flashlights or even a half dozen would arouse real suspicion. Storage batteries such as those used in cars and trucks also are restricted items. The enemy needs these to operate his communications system and there is a serious shortage of them. Naturally, the normal batteries used in a car or truck are not questionable items.

Any type of communications sending equipment is suspect. Regularly installed radio receivers in automobiles are common these days. But a car carrying several receiving sets should be investigated unless the sets are properly listed on a manifest.

All sorts of sturdy textiles as well as plastic and rubberized material which can be used for shelter in the jungle should be on the restricted list as should green and khaki cloth for clothing. If a driver passing through a checkpoint is found to have four suitcases packed with khaki cloth and no travel manifest for it, the policeman should investigate further. Many people in Viet Nam now wear khaki clothing and only what would be considered to exceed a normal amount for a particular person should arouse suspicion.

Undeclared and unlicensed firearms, of course, must be investigated immediately. A hunter with a proper permit would not necessarily be suspect and neither would someone carrying shotguns, revolvers and perhaps even a submachine gun if the duties of his job give him a legitimate reason for doing so.

A normal fuel supply for one person might not be normal for another. Many drivers, in addition to the contents of their regular gas tank, carry 10, 20 or 25 liters of gasoline as a reserve supply. This practice is not uncommon anywhere but it is especially appropriate to countries where one does not find service and fueling stations every few miles. A farmer who owns a tractor might go to a town once a week to buy fuel for use on his farm. He may buy as much as 100 or 150 liters at a time. The Police in the area would most likely know such a man and the size of his farm and whether he really is operating tractors. If they believed he was buying too much gasoline for his needs, the matter should be investigated.

Electric generators are highly useful to the Viet Cong for their communications systems, camp lighting and anything else for which power is needed. Again, it should be remembered that possession of an extra generator in a vehicle does not mean it is destined for the Viet Cong. There are many thousands of portable generators in villages, hamlets and even on scattered farms where no public power supply is available. If a man were found to have purchased a generator to install in his small shop in a village, this would not necessarily be of interest, but if the same man buys another generator a week later, the Police should look into the matter.

B. ESTABLISHING A CONTROL CENTER

To regulate the movement of people and materials, a logical system of passes and *shipping manifests* must be established to show what is being moved as well who is traveling where and for what reason. The visiting and business travel permission involving personal effects may well be decentralized to the strategic hamlet, quarter or city precinct. The control center, where people must go to fill out the necessary official forms and be issued movement passes and manifests enabling them to move from place to place legally and to transport authorized goods, is the heart of this operation. It would be established in the district chief town, probably at the district headquarters for the convenience of the public. In larger urban areas, such as Saigon-Cholon, Hue and Da Nang, control centers might be set up in Police precinct stations. The inconvennience caused those people whose point of origin and/or destination is not a district town is unfortunate. Perhaps, however, it will not be overwhelming because most traffic which is moving any distance is likely to start from and stop at least at district towns. The hamlet Security Office location for individual travel passes should present no special problem; probably the time of the Councilmen may become critical if he has a heavy personnel employment schedule.

1. *Office Layout and Procedures*

Planning the physical layout of a center for efficient service is extremely important. No standard plan can be developed because the set-up in each center will depend on location and availability of space. But one thing every control center ought to have is a big bulletin board prominently displayed on the wall with six or seven sentences in plain, simple language, enumerating points in the procedure the applicant is to go through. Any changes in rules should be reflected on this bulletin board. It might carry slogans about the resources control program which are changed periodically. In general, it has been found that receiving applications and issuing passes and permits on a mass basis is best handled by a continuous flow type of operation similar to the one used by the National Identification Card processing teams. This means the office should have an entrance on one side and an exit across the room so there is a minimum of movement back and forth. Center personnel should be organized in such a way that when a member of the public comes in, he stops at the first station, then moves directly down the line to eventually pick up his permit and leave by the exit. (See example of Bulletin Board on page 67).

The first step in the procedure will be the filling out of certain forms depending, of course, on what sort of a permit the person wants. Thus, it would be logical to have a stand or table with the necessary forms and instructions placed near the entrance. When the system first goes into effect, it would be wise to station someone at this point to answer questions and direct people where to go. Next, there should be a desk for an office staffer who fills out forms for people who cannot read and write. There must be counter space or tables off to the side where literate people can complete their own forms. The next staff member in line should be the person who examines identification cards and any supporting papers that are necessary. Here, the Communist suspect file normally would be found and all ID Cards checked against it. This inspection procedure should not take more than one minute per person unless something is wrong. Provision should be made for another section in the control center, if possible a separate room, where people whose papers are not in order or who are suspect for one reason or another are sent for further questioning and investigation. To attempt to question them in the regular line would embarrass the person, perhaps unnecessarily, and hold up the flow of traffic. There should be one station with a separate staff member to handle trucks. A truck driver would complete his shipping manifest and give it to the official who then personally inspects the truck to see that it is loaded according to the manifest. In a district headquarters station, where a large volume of truck traffic as well as automobile traffic must be handled, it would be necessary to divide the operation pretty much in two — one part dealing with bulk goods and the other with people accompanying shipments — so that the driver of a truck loaded with produce destined for Saigon does not keep waiting for interminable periods of time for five or six people who simply need a baggage pass to carry a hamper of ducks to a family reunion.

The final desk or section necessary to a control center is that occupied by the senior official who reviews papers to see they are in order and approves issuance of the pass or permit which will send the traveler on his way.

2. *The Public View*

There may be many variations in individual control centers but personnel must always bear in mind that their offices are supposed to serve the public as fast and efficiently as possible and that they should constantly seek ways to streamline the system. All of the public considerations outline in Chapter IV, «Gaining Support for the Program», should be applied in the operation of a control center. People must know what is expected of them and, in turn, what they have a right to expect from the Police authorities. Villagers and rural people who are not accustomed to contacts with officialdom often are shy and apparently very patient. However, the most patient person in the world will eventually become disgruntled and angry if he has to spend long periods standing in lines waiting for attention.

The control center office should be clean and well lighted. This is important because the public receives its first impression of the operation from the physical appearance of the office. If it is dirty and poorly run, people have contempt for the officials in charge, if not for the whole program. If the office is clean and pleasant and people are handled efficiently and politely, they will feel some satisfaction and probably even accept the rather rigorous control measures being imposed on them with a better than usual spirit.

It is a good idea to employ some women in control centers for two reasons. One is that Police manpower requirements are becoming more and more difficult to fill and the more jobs which can be turned over to women, the better. Women are certainly every bit as suited as men to control center jobs, if not more so. Another reason why women should be considered for these positions is that most of the people seeking passes and permits will be men and they usually react more favorably to being served by a pleasant young woman than by another man, providing of course, that the woman knows her job and carries it out efficiently, fairly and courteously.

3. *The Suspect File*

The National Police propose to develop, through the Criminal Bulletin Section of the National Records Bureau, a file of Communists and criminal suspects on a nationwide basis. It will consist of 7.5×12.5 cm (3"×5") index cards prepared at the Central Archives in the Criminal Bulletin Section. These cards will be distributed to all provincial and district police headquarters throughout the country and to all major transportation terminals. They will bear a photograph, if possible; one of the index fingerprints just as on the National Identification Card; the fingerprint classification and the name and curriculum vitae of the individual.

C. PREPARATION OF PASSES AND MANIFESTS

There are several fairly standard types of documents in a system of passes and manifests with variations according to need. They are: (1) the shipping manifest which is a control sheet to determine the validity or legitimacy of the movement of relatively large quantities of goods in trucks; (2) the non-commercial travel permit for individuals who want to travel themselves or who want to transport privately a single item or a few items, or carry one or more passengers; (3) the commercial travel manifest to be used by all common carries to list passengers, and (4) the local travel pass or 90-day pass for small three or four-wheel commercial vehicles; (5) the individual travel pass for travelers not transporting material other than their own effects.

1. *The Shipping Manifest*

Generally, the Shipping Manifest (see Ill. 6, pages 56 and 57) should be prepared in three copies — one to be given to the driver of the vehicle, one to be forwarded to the destination of the goods being shipped, and one to be retained in the files of the issuing office for future reference and possible investigation.

The driver of a truck carries his manifest with him and his passage through each checkpoint enroute to his destination is noted on the document. If he reaches one post and police see that his manifest bears no proper signature or notation from the previous one, an immediate investigation must be conducted to find out whether the driver by-passed the checkpoint and, if so, why. Arriving at his destination, the driver goes to the control center in the district town where he turns his manifest over to the appropriate police official, who checks it against the load itself and, if all is in order, releases the goods for delivery. Here too, the manifest is entered into the travel register. The latter is a means of keeping track of all movement in and out of the control center (see Ill. 7, following). The form, if properly maintained, will be most useful as a centralized system of information for investigative purposes. If a case needs to be followed up, the travel register in the control center should provide a starting point for the investigation.

If the truck's destination is not a district town and there is no appropriate Police authority at the destination, the driver must go first to the control center in the district town for clearance before he can deliver his goods to villages, hamlets or individuals within the district. Investigators also will be employed in each district control center to check on actual delivery of goods. Their existence and the scope of their activities should be widely publicized so that drivers who may be tempted to help the enemy, if they could do so with impunity, will know they are subject to checks even after being cleared through a control center. When a shipping manifest is received at the control center of destination from the control center of origin, it is checked against the travel registry to see that the truck actually arrived. If it did not arrive at all, an investigation is begun to find out what happened to the load. Breakdowns and delays must be expected and taken into consideration. This copy is also compared with the manifest delivered by the driver and any unexplained contradictions or discrepancies checked into.

An examination of the shipping manifest, front, shows a blank to be completed with Number and Symbol (see Ill. 6). This means that each control center should adopt a symbol and institute a consecutive numbering system for its shipping manifests. The

Original

Duplicate

Triplicate

SHIPPING MANIFEST
(front)

Number and Symbol _____

Consigned to : _____

Address : _____

Consignor's Name : _____

Address : _____

Driver's Name : _____

Address : _____

Helper's Name : _____ ID No. : _____

Address : _____ ID No. : _____

Time of Departure and Date : _____

Estimated Time of Arrival and Date : _____

LOAD :

No AND ITEM	CONTENTS
16 Crates	Lettuce
16 Crates	Carrots
24 Sacks	Potatoes
1 each	50 KW portable generator, "Alumage Magnifique", No. A-43827
55 ltres	Gasoline

Certified as Correct - Name : _____

Title : _____

Ill. 6. *Shipping Manifest form suggested for production at Region or National Headquarters (front).*

SHIPPING MANIFEST

(reverse)

CHECKPOINTS :

LOCATION AND NAME OF OFFICIAL	DATE	TIME

Ultimate Destination Arrival : _____

Location : _____ Date : _____ Time : _____

Name : _____ Title : _____

Action Indicated : _____

Ill. 6. *reverse.*

TRAVEL REGISTER

| PERMIT No. and SYMBOL | DRIVER'S NAME | ID. No. | FROM | ARRIVED || PERMIT OF ORIGIN || ACTION INDICATED |
				DATE	TIME	DATE	TIME	

Ill. 7. *One sheet of the form for the Travel Register used to record Travel Manifests, as well as Commercial and Non-Commercial Travel Products; these could be produced at Province Headquarters.*

symbol and a new number should appear on every manifest. The form should include the name and address of the person to whom the shipment is going; the name and address of the sender; and the names, addresses and identification card numbers of the driver and helper. The estimated time of departure and the estimated time of arrival should be shown. The cargo is listed on the lower half of the manifest and certified by the control center official. The reverse side of the form has space for signatures of officials at every checkpoint passed enroute to the destination. The form is complete when the control center official at the destination certifies that the shipment has arrived and what action, if any, is indicated. In the interests of speed and efficiency, police officials should work with local trucking companies in the preparation of manifests. For example, if a truck is scheduled to leave on a certain day, the driver or company employee can come to the control center earlier in the day or the previous day to pick up the necessary forms. He can take them back to his place of business to fill out and when the driver comes to the center before leaving on his trip, the manifest will have been completed and all that remains to be done is to inspect the shipment and check the driver's and helper's identification. Police at the control center of destination should very carefully compare the contents of the truck as shown on the manifest delivered by the driver with those on the copy received from the originating control center. One method of evasion would be for the driver to make changes in the manifest after he has left the control center of origin. Naturally, the load itself also must be inspected carefully to see that all is in order.

In any system of passes and permits a good deal depends on the individual judgment of the control center supervisor. He will be influenced by a number of factors, but certainly a thorough knowledge of local conditions will help him more than anything else in his determinations. He would know, for example, that a ton of rice is a normal shipment into a certain village 50 kilometers from Nha Trang. He would also know that 10 tons of rice would greatly exceed the normal needs of this same village. He would know that an established truck line was conducting normal business if it shipped a load of fish to Saigon. He would know that a dozen generators shipped to the ABC Supply Company, a legitimate sales organization in Nha Trang, was perfectly in order. He would judge that 50 radio receivers sent from an import-export company in Saigon to the Vietnamese radio distributor in Can Tho is a legitimate shipment. This official will not always make the right decision; he probably with clear some trucks which seem all right but are not. These cases, of course, must be investigated and action taken against the offenders if they can be apprehended. The important point is that the district official in charge of the control center, very shortly after he assumes the duties of this position, should know pretty well who the regular truck suppliers are and which ones might be suspicious. Naturally, he should expedite clearances for the business people who are well known to him and reliable, and be suspicious of a newcomer in the area or someone who departs from normal activity.

2. *The Non-Commercial Travel Manifest*

The shipping manifest and the non-commercial travel manifest are prepared and handled in an identical fashion. The latter is the form used to regulate the movement of small amounts of goods and of people accompanying goods traveling in cars or other small privately-owned vehicles on the highways and in small boats on rivers and canals (see Ill. 8 pages 61 and 62). It will be the third major document, along with the shipping manifest and individual travel pass, used in the system of passes and manifests and to keep legitimate traffic moving quickly and efficiently. It should not be handled in the same operation, or by the same persons as the shipping manifest, at least not in a busy control center. This is the form that every person accompanying goods and every individual boat, car, motorbike or small private station wagon or bus will use when traveling into, out of, or from district to district within a restricted area. Small private vehicles, of course, must be inspected with as much or more care than large commercial trucks before permits are issued. Small buses or station wagons used for commercial purposes, but whose routes cover several districts or provinces, might be covered either by this form or by the commercial travel manifest. Private travel by individuals within a district probably can be left unregulated, except as controlled by individual strategic hamlet councilmen by the individual travel pass.

3. *The Commercial Travel Manifest*

Shipping manifests and individual travel passes cover the movement of goods in cars or trucks on the highways and in small privately operated boats on canals. But for passengers and cargoes on common carries such as buses, trains, larger boats and airplanes, a different system and a different form — the commercial travel manifest (see Ill. 9, following) — should be used. This form concerns passengers only; manifests controlling shipment of goods on common carriers have long been in use and are fully understood by the personnel concerned. Passenger lists, of course, have always been maintained by airlines, but the resources control system would extend this procedure to all other common carriers and add the requirement that competent authority must check identification cards and determine whether there is any reason why a person should not be allowed to travel. Since airlines, boat and bus companies, and railroads operate their own terminals and depots, a separate control center operation has to be set up to handle them.

Using the airline as the simplest example, since no one can get on or off a plane except at stops, the system might work something like this: A small control center operation, manned

Original

Duplicate **TRAVEL PERMIT — NON-COMMERCIAL**

Triplicate *(front)*

Number and Symbol _____

Driver's Name : _____ ID No. : _____

Passengers' Names :

1. _____ ID No. : _____

2. _____ ID No. : _____

3. _____ ID No. : _____

4. _____ ID No. : _____

5. _____ ID No. : _____

6. _____ ID No. : _____

Departure Time : _____ Date : _____

Estimated Arrival Time : _____ Date : _____

Restricted Articles :

_____

_____

_____

_____

Ultimate Destination Arrival : _____

Location : _____ Date : _____ Time : _____

Name : _____ Title : _____

Action Indicated :

Ill. 8. *Suggested form for Travel Permit — Non Commercial; these could be produced at Province Headquarters (front).*

TRAVEL PERMIT — NON-COMMERCIAL

(reverse)

CHECKPOINTS :

Location and Name of Official	Date	Time

Ill. 8. *reverse*.

ORIGINAL   VEHICLE TYPE ....
DUPLICATE   LICENSE NO. ....
TRIPLICATE

TRAVEL MANIFEST - COMMERCIAL

NAME	ID No.	DESTINATION	DEPARTURE	ARRIVAL	REMARKS

Ill. 9. *Suggested form for Travel Manifest — Commercial; these could be produced at Province Headquarters.*

by a member of the National Police, would be established at every airport in the country. Except for Saigon and possibly Hue and Da Nang, the centers would be one-man operations because the only concern is identity of the passengers — who are they, where are they from, and whether anything is wrong with them. The airport center's officer would be supplied with the communist suspect file and each passenger's ID card checked against it as he arrives at the airport and checks in for his flight. The officer also would need a copy of the airline's passenger manifest. Since the airline already prepares such forms for its own use, the Police can use them and need make up no special document of their own. The Police officer arranges for a desk and necessary facilities with airport officials. When a passenger arrives at his desk, the officer does three things: (1) inspects the ID card presented to him by the passenger to make sure it is accurate. He does not permit one person traveling with three or four others to handle the clearance for everyone in the party; each person must present his own ID card so that the picture on it can be compared with the person carrying it; (2) checks the passenger's name against the suspect file to see if there is any reason for suspicion. If there is, the person should be taken out of the line and held for investigation; (3) compares the ID card with the names on his copy of the flight manifest, making a notation or checkmark next to the passenger's name and then sending him on his way.

Commercial passenger-carrying boats and the railroads can be regulated in much the same way as airlines, with the transport people supplying copies of their manifests. If the trains or boat lines do not use passenger manifests, they must be requested to begin making them up. To gain the cooperation of transportation company officials, it is necessary to talk with them and explain what resources control involves; how it will help them, and what they will be asked to do. As with the general public, it is necessary to convince these businessmen that the program will be beneficial in the long run and that their cooperation is needed. Acceptance of bribes from businessmen must not be tolerated. Naturally, the same courtesy and fairness as discussed in regard to the district control center applies to the centers in transportation terminals. Here too, Police officers are public servants, and it is their duty to be courteous to passengers and see that they are handled as quickly as possible to reduce the time they have to wait in line.

It will be extremely difficult to control passengers on trains and buses, since they make many stops where no facilities for control exist. It will be necessary to fence in station areas to control the ingress and egress of passengers and to station the Police check-in and check-out desks at some sort of a gate or entrance. The cost of building such station enclosures will have to be considered in the planning process for the resources control program in each province. Major railroad terminals can set up special Police desks somewhere within their stations, perhaps at the gates leading to trains. Another difficulty is that people can jump off trains and buses as they slow down and escape into the countryside. It is the responsibility of the bus driver or train conductor to report such an action immediately to the nearest police authority. This sort of thing has occurred many times in the past in war situations and, while there can be no foolproof system of immobilizing the enemy, every effort that is made in that direction helps.

Buses present the greatest problem of all in the matter of commercial transportation. Many bus lines now prepare passenger manifests, but just as many do not. Most difficult of all to control are the passengers who board the bus after it has left one major terminal, ride for a short distance and get off before another terminal large enough to have a control center is reached. Much of the control will have to be exercised by the drivers and by the regular checkpoints through which buses, like all other highway vehicles, will have to pass. (See Chapter VIII on Checkpoints). Operators of bus lines and the drivers themselves will have to be thoroughly informed of the reasons for the extra work and responsibility that is being asked of them, and well trained in the handling of manifests. It will be up to a bus driver to check identification cards when passengers board his bus at points away from terminals; he will have to maintain his own manifest for each trip on which he lists each passenger's name, his boarding point and his destination. More than any other common carrier, the driver of the bus will be responsible for checking on the movement of persons. When a bus passes through a checkpoint, the identification cards of all the passengers normally will be checked against the manifests handed to the post's officers by the driver. Goods carried on buses usually will be considered as a passenger's baggage and will not be manifested separately.

Copies of the commercial travel manifest are handled in the same way as the shipping manifest — the original is given to the person responsible for the vehicle, the duplicate is sent by other means to the vehicle's destination and the triplicate stays at the originating terminal.

4. *The Local Pass*

There is one exception to the usual rules of the manifest system and that applies to the small three and four-wheel vehicled with a capacity of six passengers or less. The little three-wheel Lambretta bus is a common sight on Vietnam's highways, but it nearly always is a local means of transportation. While they qualify as commercial vehicles, these buses do not make long trips but rather are likely to come and go over the same route and pass the same checkpoints one or more times a day, engaging in strictly local activities. It isn't necessary to require a passenger manifest for each one of these trips and to do so would create too much of a hardship on the driver and passengers. Therefore, the local pass (see Ill. 10, following) can

Oirginal

Duplicate

LOCAL PASS

Number and Symbol ....

Driver's Name : .... ID No. : ....

Address : ....

Vehicle : .... License No. : ....

Authorized Routes : ....

....

....

Hours of Operation : ....

Dates of Validity : ....

....

....

Issuing Official : ....

Title : ....

Ill. 10. *Suggested form for a driver's Local Pass; may be produced at Province Headquarters.*

be issued to the driver by the control center of the district in which he operates. This pass would be valid for 90 days and would allow officials to know who is moving about on the local roads. At the end of every 90-day period, the driver would go to the control center himself for a new pass. Only two copies of this pass need be made — one to give the driver who should keep it with him at all times, and one to be kept at the control center.

5. *The Individual Travel Pass*

The individual making a trip and carrying his personal effects is the most usual type of traveler. If he is not moving produce or material he is expedited in his travel by receiving his pass from his local Security Councilman. This official approves the travel and issues the individual travel pass from a book of standard forms. The pass permits the holder of the recorded identification to go certain point or points and return. Coupled with the ID card, most travelers are thereby closed for visits to friends, family and business. The travel pass with the ID card is the basic unit for the commercial or common carrier (bus or boat) in making up the Commercial Travel Manifest (see Ill. 11, following).

CHAPTER VII

IDENTITY CARDS AND FAMILY REGISTRATION

A. THE NATIONAL IDENTITY CARD PROGRAM

The first Viet Nam national program for identification of the population was introduced in 1938. The identification document was a simple piece of paper with the required data printed on it. It had no protective covering and was easily defaced, quick-

Example of a Bulletin Board

RESOURCES CONTROL PROTECTS OUR PEOPLE
- *** Have your ID card ready.
- *** If you are carrying commercial goods, pick up Form No. ...... from Desk No. ......
- *** If your are carrying passengers and/or goods in private vehicle, pick up Form No. ......
- *** Each passenger must pick up Form No. ......
- *** List all goods and passengers carried in your vehicles.
- *** Go to Desk No. ...... and show inspecting officer your completed manifest.
- *** Go to Desk No. ...... to get your manifest approved and stamped.
- *** Make *NO* changes yourself in your manifest between here and your destination.
- *** Be sure to follow your stated route and have your manifest stamped at each checkpoint between here and your destination.
- *** In case of accident or any circumstances beyond your control, report to the nearest Police control center.

RICE FOR OUR FAMILIES AND FIGHTING MEN

NO RICE FOR THE ENEMY

NAME ID No. Hamlet Day Month Hours Effective Destination Approved Title	NAME ID No. Hamlet Day Month Hours Effective Destination Approved Title
NAME ID No. Hamlet Day Month Hours Effective Destination Approved Title	NAME ID No. Hamlet Day Month Hours Effective Destination Approved Title
NAME ID No. Hamlet Day Month Hours Effective Destination Approved Title	NAME ID No. Hamlet Day Month Hours Effective Destination Approved Title

Ill. 11. *Sheet of a booklet with detachable form for Individual Travel Pass; may be produced at Province Headquarters.*

ly worn out and counterfeited without much trouble. Further, separate and different identification documents were issued by the authorities in each of the regions of the country and they were not uniform in size, appearance and in the data required. They did, however, serve the useful purpose of making an initial identification of the country's people. See Ill. 12, pages 70 and 71 for the original card.

In 1957, the Government decided that a new and better type of positive identification was needed and legislation was passed requiring all persons over the age of 18, male and female, to get and carry an ID card. It also was decided that everyone should be fingerprinted with two fingerprints becoming a part of the ID card and a full set from each person going into the files of the Central Identification Bureau in Saigon. Relative peace existed in Viet Nam at this time and it was believed that a card made by a simple laminating process would serve the purpose (see Ill. 13, page 72). Shortly afterwards, however, Viet Cong violence was stepped up and at least one card was found which was known to have been forged. In addition, it was found that laborers who carried the cards in their trouser pockets perspired so heavily that the card and the plastic around it deteriorated rapidly. To improve the ID card, two things were done: (1) a new card was designed on the safety-type paper which is in use today, (see Ill. 14, page 73) and (2) the old adhesive or pressure-sensitive laminating process was replaced by a modern machine operation, (see Ill. 15, below).

Ill. 15. *Modern method of machine high pressure sealing and laminating as now used in the Vietnamese National Identification Card Program issued under National Police supervision.*

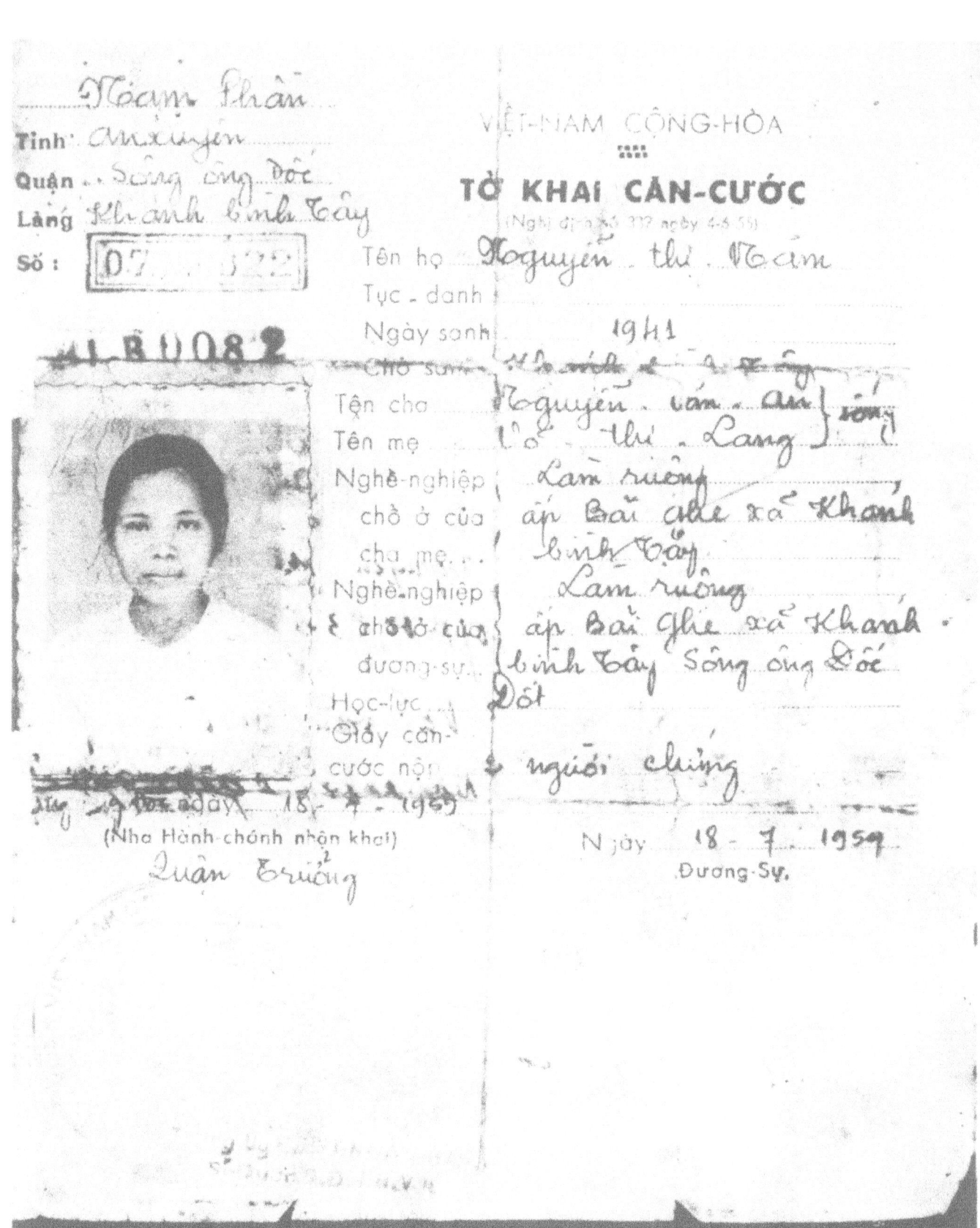

Ill. 12. *Sample of 1938 type identification document (front).*

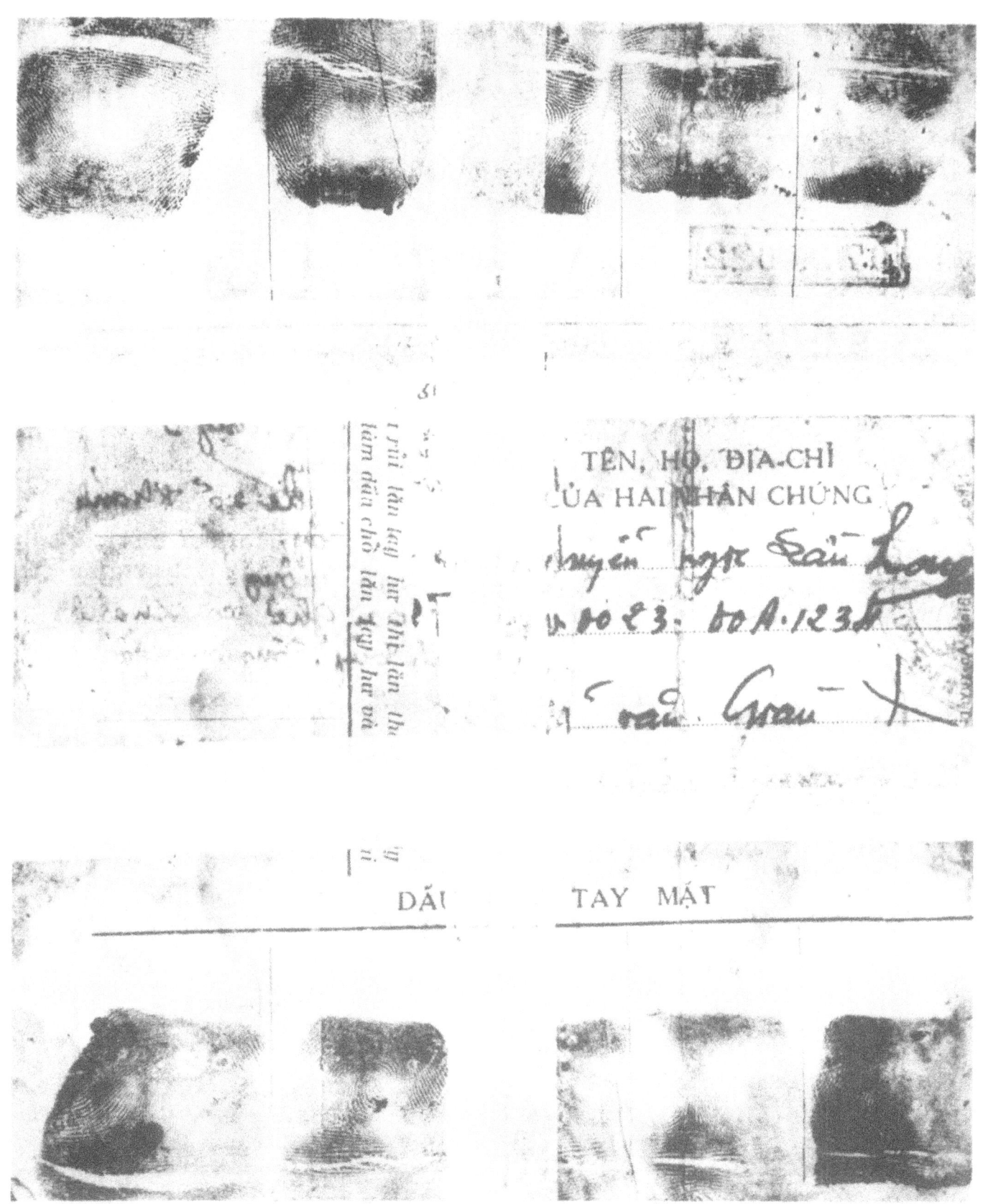

Ill. 12. *reverse.*

VIỆT-NAM CỘNG-HOÀ REPUBLIC OF VIETNAM	THẺ CĂN-CƯỚC 
	IDENTIFICATION CARD
BỘ NỘI-VỤ SỐ: No	
DEPARTMENT OF INTERIOR	

- Tên Họ .... **Names** ....
- Bí Danh .... **Aliases** ....
- Ngày năm sanh ..... **Date of birth** ....
- Nơi sanh ...... **Place of birth** ....
- Cha .... **Father** ....
- Mẹ .... **Mother** ....
- Nghề-nghiệp ..... **Profession** ....
- Địa-chỉ .... **Address** ....

Height: 1m
Bề cao: 1 th

Ngón trỏ trái / Left index

Ngón trỏ mặt / Right index

Dấu vết riêng

Distinctive marks:

Date   ngày ...... / ...... / 19 ......

Ill. 13. *Sample of 1957 type Identification Card (pressure adhesive plastic, non-safety paper); front and reverse views.*

Ill. 14. *Sample of 1961 type Identification Card (machine laminated plastic and safety paper); front and reverse views.*

The old type had its advantages in that it was cheap and required no machinery to laminate a card except an ordinary set of hand-operated rollers. But it was quickly learned that with a razor blade and a little practice, a person could easily split the two sheets of plastic apart and insert a new picture or change data on the card.

1. *Reactions of the Viet Cong*

That the Viet Cong well understands the threat to his freedom of movement and operations possible through an effective identification card program was demonstrated by his reactions to the new, improved identity card which came into being along with an efficient, countrywide system to process the population. One of the enemy's methods of attack was propaganda. The Viet Cong said, for example, that anyone who loses his ID card and is caught without it will be considered a draft dodger and sent to jail. He also complained that the ten piastres each person is charged for his card is a capitalistic method of gathering taxes from the people. Actually, through the American aid program, the United States government provided to Viet Nam free of charge all the cameras, lights and related equipment necessary to prepare the cards. The 10 piastres collected from each person by the Government of Viet Nam is just enough to cover photographic paper, chemicals, blank forms and salaries of the people who do the processing. One piece of propaganda, dated Oct. 10, 1962 and signed by the Liberation Front Committee in Ben Cat district, Binh Duong province, had this to say about the identity cards:

«They (the American and President Ngo Dinh Diem) say that they issue ID cards to the population but it is to get intelligence information about the popular revolutionary movement and collect money from the people in order to set up their domination of the people of the South.

«Our dear countrymen, we cannot let the Americans and Diem rule over us again as in 1959. Everybody, regardless of his religion, social class and tendency, has to combine his effort by all means to fight against the ID program and the concentration of the population into strategic hamlets.

«Soldiers, officers, civil servants in the Government of the South, for your own benefit, for your family, let us fight Americans, supporters of the war, and the cruel government which forces you to terrorize the population and forces your family carry plastic ID cards and to concentrate into strategic hamlets. Let us cooperate with the population to fight the ID program.»

The guerrillas employed action as well as words in their campaign against the identification program. Most people throughout the country, except in areas impossible to reach because the Viet Cong control them, have now been processed and received their cards. But during the period February 1962, to February 1963, when the big team processing campaign was underway, the enemy did such things as set up temporary roadblocks on the way into towns where the processing was underway. The guerrillas also stole cards and receipts in remote areas where Government protection was not always possible. In some instances, processing groups were physically attacked, grenades were thrown, ambushes laid. To counter these enemy attacks, the Government countered with a number of successful protective measures (see paragraphs following) endeavoring first of all to show the public the need for and benefits of an identification program and thereby gaining the people's support. A 20 minute documentary film was prepared to show in story form reasons why the program is necessary, what it is designed to do and how it works. This was shown in all motion pictures theatres in Viet Nam as a newsreel and mobile units projected the disseminating information. Leaflets, radio announcements, press, loud speaker and mobile units, all were used in the campaign to inform the public. There also was an effort to control and limit distribution of cards in areas where the situation was insecure or where the villagers were particularly pro-Viet Cong. This, of course, was a somewhat drastic measure but was only temporary and as such proved effective.

The resources control program, when operating effectively, will protect and expand the identity card program in restricted areas and, conversely, the identity card program will be a major factor in the regulation of movement throughout the country. Identification cards will be demanded at all checkpoints and before issuing any type of pass or permit for movement of goods. Such a demand is justified now that ID card processing is virtually complete for the whole country.

In one year during the emergency in Malaya, more than 55,000 cards were stolen. The government countered by restricting the movement of persons who had lost their cards and by increasing the cost of replacement in the belief that people would make a greater effort to hold onto their cards. In spite of the considerable losses, the Malayan government continued to issue the cards and continued to insist that people carry them. The program proved to be a valuable weapon in that country's fight against the Communists.

2. *Processing Methods*

During the peak of the ID card processing in Viet Nam, about 600,000 persons were handled every day. Just before a district or specific locality was to be processed, information and notices were disseminated by all available means. Generally, people were requested to come to a central registration place in a provincial or district capital where they were fingerprinted, photographed and their application forms reviewed. Everyone was given a receipt to carry until his new plastic card was ready. Naturally, it was not possible for everyone, especially those living in remote areas, to come into a province or district town to be processed. In fact, in some of Viet Nam's larger cities, it was not even practical to ask people to go from one side of the city to the other. In these cases, the Government went to the people in the form of mobile processing teams which could service one village or one fairly small region at a time.

After the pictures had been taken, fingerprints affixed to the ID cards and the cards signed, the teams sent the photos and cards to the central processing center in each provincial capital where they were put together and sent on to Saigon for laminating. Two pilot projects — the selection of one district, province or other specifically designated area to test a system or program — were carried out in Tay Ninh and Tuyen Duc. This is an important point to remember in police organization in strategic hamlets and checkpoints. A pilot operation will point up many problems and requirements which become obvious only in actual practice.

3. *Counterfeiting*

Anything that can be made can be copied. There is no such thing as a counterfeit-proof document of any kind, including money. The old ID cards, introduced in 1938, were easy to copy; anyone with the simplest printing equipment could do it. Hanoi, Peking or Moscow have the capability to counterfeit if they want to go to the trouble and expense. It would, however, be difficult and costly and in nearly every case in detectable.

To laminate the new cards, a small machine with two sets of platens or rollers was used. One set consists of heated platens between which the identification card with a sheet of clear plastic on each side is fed. The hot plastic strip then is passed through another set of rollers which imprint a raised design on one side of it. The card is hard to counterfeit because of: (1) the safety paper used; (2) the embossed design imprinted on one side of the plastic covering; (3) the plastic itself is different from most plastics and an expert examining it can readily spot the difference between it and another plastic, and (4) although the plastic can be split, it is bonded to the paper card inside so that if the two plastic sheets are pulled apart, the card itself also would be torn of in layers. This means the photograph and printing would adhere to the plastic just as printing adheres to a piece of gummed taped stuck over it and then pulled off.

B. THE FAMILY CENSUS PROGRAM

The Family Census currently underway in Viet Nam is an inventory of all families by housing unit, listing family members and the family's resources, noting the presence of Communist tendencies or affiliations, if any, and carrying the curriculum vitae of each person. When complete, the Family Census will provide a method by which authorities may make house to house checks, or a specific house check, and easily determine who is supposed to live in a certain house, something about him and, generally, where he is supposed to be at certain times of the day. Because all of this data requires several pages, especially in large families, the form used is actually a booklet and is called simply the Family Booklet (see Ill. 16, pages 77 and 78).

The National Police have an advantage in the implementation of the Family Census program which it did not have in putting the Identification

VIỆT NAM CỘNG HÒA
REPUBLIC OF VIETNAM

TỈNH .... PROVINCE
QUẬN .... DISTRICT
XÃ .... VILLAGE

ẤP .... HAMLET

KHÓM QUARTER	LIÊN GIA INTER-FAMILY GROUP	SỐ NHÀ HOUSE NUMBER

SỔ GIA ĐÌNH
FAMILY BOOKLET

HỌ, TÊN GIA TRƯỞNG ....
NAMES OF CHIEF OF FAMILY

...., NGÀY .... THÁNG .... NĂM 196....
DATE

GIA TRƯỞNG KÝ TÊN
SIGNATURE OF CHIEF OF FAMILY

KIẾN THỊ   KIẾN THỊ
CHECKED BY   CHECKED BY

LIÊN GIA TRƯỞNG   ẤP TRƯỞNG
CHIEF OF INTER-FAMILY GROUP   HAMLET CHIEF

	PHẦN DÀNH DI CHUYỂN GIA ĐÌNH RESERVED FOR TRANSFER OF FAMILY
TỚI Ở NGÀY .... ARRIVED ON	XIN DI CHUYỂN NGÀY .... TRANSFER REQUESTED ON
NHÂN SỐ .... NGƯỜI, NUMBER OF PERSONS	ĐẾN .... TRANSFER TO
	NHÂN SỐ .... NGƯỜI, NUMBER OF PERSONS
KIỂM NHẬN ATTESTED BY	KIỂM NHẬN ATTESTED BY
...., NGÀY .... 196.... DATE	...., NGÀY .... 196.... DATE
QUẬN TRƯỞNG DISTRICT CHIEF	QUẬN TRƯỞNG DISTRICT CHIEF

Ill. 16. *Official Family Booklet in the size as issued by the National Government (front).*

TRANG TRONG INNER PAGE	BẢNG GHI THÂN NHÂN ĐẾN TẠM TRÚ RECORD OF RELATIVES FOR SHORT VISIT TRONG THỜI HẠN TỪ 2 TỚI 30 NGÀY FROM 2 TO 30 DAYS (DO CHÍNH TAY LIÊN GIA HAY ẤP GIA TRƯỞNG GHI) FILLED IN BY INTER-FAMILY GROUP CHIEF OR HAMLET CHIEF			
NGÀY ĐẾN DATE OF ARRIVAL	HỌ TÊN NGƯỜI TẠM TRÚ NAMES	SỐ CĂN CƯỚC NGÀY, NƠI CẤP ID Nº, AND DATE AND PLACE OF ISSUE	Ở ĐÂU ĐẾN VÀ LÝ DO ARRIVAL FROM WHERE AND REASON	NGÀY RỜI ĐI DATE OF DEPARTURE
....	....	....	....	....

PHẦN GHI NHẬN SỐ THAY ĐỔI
RECORD OF CHANGE IN NUMBER OF PERSONS

NHÂN SỐ THÊM, BỚT NUMBER OF PERSONS ADDED OR SUBTRACTED	KIỂM NHẬN ATTESTED BY
SỐ NGƯỜI CŨ .... NGƯỜI PREVIOUS NUMBER OF PERSONS + THÊM (1) .... ADDED - BỚT (1) .... SUBTRACTED SỐ NGƯỜI HIỆN TẠI .... NGƯỜI PRESENT NUMBER OF PERSONS	NGÀY .... DATE ẤP TRƯỞNG
(1) XIN GHI ĐỦ HỌ TÊN TỪNG NGƯỜI .... RECORD FULL NAMES OF EACH PERSON	

LÝ LỊCH CÁ NHÂN TRONG GIA ĐÌNH
INDIVIDUAL DESCRIPTIONS OF FAMILY MEMBER

SỐ .... NUMBER

1) HỌ, TÊN ....
   NAMES
2) BÍ DANH ....
   ALIASES
3) NĂM SANH ....
   DATE OF BIRTH
4) NƠI SANH ....
   PLACE OF BIRTH
5) CHA ....
   FATHER
6) MẸ ....
   MOTHER
7) GIẤY KHAI SANH (HAY GIẤY THẾ VÌ KHAI SANH) SỐ ....
   BIRTH CERTIFICATE NUMBER
   LẬP TẠI .... NGÀY ....
   DELIVERED BY   DATE
8) NGHỀ NGHIỆP ....
   PROFESSION
9) SỐ QUỐC GIA DANH BỘ (NẾU CÓ) ....
   NUMBER OF NATIONAL BUSINESS REGISTRATION IF ANY
10) THẺ CĂN CƯỚC BỌC NHỰA SỐ .... CẤP TẠI ....
    I.D NUMBER   ISSUED BY
    NGÀY ....
    DATE
11) TỜ KHAI CĂN CƯỚC SỐ .... NGÀY ....
    OLD ID PAPER Nº   DATE
12) LIÊN HỆ VỚI GIA TRƯỞNG ....
    RELATIONSHIP WITH CHIEF OF FAMILY

PHẦN DÀNH GHI VIỆC DI CHUYỂN CÁ NHÂN
RESERVED FOR INDIVIDUAL TRANSFER

BẢNG GHI NHỮNG NGƯỜI VẮNG MẶT RECORD OF ABSENCES DO CHÍNH TAY LIÊN GIA HAY ẤP TRƯỞNG GHI FILLED IN BY INTER-FAMILY GROUP CHIEF OR HAMLET CHIEF				
NGÀY ĐI DATE OF DEPARTURE	HỌ TÊN NGƯỜI VẮNG MẶT NAMES OF ABSENT	ĐI ĐÂU DESTINATION	LÝ DO REASON	NGÀY TRỞ VỀ RETURN DATE
....	....	....	....	....

Ill. 16. *reverse.*

Card system into effect. This is the assistance being provided by the hamlet committee and members of hamlet construction teams. The blank Family Booklets are sent to the cadres and hamlet committee members who distribute them among the people with instructions to fill them out. They also will help those who cannot read and write to complete their forms and arrange for the family to gather at the village center of district town on an appointed day to be photographed. Naturally, there are variations on the basic plan depending on local conditions. For example, it was found that special interview groups composed of persons who were bilingual in a Montagnard dialect, had organized to work with the teams filling out Family Booklets for the tribal peoples. Just as in any other Government program affecting large numbers of people, the population must be told why this identification system is necessary and what they will be expected to do. Because it is a program which implies control, or at least surveillance, efforts to make the people understand it must be greater than in a plan whose benefits are immediately obvious, such as the building of a road or a training course on proper use of fertilizer.

Usually, when the full processing team comes into the village, the Family Booklets are complete and the team only has to review the Booklet to see that it contains the required information and that it is correct, make any necessary corrections and then turn the Booklets over to the hamlet committee to enable them to prepare the Family Control Sheet. This is the master control sheet for the hamlet, maintained by the hamlet committee, containing names of inhabitants, one or two of the most pertinent facts about each one and a photograph of each member of each family (see Ill. 17, pages 80 and 81). If possible, a first trip to announce the program and confer with local leaders and cadres should be made by the processing team or one or more members of it.

A photographer comes to the processing centre on the appointed day, takes all necessary pictures and sends them to provincial headquarters for developing and printing. One small item that will be helpful to the photographic workers in processing the hundreds of negatives will be an identification blackboard photographed into the picture of the family. Photographers employed in this work can make up a small blackboard of about 75 by 50 centimeters and carry it and chalk with them to write the family's name, the street address, if any, and the name of the hamlet and district. The blackboard also should carry date because there undoubtedly will be numerous changes in the family group requiring a new photograph. The blackboard could be prepared in advance with the items required lettered in white paint on the blackboard and a space for the photographer to write or print with chalk the data required for identification. Since it will take a few days for the photograph to be processed, the hamlet committee will have plen-

TỈNH			**PHIẾU KIỂM TRA GIA ĐÌNH**			ẤP	
PROVINCE						HAMLET	
QUẬN			**FAMILY CONTROL SHEET**			ĐƯỜNG	
DISTRICT						STREET	
XÃ			HỌ. TÊN GIA TRƯỞNG		LIÊN GIA		SỐ NHÀ
VILLAGE			NAME OF CHIEF OF FAMILY		INTER FAMILY GROUP		HOUSE NUMBER

SỐ THỨ TỰ N?	HỌ VÀ TÊN NAME	TUỔI hay NĂM SANH AGE OR YEAR OF BIRTH	THẺ CĂN CƯỚC SỐ ID NUMBER	NGÀY CẤP PHÁT DATE OF ISSUANCE	NƠI CẤP PHÁT PLACE OF ISSUANCE	NGHỀ NGHIỆP PROFESSION	LIÊN HỆ RELATION SHIP

TÀI SẢN PROPERTY			HUÊ LỢI HÀNG NĂM YEARLY REVENUE		
LIỆT KÊ DESCRIPTION	SỐ LƯỢNG QUANTITY	TRỊ GIÁ VALUE	LIỆT KÊ DESCRIPTION	SỐ LƯỢNG QUANTITY	TRỊ GIÁ VALUE
NHÀ CỬA, ĐỒ ĐẠC REAL ESTATE, FURNITURE			THÓC LÚA PADDY		
RUỘNG FIELD			NGÔ (BẮP) CORN		
RẪY ORCHARD			KHOAI POTATOE		
VƯỜN GARDEN			HOA QỦA FRUIT		
ĐÌA (AO, MƯƠNG) POND			CHĂN NUÔI BREEDING		
TRÂU BÒ CATTLE			NGƯ SẢN FISHERY		
LỢN, DÊ PIG, GOAT			LÂM SẢN FORESTRY		
HÀNG HÓA GOODS			THƯƠNG MẠI BUSINESS		
			CÔNG XÁ (TIỀN CÔNG)		
CỘNG TOTAL			CỘNG TOTAL		

Ill. 17. *Official Family Control Sheet in the size issued by the National Government (front).*

DANH-SÁCH THÂN-NHÂN ĐI TẬP KẾT (HAY CÒN Ở LẠI) NGOÀI BẮC
LIST OF NAMES OF RELATIVES IN THE NORTH

SỐ THỨ TỰ / Nº	HỌ VÀ TÊN / NAMES	TUỔI (HAY NĂM SANH) / AGE OR YEAR OF BIRTH	HOẠT ĐỘNG V.C TỪ NGÀY / DATE WORKING FOR V.C	CHỨC-VỤ NGÀY TẬP KẾT / POSITION AT BEGINNING	CHỨC-VỤ HIỆN TẠI / PRESENT POSITION	CÓ LIÊN-LẠC VỚI GIA-ĐÌNH KHÔNG / ANY CONTACT WITH FAMILY	CƯỚC-CHÚ / REMARKS

DANH-SÁCH THÂN-NHÂN ĐANG HOẠT ĐỘNG CHO PHIẾN-CỘNG TẠI MIỀN NAM TỰ-DO
LIST OF NAMES OF RELATIVES WORKING FOR V.C IN SOUTH VIETNAM

SỐ THỨ TỰ / Nº	HỌ VÀ TÊN / NAMES	TUỔI (HAY NĂM SANH) / AGE OR YEAR OF BIRTH	NGÀY GIA NHẬP V.C / DATE WORKING FOR V.C	NGÀY THOÁT-LY GIA-ĐÌNH / DATE SEPARATED FROM FAMILY	CHỨC-VỤ HIỆN TẠI / PRESENT POSI.	CÓ LIÊN-LẠC VỚI GIA-ĐÌNH KHÔNG / ANY CONTACT WITH FAMILY	CƯỚC-CHÚ / REMARKS

NHẬN XÉT VỀ GIA CẢNH / OBSERVATION ON FAMILY CONDITION	NHẬN-XÉT VỀ XU-HƯỚNG CHÍNH-TRỊ / OBSERVATION ON POLITICAL TENDENCY	
MỰC SỐNG / STANDARD OF LIVING: THIẾU THỐN / NEEDY — EO HẸP / POOR — VỪA ĐỦ / JUST SUFFICIENT — DƯ DẬT / COMFORTABLE	ĐỐI VỚI CHÁNH PHỦ QUỐC GIA / IN REGARD TO NATIONAL GOVERNMENT	ĐỐI VỚI PHIẾN CỘNG / IN REGARD TO V.C
CÓ ĐƯỢC AI TRỢ GIÚP KHÔNG? / ANY HELP RECEIVED? HỌ, TÊN / NAMES LIÊN HỆ / RELATIONSHIP CÔNG VIỆC / PROFESSION NGÂN KHOẢN / AMOUNT ĐỀU HÒA / REGULAR — BẤT THƯỜNG / IRREGULAR	TUYỆT ĐỐI TIN TƯỞNG / ENTIRELY FAITHFUL TÍCH-CỰC THAM-GIA CÔNG-TÁC / COOPERATE ENTIRELY	THÙ OÁN CỘNG SẢN (LÝ DO) / HATE V.C (REASON)
	LỪNG CHỪNG / INDIFFERENT THIẾU TIN TƯỞNG / LACK OF BELIEF THAM GIA MIỄN CƯỠNG / DO NOT COOPERATE	THIÊN PHIẾN-CỘNG (NGUYÊN NHÂN) / V.C SYMPATHISER (REASON)
CÓ PHẢI GIÚP ĐỠ AI KHÔNG? HỌ, TÊN / NAMES LIÊN HỆ / RELATIONSHIP NGÂN KHOẢN / AMOUNT ĐỀU HÒA / REGULAR — BẤT THƯỜNG / IRREGULAR	BẤT MÃN / DISSATISFACTION CHỐNG ĐỐI / OPPOSITION	THEO PHIẾN CỘNG / V.C PARTISAN BẤT LIÊN LẠC / HAD CONTACT GIÚP PHƯƠNG TIỆN, LƯƠNG THỰC / PROVIDE FACILITIES AND FOODS CHỨA CHẤP / GIVE ASYLUM
CÓ THÂN NHÂN GIÚP VIỆC CHÁNH PHỦ KHÔNG? / ANY RELATIVE WORKING FOR THE GOVERN HỌ, TÊN / NAMES LIÊN HỆ / RELATIONSHIP CHỨC VỤ / POSITION ĐỊA CHỈ / ADDRESS		

Ill. 17. *reverse.*

ty of time to complete the control sheet. When the photographs are returned in a package, they are sorted and, from the identifying data in the photograph, attached to the family booklet which is then returned to the head of family. Normally, two prints will be made. One will go into the Family Booklet which will be returned to the family, and the second onto the control sheet retained by the local authorities. This is subject to variation according to security conditions as in the National ID Card Program. If a serious enough security situation exists, the Booklet may have to be kept at district headquarters until the situation clarifies itself. This has also been true of ID cards in some instances.

C. CHECKING IDENTITY DOCUMENTS

It is a simple enough procedure to check identity documents and most members of the Police know how to do it properly. The problem which usually arises in the examination of ID cards in routine inspections, however, is carelessness, especially in comparing the picture on the card with the facial characteristics of the person presenting it. In the United States, during World War II, identity cards were required for entry into defense plants. One of the common tests of plant guards was to send in a person who sould show a card bearing a photograph of Adolf Hitler. It was surprising and disturbing to learn how many of these people were admitted without question. Failure to compare an identity card picture with the bearer of the card also has been noted in Viet Nam. At some checkpoints now in existence, for example, it has been found that officers will pick up all identity papers from passengers on a bus and take them into their post for checking. The man who looks at the identity cards never sees their owner which, of course, is a complete waste of time and effort. The following points should be remembered when checking identity documents:

1. *The Photograph* must be compared carefully with the bearer of the card and an effort made to recreate conditions under which the picture was taken. For example, most people do not wear hats when identification pictures are taken. If a man is bare headed in a picture and is wearing a hat when he presents his card for checking, the Police officer must ask him to remove the hat for comparison, or the officer can place his finger over the top of the person's head in the photograph to simulate a hat. A woman who had long hair when her photograph was taken might look quite different with a short bob. In this case, try to cover up the hair on the photograph and compare only the facial features.

Where a person has changed slightly due to age or a gain or loss in weight, it is well to look carefully at the ears, at least on pictures of men where the ears are not covered by hair. Since the identification photo is full face and not profile, comparison of the nose does not help. The ears are equally unchanging, however, and each person's are of a distinct shape. Eyeglasses change an individual's appearance. Usually, when a person has his identification picture taken, he is asked whether he customarily wears glasses and if so, he is photographed with them on. Whatever the case, the person being checked must be asked to put on or remove his glasses to correspond with the picture on his ID card. A check of an individual's age as recorded on the card is another aid to identification in cases where doubt exists.

2. *The Official Stamp* should be checked closely on all ID cards. An effective method is for the Police officer to compare the stamp on his own card with the one on the card he is checking. The official stamp is authentic in the vast majority of cases but it is a rubber stamp after all, and can be duplicated easily. Just because the stamp appears does not mean the person is carrying a legitimate ID card. What is very difficult to duplicate is the embossing on the new cards now in use and the Police are justified in placing a great deal of faith in their authenticity.

3. *The Fingerprint* is the one means of positive identification that exists on the identity card but, at the same time, only an expert can make a positive identification from a fingerprint. However, it is possible for everyone to learn enough about fingerprints to make a partial identification and provided a possible investigative lead. Fingerprints ink impressions of the friction ridges on the ends of a person's fingers and, while no two person's prints are identical, all prints fall into only a few general patterns. To take a fingerprint, an individual's fingertip is pressed onto an inked slab of glass or metal and then onto a card or piece of paper.

Fingerprints fall into three general groups of patterns, each group bearing the same general characteristics for family resemblance. The patterns may be further divided into sub-groups by means of smaller but still quite easily identifiable differences. The three divisions are:

ARCH
Plain arch
Tented arch

LOOP
Radial loop
Ulnar loop

WHORL
Plain whorl
Central pocket loop
Double loop
Accidental whorl

Enlargements of all the types of pattern mentioned are reproduced on the following pages, (see Ill. 18). These same enlargements should be posted inside the door of every checkpoint post and at every small Police station so that the Police become familiar with them. Every provincial Police headquarters has an identification bureau which is capable of producing these enlargements.

When post personnel become familiar with the general fingerprint patterns they will be able to examine

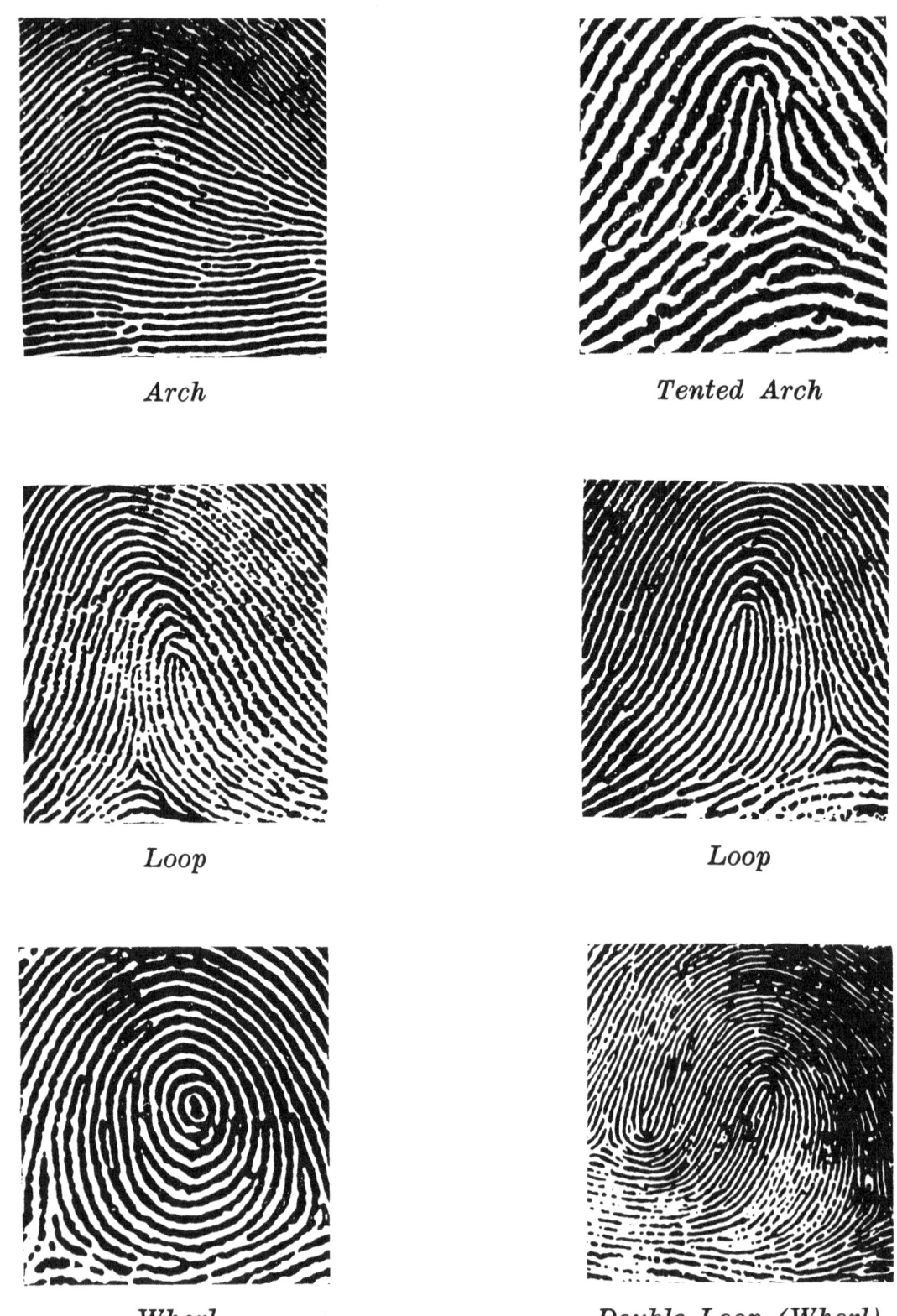

Ill. 18. *Fingerprint patterns, groups and sub-groups (from National Police poster); should be posted for reference at check points.*

prints as an aid in uncertain identifications. All the equipment necessary is the regular inked office stamp pad, which every post probably will have on hand anyway for stamping manifests, and some clean white paper on which to make the print. It must be emphasized that this cursory study will not make anyone a fingerprint expert and if positive identification by fingerprint becomes necessary, the person must be held until such identification can be made by an expert from the provincial identification bureau.

The fingerprint is included on identity cards to prevent forgeries but instances could arise where one person tries to get through a checkpoint by using another's card. If a checking officer's suspicion is aroused and he is not satisfied with the other means of identifications, he can at least make a preliminary check of the fingerprints by knowing the differences in the various types.

4. *Questions* asked of a person regarding particulars of their identity documents should be phrased as follows:

>   What is your name?
>   Where do you live?
>   How old are you?
>   Where was your card issued?

Leading questions, such as «is your name Nguyen Van Ba?», «are you 37 years old?» should be avoided.

5. *Damaged Identity Papers* may cause trouble at times. They should be scrutinized very carefully but if the holder of a damaged card can be satisfactorily cleared on all identifying points on his card — photograph, stamp, fingerprint — he should be allowed to proceed, but with instructions to report to his local processing center to get a new card. In Saigon and Gia Dinh, Tuyen Duc and Tay Ninh provinces, the old-type laminated cards are still in use. These are made with a very soft plastic and people have been known to fold them to make them fit into their wallets. Among laborers, checking officers may find cards badly damaged by perspiration, especially around the edges.

Flat rules cannot be set down on how to handle a person with a badly damaged ID card. The checkpoint officers must decided whether the card has been damaged by natural causes or whether it has been tampered with. In the latter case, it is necessary to take the person's name and the number of his card and report the matter to provincial headquarters, or even to detain the individual for investigation. Following these general guidelines, the checking officers must rely on their own judgment of each individual situation.

Chapter VIII

CHECKPOINTS AND SEARCHES

It is of little value to issue passes and permits or require people to carry identification cards unless there is, at the same time, a system of checking these official papers. In normal times, identification cards might be checked occasionally for one reason or another, but in an emergency which justifies the establishment of a resources control program, an effective system must operate to check on travel passes and manifests and to search vehicles for hidden goods. Further, the people must know about it, how it works and what the objective of the system is. Strategic hamlets, of course, are able to exercise frequent examination and thus rigid control over the comings and goings of people through their gates. Whether they do or not is another matter. Movement on the various forms of public transportation which have regular stops and terminals can be fairly well examined with the assistance of the carriers. But vehicle and craft travel on the highways, roads and canals of Viet Nam can be regulated only by efficiently operated checkpoints. This chapter describes checkpoints, how they are established and operated, and how to conduct searches.

All ways and means of transportation must be taken into account in a system of resources control; they can be divided into two main categories even though many similiar methods and procedures apply to both:

(1) Car and truck travel on the nation's highways and roads, barges and small boats navigate on rivers and canals. Control is enforced through examination at checkpoints of shipping manifests, travel permits, passengers, cargo and vehicles.

(2) All forms of transportation having terminals, depots and regular stops. Here controls are enforced by processing lines at loading points to verify the system of passes and manifests. These «stops» are included for the railroads, airplanes, commercial boats and buses as described in Chapter V. Buses, of course, travel on the highways and are considered briefly in this chapter but the problems involved in examining and controlling the passengers and goods moved about in this manner cause them to be placed in the second category.

A checkpoint is an arterial post manned by a predetermined number of men to examine vehicular and pedestrian traffic. The policemen assigned to the post maintain a constant vigil over all passing traffic and may stop conveyances or individuals for search purposes according to a constantly changing pattern of spot checks and inspections, or according to a special security situation which may exist in a particular areas at a particular time.

A. CHECK POINT CRITERIA

1. *Choosing a Location*

Using the province, with its division into districts, villages and hamlets, as the basic unit in establishing checkpoints, the responsible authority first considers possible locations at which posts may be established. To do this properly, the official must have maps available to him and a knowledge of how to read them. The layman generally uses no more than two types of maps: the plain map and the contour map. The first shows only the flat features of the land such as the coastline, rivers, major highways and railroad lines and the location of towns and cities. It also shows the geographical divisions of an area such as provinces and districts and might mark administrative and military divisions as well. This kind of map is not considered adequate for use in planning the location of road blocks or checkpoints. A contour map, on the other hand, shows relative curves on the surface of the land so that mountains, hills, plateaus and lowlands are thrown into relief and an actual picture of the terrain evolves. It is essential to study this kind of map because geography and terrain are all important in deciding where to set up a checkpoint (Ill. 19, page 88, should be followed in reading the discussion on «Choosing a Location»).

Maps should be studied, first of all, to try to see ways in which a Viet Cong might try to get around established points. Secondly, the responsible authorities should study the major flow of traffic in their areas so they will understand where it goes and where it comes from. There is no reason, for example, to establish a major checkpoint on a road where traffic is very light; the control problem will have to be handled another way. Since there is no substitute for first-hand knowledge of an area, Police officials responsible for setting up checkpoints should make personal reconnaissance trips to proposed post locations. There may be something, not obvious on a map and not known to the Police, which can be learned in an on-the-spot survey, something that might affect the decision to establish a checkpoint or the amount of protection needed for it.

Two major considerations govern the location of checkpoints. They are (1) vulnerability to attack, and (2) the physical requirements of the post itself. Although each situation is different and must be studied separately before a decision on location can be made, certain basic principles may be set forth as general guidelines. They are good rules to remember but, like all rules, they may be broken if good reasons exist to do so and if the necessary protective measures are taken.

a. A check point rarely should be set up in a narrow ravine or valley where the guerrillas could easily shoot down on a hard-to-defend post. If, by nature of the terrain or location of the roads, the Police are forced to place a checkpoint in a ravine, they will require military assistance to guard the peaks around the post and provide adequate protection for it.

b. A checkpoint should not be located in heavy jungle where, again, it would be vulnerable to enemy attack. If a point must be placed in a heavily forested region, the area around it should be cleared for a reasonable

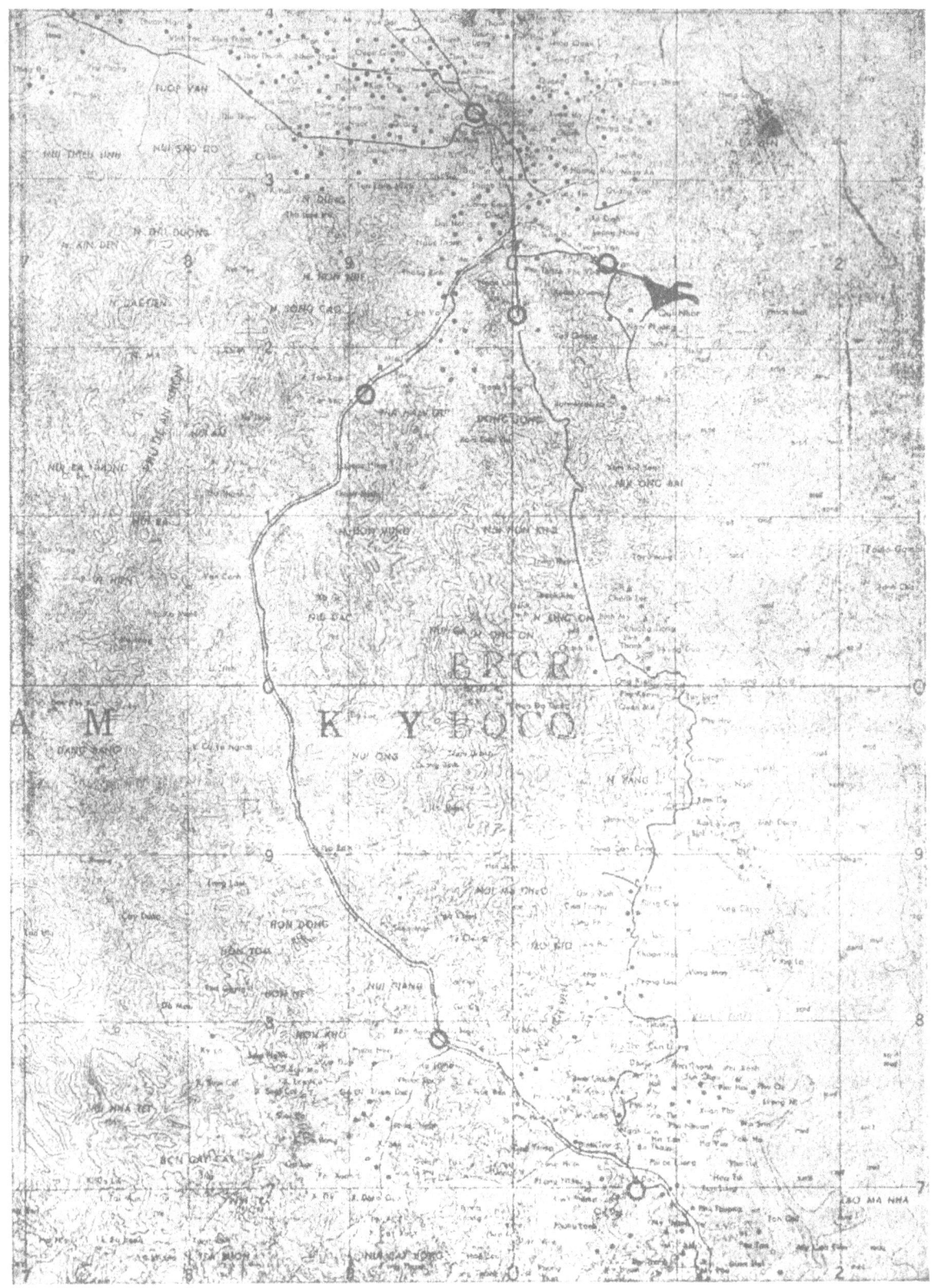

Ill. 19. *Use of map in check point selection; unless reconnaissance would show reasons not easily read from the map, the O marks indicate locations desirable for thwarting by-pass, for defense and for furthering traffic flow.*

distance so the post is defensible.

c. A checkpoint should not be located near a bridge if it can be avoided. An extremely difficult and hazardous traffic situation can result if vehicles are backed up for any distance on bridges.

d. The ideal checkpoint is established in open country and on high ground, allowing the officers manning the post a long clear view of the surrounding country. At such a post the police will be able to see anyone who tries to bypass the checkpoint and with long straight stretches of road, the traffic problem, particularly on main highways, will be decreased appreciably. The latter is important for the sake of good public relations, among other reasons. Resources control is not going to be popular with the people but the situation will be aggravated even more if motorists and passengers have to wait in long lines to pass through a checkpoint.

e. A checkpoint must have turn-off space. This means providing extra room along the highway where automobiles, trucks and buses can park if a complete search is to be made rather than having them remain on the road to tie up traffic. Space must be provided on both sides of the highway so that cars are not forced to turn off in front of oncoming vehicles, a hazardous practice (see Ill. 20, below)

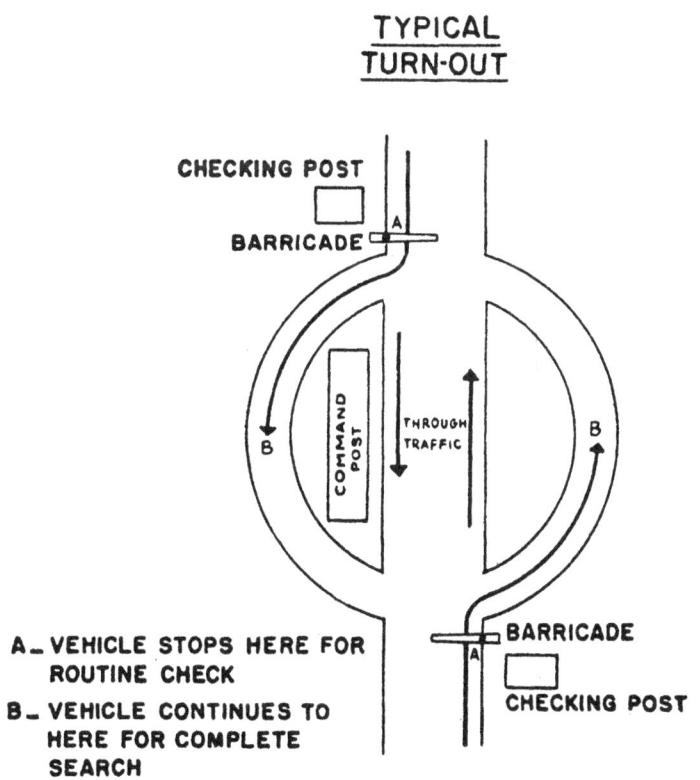

Ill. 20. — *Diagram of a method for providing turn-outs for vehicles to be completely inspected; the checkpoint defended area can include several successive turn-outs, but at least two are needed to insure safe traffic flow.*

An exception to this would be the secondary road with very little traffic. Here a car or truck can be searched right on the road and other vehicles can pass around it without creating a traffic jam. On a major highway, however, an area large enough to provide turn-off space on both sides of the road must be selected for the checkpoint. For heavy traffic conditions several sucessive turn-offs may be needed. The turn-off should be long enough to handle the largest piece of equipment that reasonably may be expected to come along. The length, width and composition of the roadbed for the turn-off are matters to be turned over to highway personnel in provincial public works services. (Exhibit of open area point).

f. An effort should be made to set up a checkpoint along a highway which limits or restricts traffic. Such a road would be one running through an area where the surroundings make it difficult for a driver to leave the road before reaching the checkpoint. For example, an ideal spot would be on a long straight stretch of highway running through swamp or marsh land or along the seacoast where it is virtually impossible for a car or truck to turn off the road for many kilometers. The point chosen would need solid inslands of some sort to serve as turn-off areas.

g. Checkpoints must be established a reasonable distance apart. There should be no more of them than are absolutely essential to control traffic both because of inconvenience to the public and because checkpoints are costly to operate in terms of equipment and man power. There is no flat rule on what a reasonable distance is; each province has its separate problems. District Police will have to solve them within the framework of the established principles. Further, the Police will have to consider the surrounding provinces as well as their own. It would be foolish for one province to have a checkpoint one kilometer from its border and the neighboring one to have another just inside its boundary. There is little similarity between province borders and national borders with foreign countries where immigration and customs checkpoints must be operated. There is no reason to believe that a provincial boundary automatically requires a checkpoint.

2. *Mobile and Surprise Elements*

There are two basic kinds of checkpoints, fixed and mobile. For maximum effectiveness, the two are used simultaneously. In any system of fixed checkpoints, ways are found to get around them and mobile patrols are the most effective way of combating this evasion. A patrol should cover the area immediately surrounding a checkpoint so that it can observe and stop drivers who try to turn around or otherwise evade the post. Motorcycles, automobiles or jeeps may be used but all patrolmen should be thoroughly familiar with the highway, road and trail system in the checkpoint area so they will know where to expect people to go. The patrol would operate as any other patrol system and it is sufficient here to say that in a good operation, patrolmen would know where certain traffic usually goes or is supposed to go. They would know where trucks should travel, whether they are loaded with cabbages or gasoline, and if they saw a truck or any other vehicle on a road where it has no apparent reason to be, they would have reason to stop and conduct a search.

A second function of these patrolling units would be to set up temporary checkpoints. They would establish them according to the principles contained in this chapter but with the added element of surprise so as to trap a vehicle trying to evade a fixed checkpoint. The surprise element, of course, is also present in the system of patrolling roads and trails around established checkpoints. Enemy guerrillas will learn quickly where the fixed points are since no effort will be made to try to hide them; rather they will be well advertised in an effort to avoid serious traffic problems. The Viet Cong has an advantage because it usually is impossible to know where he will attack next. In the mobile checkpoint and patrol system, the Police should endeavor to appear with equal suddeness.

a. Dangers of Fixed Checkpoints

Certain physical dangers are inherent in fixed checkpoints. The enemy will know where they are and that they are manned day and night. This enables the Viet Cong to plan attacks on checkpoints and this they are certain to do, particularly those on major highways.

Picture a typical checkpoint on a major highway near a large town. No matter how fast and efficiently the Police handle the operation, a number of cars and buses are certain to be lined up waiting for the minimum check which usually is just a look at the papers of each person and a glance into the trunk and glove compartment of each vehicle. Suppose the line consists of a gasoline truck, another truck loaded with inflammable material and several cars full of passengers. An attack, hitting the trucks first, could start a deadly fire killing dozens of people. Thus, it is essential to plan carefully with local military units because they will have to provide the main defense of the point. Checkpoint personnel must maintain their own self-defense and alert systems in coordination with military defense, since surprise by guerrillas is axiomatic in their attack. For example, some of guerrillas will attack within the check point where police are concentrated, while others will use fire and movement to overcome the defenses manned by military.

b. Dangers of Mobile Points

The dangers in mobile points are not to the patrol units but to the general public. It is common knowledge that the Viet Cong set up their own road blocks or checkpoints in an effort to capture people and supplies. As a result, people very naturally are terrified at the sight of an unexpected block on the road ahead of them. The Police, therefore, must make every effort to identify mobile checkpoints so that the public can distinguish between legitimate government operations and Viet Cong traps.

The Viet Cong now have the uniforms and equipment necessary to establish road blocks and impersonate Army or Police personnel. There are a number of things which can be done, however, in establishing mobile points to let people know they are legitimate. These include setting up checkpoints only in areas where it is absolutely certain that the Viet Cong cannot come in and do the same thing themselves, and the use of equipment such as bright lights at night or large but easily movable signs telling the public that a checkpoint is ahead. The use of any symbol that the Viet Cong cannot duplicate or the frequent changing of symbols also is a possible device.

(*NOTE:* Care in handling the public seeking to avoid a mobile checkpoint is mandatory. The population has been warned that government points are only to be found in areas under full governmental control such as administrative centers; and that those people meeting checkpoints away from such governmental areas should avoid the block as it is in all probability a VC operation.)

B. OPERATION OF A CHECKPOINT

Equal in importance with the location of a checkpoint is its staffing and efficient operation. Each person maning a checkpoint, fixed or mobile, must know his traffic control, search, record and protection job thoroughly, be methodical and move quickly to keep traffic delays to the minimum. Equally important for survival is the ability to participate in alerting and defending againts VC attack.

1. *Personnel*

A minimum of three people, not counting security operations, are required to maintain the search operations at a checkpoint, even the smallest one. There must be two officers who do the actual checking and searching and an officer in charge. Individual judgment, based on the amount of traffic on the road or highway in question, must be used in assigning personnel to a checkpoint, but generally this pattern should be followed:

a. Small Roads.

Vehicles may be stopped right on the road or there can be a small turn-off area if convenient. It is presumed, however, that traffic is so light that only one line of traffic will need to be handled at a time.

b. Secondary Roads with Turn-offs.

Checkpoints on these roads may require only the minimum staff of three but increases in personnel, based on the amount of traffic, may be decided upon by responsible Police authority. For example, if two checking lanes have to be set up, two searchers would be required on both sides of the road who, with the officer in charge, would total five men. Or, even with one lane, two men may be needed in the turn-off area to conduct thorough searches and two more to remain on the road for the quick checks of all passing vehicles. With the officer in charge, this again would total five. It should be emphasized that, based on the minimum requirement and on traffic considerations, the responsible local Police official must determine personnel requirements for these posts.

c. Major Roads and Highways with Turn-Offs and Heavy Traffic.

Checkpoints on such arteries need at least nine men. There should be four on each side of the road — two conducting thorough searches on the turn-off and two doing the quick on-the-road checks required of all other vehicles. The ninth man, of course, would be the officer in charge. Assuming 12-hour shifts, a major checkpoint, as described here and operating 24 hours a day, would require a minimum of 18 men. No allowance for days off is included and should be added for efficient operation.

The requirements outlined above show that provincial police officials must coordinate the plans of all their districts so that manpower needs for an entire province can be calculated in advance. Personnel requirements should cause responsible Police officials to be extremely cautious in their recommendations and decisions on the number of checkpoints to be set up.

The number three is set as a minimum on even the smallest checkpoint for reasons of efficiency and for self-defense within the search sector of the post. One policeman is in command and the other two conduct the searches. The officer in charge should seldom take part in actual searching but should be responsible for the control of travel past the checkpoints and protection of his two colleagues; as they check papers and search vehicles or individuals, he must be alert for anything that would mean danger to his men. His gun is loaded and holstered but he is prepared to use it if necessary. The searchers are both armed as well and their guns are slung or holstered leaving their hands free for the search. Men at a checkpoint must always be on the alert and prepared for the time when a truck passing through the point will not be driven by an innocent citizens but by a Viet Cong guerrilla, perhaps carrying amed passengers.

Regular checkpoint personnel all should be uniformed Police officers since this is a civilian operation under the jurisdiction of the National Police. However, because of the emergency situation with its tremendous demand for manpower, it is possible that the civilian security service simply will not have enough men to perform its task. It would then be necessary for Police officials to ask the province chief to call on the military — either the regular army, the Bao An (Civil Guard) or the Dan Ve (Self Defense Corps) — to aid in the manning of checkpoints. At the posts, however, the military would be under the control of the Police unless they were located in an area of battle where the military always takes precedence over civilian authority.

2. *Barricades, Roadblocks and Lighting*

If practical, movable hurdles or barricades should be set up by which movement is controlled. There are various kinds of simple roadblocks:

a. The conventional barrier pole or simple lever on a fulcrum with a counter weight at the free end which is raised and lowered by manual control. It is good because it is simple and inexpensive to make. All that is needed is a pole, a post to mount it on and a heavy rock, piece of metal or even a bucket filled with sand or concrete to use as the counter balance. The barrier pole, with a short supporting rod, can be made of bamboo.

b. A plain wire, rope or chain stretched across the road. The drawback to these barriers is that they are difficult to see; if they must be used, red flags always should be hung from them so motorists can see and recognize them at a distance.

c. A temporary barricade, to be used either at a mobile checkpoint or for a limited period of time until a permanent one can be installed, is a concertina roll expanded, or if more time permits, a temporary series of three barrels or short rows of barbed wire on an «X» frame placed so that vehicles must slow down almost to a stop in order to pass through them. One distinct disadvantage of this type of barrier is that unless the road is very wide, traffic is restricted to one lane and if is at all heavy, cars will always be waiting to proceed in one direction while those traveling the opposite way are driving through the barrier. This can be partially solved if the two sets of barricades in each pair are set far enough apart so that two or three cars can pass between the sets and stop to be checked (see Ill. 21, below).

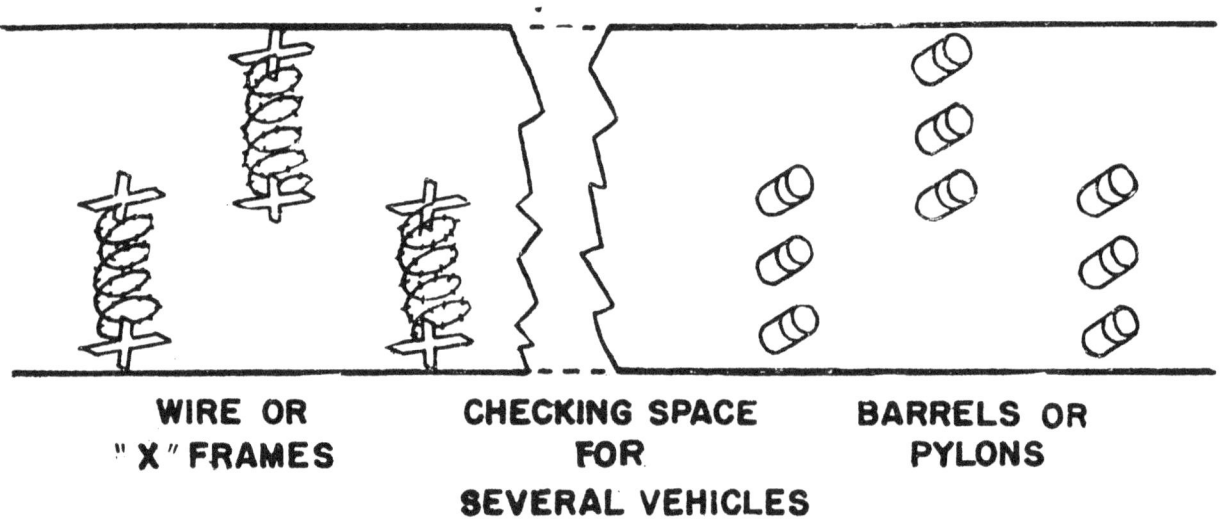

WIRE OR "X" FRAMES   **CHECKING SPACE FOR SEVERAL VEHICLES**   **BARRELS OR PYLONS**

Ill. 21. *Diagram of a method for halting traffic for inspection using movable obstacles; a check point so established would usually be temporary (mobile check point) as traffic flow is restricted.*

Strict crowd control must be exercised in order that officers performing checks and searches are not crowded by persons waiting to move through a checkpoint. Crowds will occur mainly at points near cities or major towns where bicycle and foot traffic is heavy. Facilities to handle such crowds would mainly consist of a simple fence or wire barrier at the side of the road marking off an aisle through which foot traffic and two and thre-wheeled vehicles, except for the small Vespa buses, would pass.

There is division of opinion on lighting. One view, found particulary among the military, argues that a brightly illuminated post offers a clear target to the enemy. The other, while agreeing that this is true, says that since checkpoints must be operated at night, the Viet Cong's favorite time to travel, they also must be adequately lighted to conduct checks. Light is required for searching and, perhaps even more important, the driver of any private or non-military vehicle on the road at night will feel confidence at the sight of a lighted checkpoint and identify is as a legitimate one. Coming upon a post in darkness, even the most innocent driver might panic, use fire-arms, or try to drive through the barrier or, if possible, turn quickly around and head back in the direction from which he came. On the other hand, an illuminated checkpoint in an area dominated by the Viet Cong would be fool-hardy unless defended. In all cases lighting must be fully coordinated with the security force so as to assure that loss of night vision, shadows, and exposure of defense is minimized. Individual judgement must be exercised and the best cooperation established between the Police and the military. The Police must depend on the military for protection and patrol of checkpoints, especially at night.

3. *Spot Checking*

Ideally, to insure that no illegal goods leave villages, districts or any authorized area, every person and vehicle should be searched. Practically, this is impossible because of the time involved, the interference with normal and legitimate business, and the intolerable traffic jams which would result. It is necessary, therefore, to carry out selective searching, making sure that the element of surprise is always present, that persons passing through checkpoints never know who is going to be searched.

The majority of vehicles passing through a checkpoint are examined as follows: an officer inspects the papers of all occupants of a car, truck or bus to see that they are in order and, if the checkpoint is of such size that it carries a file or index of wanted people, he takes the papers into the post's building to check them against any such list. Another officer looks in the front seat of the vehicle and on the floor; he asks the owner to open his glove compartment and trunk and inspects them; if a trunk contains baggage he opens it and makes a quick check of the contents. This all should be done rapidly, taking not much more than a minute for a private vehicles, 5 minutes for a bus. Even in this briefest kind of inspection, one checkpoint group can check only 60 cars or 15 buses an hour.

Selective searching, involving the element of surprise, is what is called *spot checking* in Police work. It means simply that vehicle at variable predetermined intervals are stopped and detained for thorough searching.

The commanding officer of a post, at the beginning of his shift, will determine, for example, that every 12th vehicle will be directed to put onto the turn-off area to be thoroughly searched. The interval must be changed during every shift — some shifts it may be the 10th car, or the 11th, or the 7th — or it will become known that at Checkpoint A in Bien Hoa province, the Police search every 12th vehicle. This would allow any one wanting to pass the checkpoint and avoid the chance of a search to take steps to see that he is not # 12. If the officer establishes the number at the beginning of his shift, he should change it the next morning when he returns to work. He may even change it during a shift if there is some reason to do so. Only experience can show how often spot checks should be carried out or what the interval in vehicles should be. An officer must learn how long it will take his men to conduct a complete search and establish from a traffic count how many cars pass the checkpoint every hour. With this knowledge, he is able to work out what a reasonable number of cars to be stopped for a full search in a given period of time would be.

The first thing to do after requesting a driver to park his car or truck in the turn-off area and advising him that he, the other occupants of the vehicle and the vehicle itself are going to be searched, is to try to allay the fears and suspicions of the people about to undergo the check. Usually, their reaction will be, «Why have I been picked for a search?» «What have I done?» It is up to the checkpoint commander, who counts and selects the cars for spot checks himself, to courteously explain that the search is part of a routine procedure to check vehicles selected according to a varing numerical pattern with no prior knowledge of who is driving or riding in them. It should be explained that neither the driver nor any of the occupants of the car are being accused of anything, again stressing that the procedure is routine and asking the cooperation of all in the car. This done, the officers should examine the papers of the vehicle's occupants, give them a quick body and clothing search and then give the automobile or truck a thorough spot check. As always at a checkpoint, a careful watch should be kept for any suspicious actions: attempts to evade a search, undue uneasiness on the part of any person, or earlier, an attempt to avoid the checkpoint altogether.

4. *Suspicious Vehicle*

Suspicious vehicles must be treated somewhat differently from the average bicycle, cart, car or truck stopped and searched in a spot check operation. Suspicious vehicles are those which have attempted to turn around short of the checkpoint; those in which something, such as an unaccounted for pistol, has been found in the quick search; vehicles about which the checkpoint has had advance information, and those which for many and varied reasons cause a checkpoint officer to be suspicious. There should be no iron-clad rule about the numerical pattern in spot checking. If a suspicious vehicle tries to pass, it must be checked even if the regular pattern then in effect has to be abandoned.

The officer in charge must make the decision on the extent of the search of a suspicious vehicle. He bases it on what the searchers report they have seen or found which causes them to suspect something wrong, or on advance observation or information. A suspicious vehicle may be anticipated and its inspection planned for, or it may arrive suddenly and unexpectedly; it may have to be searched either at a fixed or mobile checkpoint or at any point along the road where a patrol may have reason to halt it. While courteous conduct still must be observed, police officers understandably have to use firmer methods when they suspect they may be dealing with enemy agents or sympathizers who might be armed. The following procedure, again using a minimum of three men, should be followed after the vehicle has been halted:

a. Searcher ≠ 1 will approach the vehicle from the driver's side, open the driver's door and request him to leave the vehicle;

b. No. 2 will approach the vehicle from the other side and slightly to the rear; he will keep any other occupants of the vehicle under careful observation;

c. No. 3, the officer in charge, will be armed, if possible with an automatic weapon, which he will hold in a ready position. He will stand off to one side of the vehicle always maintaining a clear view of the driver and not allowing ≠ 1 or ≠ 2 to cross his line of fire. No. 3's part in the operation in purely defensive and he takes no part in the examination of documents or search.

d. The driver of the vehicle will not be questioned concerning his identity or requested to produce documents from his person until he has been given a quick body search by No. 1.

e. After the driver has been searched and his papers examined the other occupants of the vehicle, if any, should be asked to step out of the car one at a time. They are then searched in the same way as the driver and their documents checked.

f. The vehicle is searched thoroughly according to the instructions for its particular type.

If, after the search, suspicion is still unresolved, or if it is confirmed, the vehicle with its occupants will be conducted under direct Police supervision to the closest district headquarters, in most cases, for further investigation.

5. *Official Vehicles*

The search of official vehicles is a sensitive matter which causes trouble anywhere in the world. The following might be applied as general guidelines:

a. As a practical matter, it is common sense not to attempt to search military vehicles. Obviously, if a convoy is traveling down the road, it should be allowed to pass unchallenged through a checkpoint. As for isolated military vehicles, one solution is to ask the military to station their own men at checkpoints to search military jeep or trucks. If this is impractical, possibly the province chief or provincial police chief could tactfully discuss with high military authorities the possibility of having regular checkpoint personnel search military vehicles. A good case for doing so can be made if the Police have evidence to show that the Viet Cong have used what appear to be military conveyances complete with false license plates and other identifying marks. Also Viet Cong can hide contraband on a military vehicle either through pressure on the individual military or by deceit as to contents of transported goods. Even though a uniform is a form of identification in itself, military men can certainly be asked to show their papers, especially in highly restricted areas.

b. Vehicles bearing diplomatic or no tax license plates normally will not be searched under restraint. There is no reason why occupants of these vehicles should not be asked to produce their identifying documents but, since many diplomatic people are highly sensitive about their rights and privileges in the countries where they serve, the Police should be very careful in exercising restraint while dealing with them. Members of the Polish Communist delegation to the International Control Commission, for example, would look for instances of even the slightest discourtesy or infringement of their rights. Checkpoint police should, therefore, thoroughly inform themselves on how they are to handle cars with diplomatic or no tax plates. This may vary from province to province, depending on the security situation in each. A good «eye» search can be made while conversation is made in a courteous manner; frequently explanation of the local emergency, or Viet Cong tricks in getting rides in diplomatic or non taxed vehicles, will bring cooperation with police. The mere statement Viet Cong have mined parked cars helps in getting driver's assistance to a search.

c. Provincial authorities in official cars are another category to consider. An effort should be made to convince the province chief that, in order to set an example for all lower provincial officials as well as private citizens, he should not only allow his car to be stopped and his identity documents checked, but should publicly demand it and make sure his people find out about it. Unless he is a new chief, he was, in all probability, the first person in his province to get and carry a card in the National Identification Card Program. In doing so, he set an example which everyone else was expected to follow; leadership of this sort is even more important to the success of a resources control program. From the province chief's own standpoint, he has an unassailable argument to use on provincial officials who cone to him to complain that they are stopped and required produce identification documents in spite of the fact that they are riding in official cars. There is little an indignant official can say when the province chief himself announces that he always permits himself to be examined at checkpoints. The province chief may also be approached on the basis that checks of his vehicles reduce the possibility of Viet Cong sabotage or assassination. A fundamental principle of any identification system is that *there are no exceptions.*

A word of warning about young people might be in order. This is in no way a flat rule, but it is wise to be suspicious of younger people since it has been learned by experience that they are the ones who take most of the chances and do most of the transporting of contaband. They have less judgement than more mature people, and experience shows that if carryng firearms are more likely to use them without regard to the consequences.

6. *Buses*

Although buses already have been treated in Chapter V on Passes and Manifests, it is necessary to mention them briefly here. It is true that a bus has regular stops and terminals but it is also quite possible that one might stop to pick up a person who flags it down along the road. Also, passengers quite legitimately can ask a driver to stop and let them off if the bus passes close to their destination. Therefore, in a checkpoint operation, buses must be checked in the same manner as cars and trucks. If a bus happens to fall into a checkpoint's numerical pattern for spot checks — if it is the 10th vehicle on the shift when every 10th vehicle is being checked — it must be stopped, the papers of all passengers checked, the passengers given quick body searches and the bus itself searched thoroughly.

Checkpoint personnel may be sorely tempted to let a full size bus, loaded to the roof with people and produce, go through with merely a cursory check, even if is vehicle # 10. But this is a temptation which must be resisted; exceptions other than those allowed for very sound reasons cannot be condoned in a checkpoint operation. If buses customarily were allowed to proceed with only the briefest checks, the enemy would soon know about it and regard it as his safest means of transportation.

C. WATERWAYS

The control of the movement of population and materials over marine routes, both on inland waterways and along coastlines, is fundamentally the same as for vehicular traffic over highways. A barge and a boat are vehicles, designed to carry people and things from one place to another, and over reasonably defined routes. Certainly, the whole system of resources control would be subverted if adequate measures were not taken to inspect and regulate marine traffic.

Relatively narrow and well defined marine arteries, such as rivers and canals, require fairly simple control measures such as static checkpoints on the banks, supported by mobile check points and patrols in boats. The static point on shore should be equipped with a cable or stakes narrowing the channel, searchlights and a method of hailing passing boats. One major drawback to the shoreline checkpoint, coupled with a wide channel exists when a «chase» boat is not present at the post. It then becomes necessary to shoot at any boat which does not answer the post's summons, possibly killing or injuring innocent people. A summons can be innocently ignored if the boat crew does not hear or understand the order. Aside from this necessity, instructions for operating the river or canal checkpoint with very few minor exceptions obvious to the Police on the scene, are the same as for those on land.

Large open areas, such as the ocean, bays and lakes, present a different problem, but it too has been confronted and solved in other places. In the late 1940's, with the tremendous increase in oil production and attendant facilities in the over water operations of the large oil companies in Lake Maracaibo, Venezuela, South America, piracy and armed hold-ups created a serious and expensive problem. In this lake, 150 kilometers long by 40 kilometers wide, armed bandits were attacking and subduing whole drilling crews and making off with all sorts of saleable gear and supplies, including cement, a product greatly in demand. Three patrol boats were assigned to rove the lake during the hours of darkness, with certain crew members holding powers of search and arrest. Systematic spot checks of all boats and searches of suspected craft or those appearing in sensitive areas broke up the menace in a period of about a year. But it was necessary to continue the patrols on a selective basis in order to prevent recurrance of the problem.

These methods, varying only superficially and in degree, have been used universally to bring marine smuggling almost to be standstill.

D. SEARCH OF VEHICLES

Certain basic methods and techniques exist for searching various types of vehicles including cars, trucks (light and heavy goods), motorcycles, bicycles, pousses and motorized cyclos. On Ill. 22, pages 101, 102 and 103, please note control search areas for the various types of motor vehicles encountered in Viet Nam. In general, these methods should be followed in all thorough checks, including spot checks of every 5th or 9th or 12th or 16th vehicle, however designated.

1. *Automobiles* should be checked in the following places:
    a. Sun visors;
    b. Dashboard compartments;
    c. Behind dashboard (a document or small weapons easily can be placed between the wires);
    d. Under the driver's seat;
    e. Between the driver and front passenger seat;
    f. At the back of driver's seat, i.e., between the back of seat and bottom of back rest;

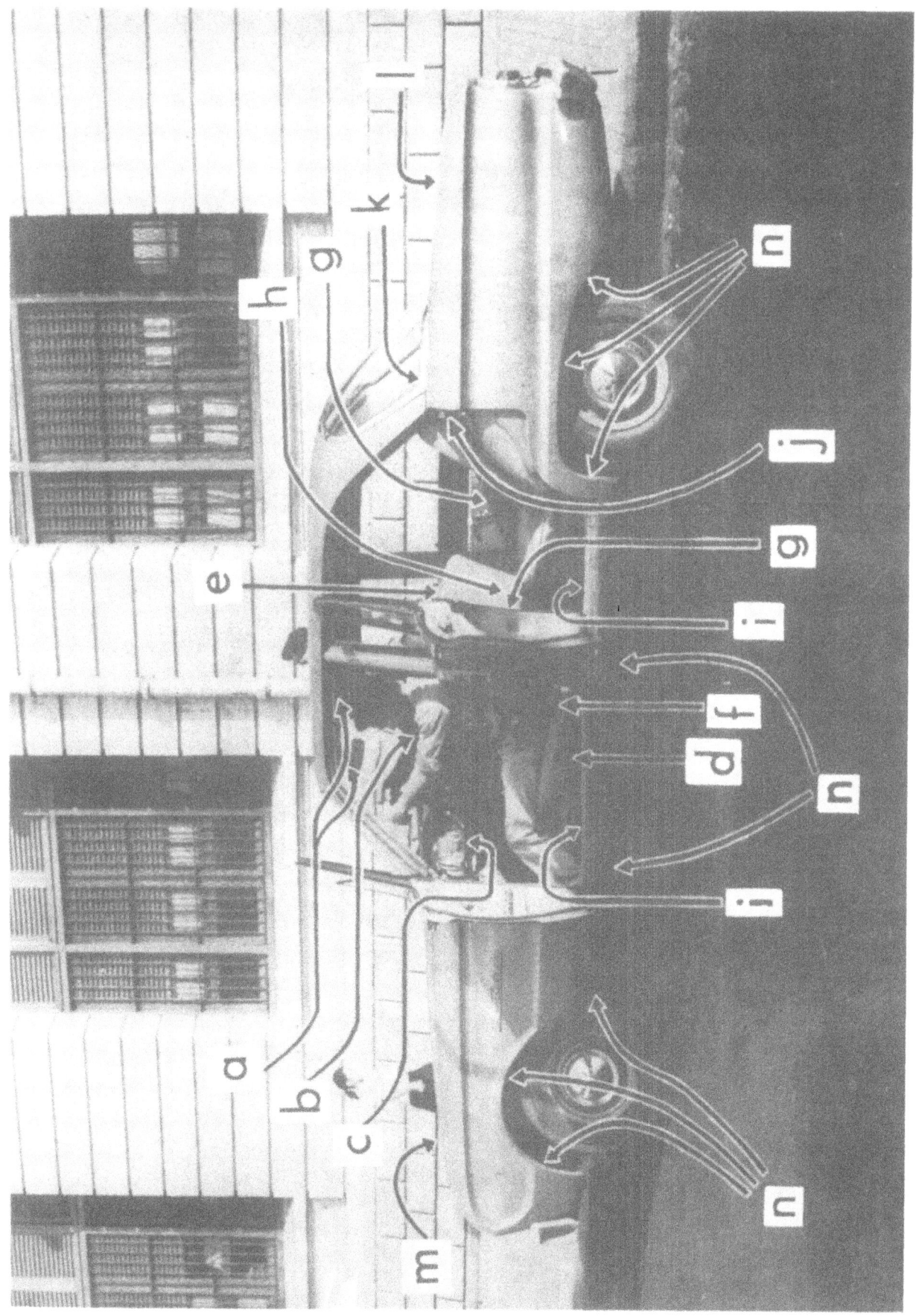

Ill. 22. Types of vehicles that check point searchers should be prepared to search thoroughly.

— 101 —

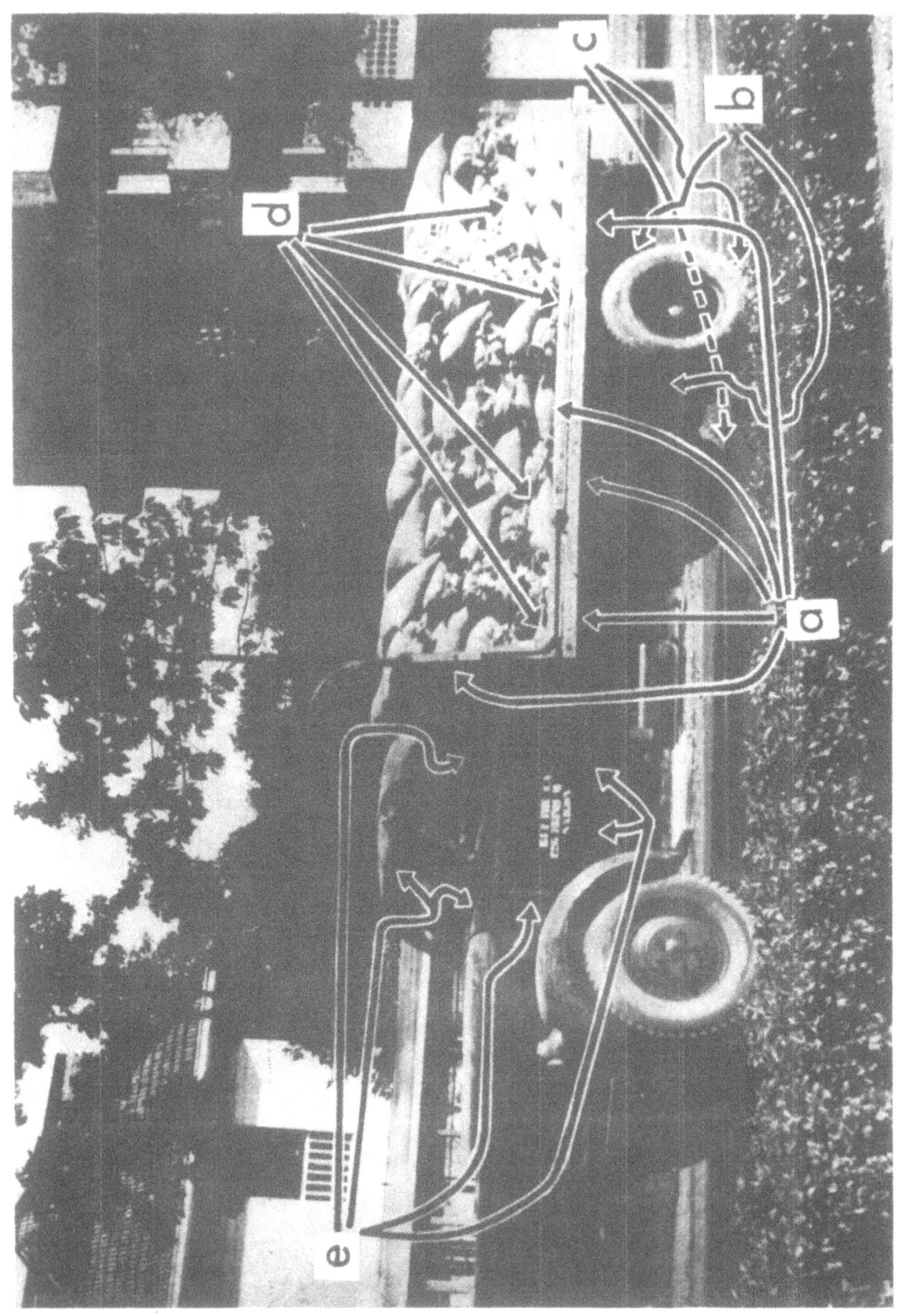

Ill. 22. cont'd

Ill. 22. cont'd

g. Door pockets;

h. Behind front seats;

i. Under any moveable mat in the car;

j. Back seats;

k. Rear window panel shelf;

l. The luggage compartment;

m. Under engine hood and spare wheel compartment;

n. Under mud guards and running boards.

In addition, all loose baggage in the vehicle or trunk should be carefully but quickly examined. Particular attention should be paid to umbrellas, newspapers, magazines and any seemingly innocent parcels, any of which may easily be used as simple means of concealment.

2. *Trucks (Light and Heavy Goods)* are searched in a manner similar to that adopted for cars but with the following additional points to watch for:

a. Wooden body construction. In trucks with wooden body construction, it is very simple to make effective places of concealment by the addition of enclosed panels or false bottoms, or the boarding-up of space between the battens supporting the floor. The sides of trucks may be prepared in a similar manner.

The best methods of search in such cases are close examinations from all angles and careful measurements.

b. Twin rear wheels. The chances of concealment between the twin rear wheels are small but the area should be examined carefully.

c. Wooden blocks (chocks). Nearly all commercial vehicles, particularly those of the heavy class, carry wheel chocks which are placed under the rear a truck have to stop on a steep gradient. These chocks are generally square or triangular and through regular use become dirty, worn and greasy. Usually they are thrown in the rear of the truck or carried in the driver's cab if the vehicle is loaded. Such blocks can be hollowed out to become good places of concealment and always should be examined carefully.

d. Gunny sacks and baskets. All gunny sacks and baskets should be lifted up and searched. A common subterfuge is the concealment of articles under a heap of gunny sacks in an apparently unladen vehicle.

e. Driver's cab. Particular attention should be given to searching the driver's cab which is done according to instructions for an automobile.

3. *Motorcycles* are comparatively easy to search but attention must be paid to the following:

a. Gasoline tank. It may be divided, one division being false. If suspicion is aroused, it may be necessary to drain the tank.

b. Tool box. It should be opened, all tools removed and examined.

c. Rubber handle grip controls. A few moments may be well spent on examination of the handle grips.

d. Footrest supports. Examine footrests and machine supports, the latter bein the hinged devices used to support a parked motorcycle in upright position.

e. General. Lamps, mudguards and all hollow or tubular constructions should be examined. A search also should be made under the seat.

4. *Bicycles.* The following should be checked carefully:

   a. Handle bars and rubber grips;

   b. Bells;

   c. Lamps, dynamos, behind reflector glasses;

   d. The seat;

   e. All tubular frame work, particularly open ends and joints;

   f. Area beneath mudguards.

In the case of very old bicycles, certain parts of the frame or the pedals may have been damaged and been repaired with wire or string. Or they may merely appear to have been damaged. Remove and examine parts.

5. *Pousses and Motorcyclos* should be inspected in the same way as bicycles, plus a check of all tubular construction attached to the passenger's hood.

   a. Remove all tapestries, padding, and other materials used for seat coverings and examine these materials and the area underneath.

   b. If a vehicle has a shelf or tray containing sundries underneath the seat, perhaps with a waterproof cover, remove it and examine each item, paying particular attention to the area in back of the shelf and underneath it.

   e. Examine the roof, taking considerable care with edges.

   d. For proper examination, the vehicle should be turned on its side.

E. SEARCH OF PERSONS

Searches of persons fall into two basic categories: quick searches and strip searches. Human beings are not thoroughly searched so readily as are vehicles; in a spot check operation, for example, vehicles at regular intervals are thoroughly searched but their occupants are given only quick body and clothing searches. Only when there is a specific and compelling reason to do so, should an individual be strip searched. It is an extreme measure which wounds the dignity of a person if he is innocent and which also takes a great deal of time. Reminder is made here against the search of a female by a male.

1. *The Quick Search*

The quick search is one in which the searcher runs his hands over a person's body to determine whether any offensive weapons — pistol, hand grenade, knife or other — might be concealed within his clothing. It is the same search that a police officer uses as part of a routine arrest and would be employed at checkpoints in spot checks and to examine occupants of suspicious vehicles.

The first thing to be done in a quick search is to ask the person to hand the searching officer his papers, his identification card and his driver's license, all of which are checked against a list of suspects if the checking authority has access to one. It is wise to make a habit of asking the individual being checked to hand the officer his papers, identification card and driver's license only, and not turn over his entire wallet which may have money in it and leave the police open to accusations of taking some or all of it. To search the man, the officer simply runs his hamds up the down his body, feels around the waist and up and down the legs, both inside and out. It is best to make the search from the rear.

If the person to be checked is under suspicion or is driving or riding in a suspicious vehicle, he is searched before presenting his identity documents. He is requested to get out of his vehicle and stand facing it with his hands resting on its roof or side while searcher ≠ 1 quickly but thoroughly runs his hands over the individual's person from head to foot. The search must include the region under arms, inside the thighs and crotch and the stomach. Clothing should not be patted but should be rolled between the fingers, otherwise any small flat object such as a knife might be overlooked.

It should be remembered that in suspicious situations, the Police officer's greatest advantage is the element of surprise. This is why drivers and occupants of suspicious vehicles are searched immediately upon being stopped and only afterwards asked to present their papers. The immediate search (1) protects the Police in case they encounter armed individuals, and (2) helps prevent a person from disposing of contraband he may be carrying.

2. *The Strip Search*

The strip search involves removing all of a person's clothing and examining it and all parts of the body. It is used only when reliable information or signs indicate that the person is carrying contraband of one kind or another on his person; the nature of the search should make it clear to any officer that only very serious circumstances dictate its use. Nevertheless there are instances when it should and must be employed and this is how it is done:

An uncommonly large checkpoint may have sufficient quarters to conduct a strip search on the spot but it is more likely that the individual would have to be escorted to the nearest district or police office. Proceeding in a logical fashion, the searcher begins at the top of the head and works down to the feet with the clothing checked first. Each garment is removed one by one and handed to the searchers by the individual himself. The clothing is searched as follows:

a. Hat. Look under the hatband and feel carefully under the lining; if anything suspicious is noted the lining will have to be lifted up. Hold the traditional Vietnamese conical hat or a straw hat of any kind up to a light to see whether anything is written on the straw.

b. Coat and Shirt. Take them one at a time, removing all items from the pockets and putting them aside for examination later. Search the clothing carefully being especially alert for unusual thicknesses. If the seams of the coat, for example, seem heavier or thicker than they should be, further exploration is indicated. As with the hat, it may be necessary to gently rip a seam so as to lift up the lining of a coat and look underneath. This should never be done haphazardly because the officer will have to see that the person's coat or hat is sewn up again whether he is a criminal or not.

c. Belt. A great many people try to conceal items in belts. Most belts consist of two thicknesses of leather put together and sewn at the two edges. It is no trick at all for an enemy agent to split a belt apart and secret a message or a map overlay inside it, then sew it up as it was before. But again, a man's belt should not be opened unless something suspicious is felt inside or unless there is strong evidence againts him.

d. Trousers. Remove contents from the pockets as was done with the coat and shirt. The trousers are examined in exactly the same way as the coat with special attention given to the cuffs.

e. Shoes. The toes of shoes should be checked carefully and if any indication exists that heels or soles have been pried apart and replaced, the police officer should do the job again himself. There is plenty of room in the heels and toes of shoes to hide small items.

f. Socks and Underwear. Socks are removed one by one and handed to the searching officer. They should be turned inside out to be sure nothing is hidden in the toes. Underclothing is rolled between the fingers and examined in the same way as coats, shirts and trousers.

When the man has removed all of his clothing, his body is searched carefully, beginning with the top of the head. Often an enemy agent or a criminal will conceal small bits of metal in his hair, where they will stick readily, in the hope they can be used to pick simple locks in prison cells. The searching officer should look in the man's mouth and, if he thinks it necessary, run his fingers around the inside and outside of the gums to see if anything is concealed there. Look in and behind the ears; inspect the man's back. A careless examination would not detect a piece of flesh colored adhesive tape beneath a shoulder blade which might be used to conceal something. Look at the arm pits. Ask the man spread his legs and lift up his genitals so the searcher can look at his crotch. Anal orifice search can best be done by a hospital attendant or doctor. Look between all the toes and examine the soles of the feet.

Finally, the searchers turn to the man's belongings which have been removed from his pockets and spread out on a flat surface. Each item should be examined carefully.

3. *Searching Women*

In general, checkpoint officers should not search a women, even with quick search techniques; they must be satisfied with an examination of her papers. However, if suspicion exists or is aroused and if the woman is in the company of other persons who are being searched, the Police should request that she hand over her purse so they can empty its contents onto a flat surface and examine them carefully.

This must be done in her presence to avoid accusations that something was stolen from her. Also, if the situation occurs at night, an officer might ask a woman to stand in front of automobile headlights and turn slowly around so that her form will be clearly outlined. Any thing other than the usual curves of the female form should be regarded with suspicion and an explanation required.

If further searching is necessary or if a woman is in the company of men who require the strip search, then a female police officer or practical nurse must be found to conduct a thorough search of her person. Probably, the woman will have to be escorted to the nearest town for this. The policewoman or nurse who performs the task should be instructed to check the **woman's hair carefully and body cavities where articles can be concealed.**

CHAPTER IX

FIRE PREVENTION AND PROTECTION FOR THE RURAL POLICEMAN

Organization of fire fighting brigades and increased knowledge of how to prevent fires and how to cope with them when they occur is very important to the rural policeman, both for humanitarian reasons and to counter possible Viet Cong activities. To set fire to enemy positions is a worth while tactic in any type of warfare.

A favorite technique of the Viet Cong is to set fences afire with the result that the flames often spread to the small, thatch houses inside. In old, indigenous hamlets, these tend to be set very close together. The danger is especially great in the dry season when the thatch ignites and burns easily. Besides firing fences, it is relatively easy for the enemy to burn out a village by shooting flaming arrows, tracer ammunition or tossing two or three incendiary flares onto thatch roofs.

It is much more desirable, of course, to prevent fires than to fight them. Fire prevention means taking those actions before a fire occurs which will prevent it from starting, or, having started, from spreading rapidly. Among preventive measures are the lighting of fires in kitchen areas only, using only matches or flints and no petroleum products, the separation of buildings in a new village or hamlet, removal of obvious hazards such as piles of combustible material, and a public education program to instruct people in elementary fire precautions. The latter includes recognition of hazards and placement of buildings so there is sufficient space between them to hamper the spread of a fire.

Because fires will break out from time to time in spite of preventive measures, there must be capability for fire protection as well as prevention. Adequate fire protection in a hamlet or village simply means the ability of inhabitants to put out a fire once it has started or to prevent if from spreading to other areas. This capability requires training volunteer fire brigades in methods of fire fighting, setting up an alarm system and teaching people how to use it, and maintaining a stock of simple materials to use as extinguishing agents.

The strategic hamlet is a small farm community with no industry to speak of, and small danger of fire, except as may start accidentally, or as is brought in from the outside. At the same time, all fire prevention measures and all fire fighting will have to be accomplished with the materials at hand in the village and by the people who live there. There will be no commercial-type extinguishers, no fire trucks, no hose lines, no pumps. It would be less than fair to teach the people the use or desirability of these modern pieces of equipment since they have no chance of getting them. There may be more than 11,000 strategic hamlets in Viet Nam when the program is completed and the Government obviously cannot afford to place a fire truck in each one.

The other limitation on rural fire fighting programs is manpower. Hamlets will have no paid firemen to operate their fire prevention programs or fight the fires once they start. Regular fire departments are high-priced, social protective means, albeit necessary ones, employing professional firemen as one of the expenses that go with the big cities, big industries or big installations. The solution for Viet Nam is the same as that practical and inexpensive one used in small towns and villages all over the world; formation of groups of volunteer firemen made up of local people who are taught the rudiments of fire prevention and protection and who organize themselves in such a way that when a fire breaks out the brigade can act quickly and efficiently, each man knowing where to go and what to do.

To understand how to fight fire, recognize hazards and institute preventive measures, one must understand thoroughly what fire is. It can be thought of as a triangle in which the three sides are represented by heat, combustible material and oxygen. The absence of any one of the three means no fire can start and removal of any of the three from a fire already burning means that it will go out. The fire triangle (see Ill. 23, below)

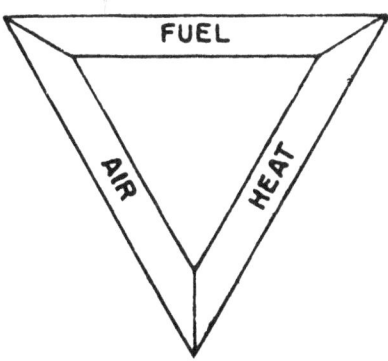

Ill. 23. *Fire Triangle.*

can be effectively used in training classes conducted in rural areas. To use it in demonstration, an instructor simply builds up a small pile of combustible materials in the open air to insure plenty of oxygen, and sets a match to it. He is able to start a fire because of the presence of the three necessary elements: fuel, oxygen and heat of sufficient intensity to bring the fuel to combustion point. If the demonstration takes place in a classroom, the instructor can use a few matchsticks or toothpicks for fuel and build the fire on a small plate. To demonstrate extinguishing methods, the instructor should pull some of the fuel away to show that without combustible material the fire will go out. He should have water at hand to pour over the flames and explain that the fire was extinguished for two reasons: (1) water decreases the heat necessary to maintain fire and (2) water creates a blanket of steam which cuts off oxygen. These two factors, plus its usual availability make water the best of all extinguishing agents.

1. *Types of Fires and How to Fight Them*

Fires are classified internationally into a few general categories; it is necessary to know what type of fire one faces before one can cope with it effectively.

Class A fires are the most common and will be found more frequently than any other in strategic hamlets. They are fueled by any ordinary combustible substance — wood, thatch, paper, grass and innumerable others.

Class B fires are those with oil, gasoline or any kind of petroleum as fuel. Occasionally these fires will occur in strategic hamlets because some people cook with kerosene and use it for cleaning and lighting.

Class C fires are those caused by short circuits or some other deficiency in an electrical system. These have not been much of a problem so far in strategic hamlets but, with the expansion of electrical systems throughout Viet Nam as part of the national economic development policy, hamlet people should be prepared for such fires.

Water is the best single extinguishing agent for a Class A fire and is available in every strategic hamlet. Another effective agent, usually in plentiful supply, is sand. It can be used on small Class A fires where it is possible to cover the flames completely but it is best used on petroleum fires, (Class B). If the fire can be caught before it spreads to buildings and confined to pools of oil or kerosene burning on the ground, fire fighters should shovel sand on the fire until it is blanketed completely and the flames smothered. Sand is also the best material available in a strategic hamlet for extinguishing the rare electrical fire, (Class C).

Water never should be used on an electrical fire since it is a good conductor of electricity and a person can easily shock himself. Instances of fatality have been reported in attempts to extinguish electrical fires with water.

Another agent is the commercial

chemical fire extinguisher. It will not be found in most strategic hamlets but Police will come into contact with it at checkpoints on major highways. Heavy vehicles, such as trucks carrying oil, gas or any other highly inflammable substance, often are equipped with chemical fire extinguishers. The drivers know how to use them, but Police at least should be aware that nearly all oil trucks, for example, carry these pieces of firefighting equipment.

A fourth method of fire control, one which perhaps is most pertinent of all to strategic hamlets, is separation. If a house or any other structure in a hamlet catches fire and the flames cannot be controlled, the major fire fighting effort should be directed toward isolating the buring structure so that the entire village does not go up in smoke. All thatch and combustible materials around the building should be removed. A shallow trench might be dug quickly around the building and filled with water or, if the fire has not progressed too far, pieces of the burning material can be pulled out and taken off to an open space to burn themselves out harmlessly. If the fire has reached considerable size, the best that can be done is to remove all combustible materials possible from the path of the flames.

2. *The Volunteer Fire Brigade*

A volunteer fire brigade is composed of people within a village or hamlet who, in case of fire, have no other assigned duties but to take charge of fighting the fire. A chief of the brigade should be appointed in each hamlet. For training purposes, it would be a good plan to gather fire chiefs from a number of hamlets to attend district or provincial training courses of an extremely basic and practical nature. The chiefs would then return to their hamlets and organize a brigade, choosing people who are young and strong enough to do the hard work involved in putting out a fire. Many women are made strong by their work in the fields and they should not be overlooked in formation of a brigade. The recruits should receive the simple instructions contained in this chapter as well as anything the chief learned in his training course. An index to the number of persons required to form an efficient brigade might be the number of people in the hamlet militia or combatant youth corps. The number will vary, of course, from hamlet to hamlet because of variations in size, both area and population, but the size of the local defense corps is, at least, a good approximation.

The volunteer or recruited firemen would be organized into what are sometimes called bucket and shovel brigades. Members of bucket brigades would carry water from the hamlet's well, reservoir or stream, if there is one, to others who would move close in to the fire and throw the water on the flames. Women could be organized into units carrying the customary two buckets on a pole across the shoulder. Using this method, a large quantity of water could be brought to bear on a fire in a very short time. Men would comprise the shovel brigade and perform the heavy work of shoveling sand on the fire or digging trenches or pulling burnable materials out of the path of the flames. They also should be the ones to actually throw the bucketsful of water on the flames and, in a Class A fire, would do the necessary separation to keep it from spreading. Women sould not take part in some phases of fire fighting for two reasons: (1) their clothing is loose and could easily catch fire itself and (2) their long hair makes it very dangerous for them to move within close range of flames. Men fighting a fire close in should wet down their clothes.

To be successful, a volunteer fire brigade must hold regular practice drill. In this way a real capability is developed as another weapon against the communist guerrillas.

Chapter X
EVACUATION, ALARMS AND CURFEW

As applied to a strategic hamlet striving to develop methods of defending itself in a guerrilla war, evacuation may be defined as the removal, according to plan, of non-combatants from an area under attack by the enemy to an area of relative safety. The same evacuation may be needed in the face of disaster caused by flood, conflagration, typhoon, tidal wave, earthquake or even cattle stampede and sudden plagues.

To conduct a successful evacuation, or at least to carry one out with a minimum of problems, confusion and panic, planning is essential. No amount of planning, of course, will guarantee that all problems will have been anticipated, all eventualities taken into account, or that all details of the plan will have been followed as intended. But thoughtful, careful plans, made before the shooting starts or the diaster strikes and supplemented by drills and practice sessions, will pave the way for as calm and efficient a movement of people as is possible and bring a large measure of success to an actual evacuation conducted under battle or other emergency conditions. To protect the people of a hamlet, the non-combatants, and move them away from the fighting or other danger, is the objective of an evacuation plan.

Just as schools conduct fire drills and ships conduct abandonship lifeboat drills, so the people of a strategic hamlet should be drilled in evacuation procedures. Without sound planning and practice, panic is likely to overtake the people in an emergency and cause an inestimable number of deaths and injuries.

All that can be expected is to obtain what is sometimes called a «posture of readiness». This simply means that a person or group of persons stand ready for something they think will happen in a certain way. They hope the thing will not happen, but they feel there is a very good chance that it will. Under current conditions in Viet Nam, it is believed wise for the people in strategic hamlets to maintain a «posture of readiness» and be prepared to evacuate the locality if necessary.

It should be made clear that the

kind of evacuation planning and organization dealt with in this chapter apply to hámlets and small villages and should not be regarded as any kind of a guide to what to do in case of an aerial attack on, or major fire in Saigon, Hue, Nha Trang or any other city or large town.

A. ORGANIZATION

A hamlet evacuation committee is a voluntary group of citizens who, as in fire fighting and hamlet defense, work together in an organized manner for their own welfare and protection. The responsibility for establishing such a group lies with the hamlet administrative committee, particularly the member in charge of security.

The security member must make absolutely certain that each person in the hamlet's evacuation organization is assigned definite duties and responsibilities and that each understands clearly what they are and how he is to carry them out.

The organizational structure of an evacuation may be divided into three main sections: (1) *Welfare;* (2) *Policing and Fire Protection;* (3) *Wardens, Alarms and Communications.* Certain of these functions, such as policing, may be similar or identical to those operating in the regular, day-to-day life of a hamlet, but in an emergency where evacuation of the population is concerned, all of the hamlet operations are directed toward one objective only: the safe, quick movement of people. The hamlet committee is responsible for appointing chiefs of the three sections.

One of the first rules of evacuation is that there be established alternate sites to which the people will move and alternate routes to get them there. It would be quite in character for any guerrilla band to feint, to make a false attack, hoping that the people of a hamlet or village will evacuate according to plan and walk right into their ambush. If an attack has begun or is imminent and there is the slightest reason to suspect that the enemy may be aware of a hamlet's evacuation plan and is lying in wait for the people to move out, runners or small patrols should be sent to investigate the evacuation routes. They might return to conduct the inhabitants out or they could use visual communications to warn the people back or encourage them to come ahead. Further, an evacuation route sometimes may be cut off by the enemy, whether he knows about it or not, and it is essential that an alternate escape route exist.

Similarly the movement of fire, flood waters and high winds is unpredictable. Again, therefore, alternate havens and routes are mandatory.

Another point, perhaps obvious but important, is that all who are assigned specific duties in the hamlet must stay at their posts as long as possible or until their jobs are completed. The hamlet militia or combatant youth have the duty to stand and fight for the hamlet and, if they can, prevent it from being overrun; certain members of the evacuation organization will also be required to stay in the hamlet as long as possible. These would include police and fire fighters and those assigned to assisting the old and the very young in the evacuation and insuring that no one its left behind. These too, should only leave when they complete their assignments. If the hamlet is about to fall to the enemy, all go, including the defenders. Likewise evacuation in the face of disaster is not a signal to cease efforts to control fire or build dikes or continue rescue.

1. *Welfare*

Welfare forms the largest and most complex part of evacuation planning. There always are a number of elderly people, women and children who must be looked after as well as those of middle age and younger, conducting the actual evacuation and/or fighting, who may be hurt and require medical attention. In an emergency situation requiring evacuation, it will be found that medical needs increase, due to both sickness and injury. Every hamlet, shortly after it is established, should have at least one person trained in elementary medicine or first aid. This individual should be appointed to take charge of the medical needs of the people when they have safely reached the relocation site. He probably also should be the one to organize and direct a group which would establish some kind of a temporary sanitation system. The latter is essential because disease germs can breed and spread quickly through a temporary camp-like living area, bringing sickness and death to the people.

Plans must be made to shelter and feed the people when they are moved from their homes to a new area. One person should be assigned to form a group responsible for obtaining food supplies, another to direct the erection of simple temporary shelters.

Social services cover a wide area, obviously. There are innumerable contingencies, only some of which will be anticipated. If, for example, the head of a household is killed or injured in an attack or dies in a flood, someone must be there to assist the wife and mother who may have both old people and young children to look after. There will be the problem of money. The hamlet administration must continue to operate in the new area and it will need money; many of the people may have none. Someone must be placed in charge of conducting the hamlet finances in the evacuation area until the normal situation is restored.

In general, it should simply be remembered that people evacuate their homes to avoid attack or disaster and most likely they have to go to some place away from their usual facilities for taking care of themselves. The function of the *welfare section*, therefore, is to provide the people with the necessities to permit them to exist in reasonably healthy and comfortable circumstances for a short period of time.

2. *Policing and Fire Fighting*

Police functions in an emergency are basic and fairly well known to any policeman, even one with a minimum of training. In an evacuation the police must try to maintain order, prevent looting and generally direct and assist the population so that it can move out efficiently. However, the chief of this section of the evacuation organization probably should appoint extra men to act as police during an evacuation. It should be the duty of the hamlet police officer to instruct these persons in advance in the elementary police methods which the situation might require.

Fire fighting is covered in Chapter IX and the volunteer brigade described there should be assigned to work out special plans which would go into effect in the event of an attack or evacuation. Naturally, the brigade should be given discretion to do what it considers best in the differing circumstances of an emergency.

Rescue operations also may be required in some instances and the police and fire fighters should be responsible for them. They would mainly involve saving people from burning or collapsed buildings and moving out sick or wounded individuals who are unable to move under their own power.

3. *Wardens, Alarms and Communications*

The chief of the section on alarms, communications and wardens is responsible for gathering a group of reliable people who will plan and practice alarms, operate radio communications, if they exist, and who will be suited to the job of «running» messages or carrying them by bicycle.

a. Wardens

This section should institute a system of area wardens in which dependable persons are made responsible for notifying the people in designated parts of the hamlet of the emergency and giving any instructions issued by the evacuation committee and supervising their execution. Usually a warden is responsible for a relatively small area and his own house and family usually is included.

In addition to notifying the hamlet residents, a warden should check to see who needs help, supply assistance himself, if possible, and insure that the inhabitants of his area are following instructions and preparing to evacuate in accordance with the plan.

b. Alarms

Something which must be emphasized to the inhabitants of a hamlet about an alarm system is the seriousness of setting it off. In the English language, an expression has come into being in this connection which says, «don't cry tiger». The story behind it is this:

A boy in a small mountain village kept cows in a nearby meadow for the villagers and one day he decided he would play a trick on them. He came running to the edge of the field, shouting «Tiger, Tiger, Tiger!» The villagers heard him and rushed out to help him round up the cows and fight off the tiger. Looking around them the townspeople saw the boy was laughing at them and they realized they had been fooled. The boy played his trick again, and still again, and both times the villagers came running. One day, the boy did see a tiger creeping along the edge of the wood and now he shouted out in real fear, «Tiger, tiger, a tiger is coming!» But the villagers, thinking the mischievious boy was up to another trick, paid no attention to the warning and went about their work. So, unhampered, the tiger jumped among the cows and killed them and the boy alone was helpless to stop him.

The moral of this simple fable is only that people pay no attention to an alarm if they hear false ones over and over again. In a hamlet, those responsible for alarms must make the system as foolproof as possible so there can be no mistaking the meaning when the alarm sounds. The authority for giving an alarm should reside with the hamlet chief, or his deputy if the chief is away when an emergency occurs.

There are a number of very simple items which can be used as alarms, the principal criterion being that they can be easily seen or heard by all persons concerned. Generally, alarm devices fall into four types: (1) Metalic, including bells, gongs, a metal triangle and many others; (2) Percussion, such as a drum or hollow wood like bamboo, (shooting should not be used as an alarm); (3) Wind, such as a siren bugle or a whistle, and (4) Visual, such as flags, flares, lights.

Easily understood signals for each type of danger must be established and exercised. A general recall signal must be included to rally the people to return to the hamlet. Finally an end of danger or secure signal is needed.

c. Communications

In an evacuation, as in almost any type of emergency, some sort of communications system is necessary. In a strategic hamlet only the simplest means, involving the least equipment, should be considered because most hamlets do not have telephones, radios and the more complex modern devices.

With the assistance of the American Aid program, the Government of Viet Nam is in the process of installing radio communications between hamlets and nearby military installations or district towns. In many areas, especially where hamlets are likely to come under enemy attack, these simple transmitting sets have been installed. But elsewhere and in the event of emergencies, such as the radio going out of order and no one available to repair it, other methods must be used.

Evacuations require emergency communications systems of a temporary nature rather than anything which might be set up for daily use. Four types are generally considered:

(1) Physical — the messenger. This is one of the oldest types of communication, used in the earliest times to carry messages from one point to another. Runners still perform this task in primitive societies and, in fact, all societies when other means fail. Horses, of course, carried the messengers where available and, as the world became more mechanized, bicycles and finaly motorized vehicles came into use.

(2) Visual. This type of communication is used for the transmitting of messages as well as for alarms. Some of the methods are the use of smoke signals, flags, semaphore, flares and flashing lights. In this system, of

course, pre-arranged signals must be used so the person receiving the signal can understand the message.

(3) Audible. Also used for alarms and also depending upon pre-arranged signals, this means of communication includes such devices as auto horns, sirens, whistles, gongs, hollow wood, bells and drums.

(4) Electronic. Facilities for telephone and radio communication, as mentioned above, are not likely to be found in most strategic hamlets. If, however, a hamlet is equipped with a radio transmitter, it also will have at least a few persons who know how to operate it. Naturally, they will play an important part in any emergency operation and in an evacuation their sole duty should be to establish contact with the village, the district or the nearest military, Bao An or Dan Ve unit.

d. Alerts

Alerts, by which the people are informed of the stages of an emergency, go into effect according to previously established criteria which have been well publicized among the inhabitants or a hamlet. The alert conditions might be as follows:

(1) Grey Alert, given immediately upon learning of the possibility of attack or emergency. Under it, farmers should return from the fields, mothers should round up their children and move them into the houses and the evacuation organization should move into operation with each member prepared to go to his assigned duty post. This action is described as the general recall and that an emergency is foreseen.

(2) Yellow Alert, sounded when it is believed by the responsible officials that an attack or emergency is imminent or taking place but evacuation is not yet needed. At this time, the people should gather up their gear and prepare for evacuation. All members of the evacuation committee should immediately go to their stations.

(3) Red Alert, given when the attack or emergency requires evacuation which begins immediately.

(4) All Clear, signaling an end to the danger. Sounding of the alerts, as the alarms, should be the responsibility of the hamlet chief or his deputy. During the day, first news of an impending attack or diaster might come from specially designated lookouts, from farmers working in outlying fields or someone approaching the hamlet from another area. The hamlet police would be the first to see a fire, a rabid dog or cattle stampedeing. They should report at once to the chief. At night, with most hamlets guarded by a militia force, a guard in a watchtower would probably be the first to spot an assault force or notice a fire. He may be authorized to sound the alarm for an alert for evacuation without waiting to inform the hamlet chief.

B. TRAINING

The entire population of the hamlet must be trained for evacuation. Training falls generally into two types: classroom and drills. The first is for all persons who have a definite role to play in the evacuation organization. The wardens, firemen, those assigned to police detail and all members of the committee should meet with the hamlet security chief and the heads of the three evacuation sections for an informal lecture on the plan and an outline of the duties and responsibilities of the various sections and groups. Most organizations would find it necessary to hold several of these sessions to discuss problems and perfect the plan.

The second type of training involves the practice sessions and drills necessary for the entire population of a hamlet. These drills are actually mock evacuations in which the people go through all the motions of a mass movement, beginning with the first alarm all the way through to the all clear signal. It can readily be seen that people must know what to do, almost automatically, when an alarm is sounded or an alert declared in order to maintain the important posture of readiness. More often than not, there will be no time for wardens and other evacuation workers to re-instruct people in their movements, especially when a state of fear and tension, inevitable in an emergency and ever ready to turn into panic, prevails. The only way the people can learn what to do is for them to actually go through the actions; verbal instructions are not enough.

Another reason for drills is that evacuation officials as well as the people themselves will be able to see errors in the overall evacuation plan and correct them. Seldom is a plan worked out so perfectly on paper that needed improvements cannot be observed in practice.

A third reason is simply to create interest. While drills must not be held so often that they disrupt daily life and cause grumbling and complaining, they do provide action and demonstrate to the people that something is actually being planned for their safety and that they are being taught how to carry out that plan. This is especially true in areas where Viet Cong hostility is open and causing daily apprehension to the inhabitants of strategic hamlets. Whenever drills are held people should be told previously that an emergency does not exist. Although not always done, the scheduling of drills in initial training, helps to make the drill less confused. Surprise drills are the last phase of training.

C. CURFEW

Curfew, or the restriction of movements of people within specified hours, relates to the protective measures for strategic hamlets covered in this chapter. Usually, the purpose of a curfew is to permit loyal combat forces to identify and take action against the enemy by operating on the assumption that the only unauthorized person moving abroad within the restricted hours is the enemy. Curfews usually are imposed during the hours of darkness which is when clandestine or guerrilla forces tend to operate.

Curfews can be divided into two types for the purposes of this text: (1) one involving a specific area such as a district, a city, a series of hamlets or sometimes an entire country, and (2) the arterial curfew dealing only with movement along highways or other transportation arteries.

During curfew hours, the persons authorized to move about outside the imposed limits are the military, the Police and firemen. All should be in uniform and thus easily identifiable; even these security forces must be instructed to attend strictly to their duties and stay within their duty areas during the curfew. Those involved in essential or emergency services, such as doctors and medical personnel, must be allowed a certain freedom to move about. For their own protection the security personnel have a constantly changing series of recognition signals. Usually verbal signs and countersigns are used. However, a series of moves may be used by a person or groups approaching a gate.

The ordinary citizen who finds it absolutely necessary to go out should be instructed to carry his identity card and a light. If security forces stop such a person, they should examine his identification and ask his errand. If it is legitimate, the best approach is to escort him to his destination and home again, if sufficient personnel is available.

As in every other aspect of the strategic hamlet and resources control programs, it is important to explain the reasons for a curfew and what it will do to protect the people as well as what they must do to implement it. The same is true for evacuation but its purpose, of course, is almost instinctively understood. Here, instruction in method of operation is more urgent and necessary. However, it is important to explain to the people that if the enemy forces the evacuation plan to go into effect, the police, firemen, wardens and other members of the evacuation committee will be in full charge. Their orders will have to be obeyed quickly and without question in order that the evacuation get underway quickly and as smoothly as possible. The people should be assured that any dishonest action on the part of any member of the evacuation committee will be dealt with firmly by the hamlet authorities.

PART III
THE MALAYAN EXPERIENCE
CHAPTER XI
THE REPORT

A. PURPOSE

The purpose of this report is to record for police administrators and serious students a summary of the actions taken and the part played by the Royal Federation of Malaya Police in the successful defeat of the communist guerrilla activity by that nation. In achieving that purpose, examination was made of the Police organization there, the methods used in resources control and rural internal security, a brief review of the police and the resettlement of the rural population, and similar matters. To do this, the writer paid two, one-week visits to the Federation of Malaya in May, 1961 and November, 1963, where, through the cooperation of the Police, this report was made possible. The bulk of the information was obtained by direct interview with Police and other government officials at various levels, private citizens, and from observation. The result so far has been the publication of one paper, «The National Identity Card Program — The Federation of Malaya», published Saigon, October, 1961; a pamphlet, «Control of Population and Material Movement», published Saigon, February, 1962; a seven weeks training course given to forty-two police instructor-students representing all provinces in Viet Nam, at Nha Trang, Viet Nam, July-August, 1962; three one-week (44 hour) courses given in the Phu Yen Province, Viet Nam, for 300 temporary rural constables, plus two 16 hour supervisory sessions; two one week (44 hour) and two 16 hour training courses for PsyWar ARVN officers and NCO's at the PsyWar training center in Saigon; a position paper concerning Resources Control and Rural Internal Security for the Public Safety Division, USOM/Saigon, dated Dec. 7, 1962; and of course, this report.

B. HISTORICAL SUMMARY

Following World War II, the Federation of Malaya returned to its prewar state as a British protectorate. During this period of reconstruction, the communist elements in Malaya, former allies against the Japanese, turned against the British government. With carefully hoarded weapons and supplies, they began in June 1948, a long series of murders and depredations aimed particularly at British rubber planters, tin miners, and government officials, but also including anyone else within range.

On June 18, 1948, the British declared Malaya in a state of «Emergency», which Emergency — the situation will be referred to as such hereinafter — was to last until July 31, 1960, when it was discontinued by the new Federation of Malaya government which had peacefully achieved its independence from England on August 31, 1957.[1]

Thus, Malaya's counter-offensive against the communist guerrillas was conducted in two phases: first, under the direct control of the British protectors; and finally, by the young, independent Federation with collaboration and advice from their former British rulers, in the fields of military action, resettlement of vulnerable population, and rigorous checks on traffic of people and supplies between cities and villages.

The initial approach was similar to that used in Viet Nam with the resettling of population groups into 510 New Villages (Strategic Hamlets) operated by civic action groups under general supervision of the Resettlement Administration. General rehabilitation and improvement of the villagers' lot was part of the program. Initially unpaid volunteer police were tried, too, but the idea was discarded.

It was soon realized that resettlement rehabilitation and military operations were not enough, and that it would be necessary to control the guerrilla's capabilities as to supply and

---

[1] It may be of interest to note that on the day this is being written the new Federation of Malayasia was officially declared a new nation.

communications. Accordingly, what was first called a «Food Denial» program was implemented under the direction of the Resettlement Administration with the Police Force having the responsibility for its enforcement.

Facing up to the problem squarely, the British imported some 300 plus of what were called the «Palestine Sergeants», although there were many officers and men from other places included, but all were British with experience in guerrilla warfare. There were some 150 British officers in the regular police force key positions. The initial police strength of 20,000 men, was raised to 30,000, including the paramilitary Police Field Force, augmented by 41,000 Special Constables, or temporary paid police, recruited and trained for the duration of the Emergency and supervised largely by the «Palestine Sergeants», aided by the regular British police officers. These 41,000 Special Constables were responsible for, under Police Force directives, Resources Control and Rural Internal Security.

The program encompassed such things as National Identity Cards; Tenant Registration (in Viet Nam it is called «Family Census»); static and mobile check points; food and critical supply control; supply control patrols and investigation; central food storage, and in one critical area central cooking was established; New Village internal security, including a national nighttime curfew in 75% of the country.

This then is the historical summary; the details follow concerning the things done in Resources Control and Rural Internal Security.

C. ORGANIZATION OF THE MALAYA POLICE - INTRODUCTION

The responsibility of the administration of the Government of the Federation of Malaya is distributed between 12 Ministers, headed by the Prime Minister, and the administration of the Police Force comes under the portfolio of the Minister of Internal Security.

The Royal Federation of Malaya Police is the instrument of the Federation of Malaya Government for the maintenance of Law and Order. Its authority stems from the Police Ordinance 1952 which lays down its statutory duties and responsibilities.

The functions of the Force are defined in the Ordinance, 1952:

«The Force shall, save as provided in Section 25 of this Ordinance, be employed in and throughout the Federation for the maintenance of law and order, the preservation of the peace, the prevention and detection of crime and the apprehension of offenders, and for the performance of such duties, police officers may carry arms in accordance with the Standing Orders.»

1. *History*[2]

Originally each State of the Federation had its own Police Force. The earliest of these in Penang and Malacca date back to 1806 and 1824, respectively. After 1867 Police Forces were gradually raised in the remaining States, beginning with those of Perak, called the

---
(2) Taken from a Police College lecture.

Perak Armed Police, Negri Sembilan and Sungei Ujong (now part of Negri Sembilan) in 1874, Selangor in 1875 and Pahang in 1888. These became the Federated Malay States Police in 1896, while at various dates between 1896 and 1920 State Forces were raised in Johore, Kedah, Perlis, Trengganu and Kelantan, the last known as the Kelantan Military Police.

In 1946 all these separate Forces were merged into the Malayan Union Police, renamed in 1948 the Federation of Malaya Police. In 1958 the title «Royal» was conferred and the Force became known as the «Royal Federation of Malaya Police». Only three other Police Forces in the Commonwealth have been similarly honoured with the title «Royal».

The Malayan Police have always had a para-military role, having been used to supress disorders in Perak in 1875, in Selangor and Sungei Ujong in 1876, Rembau (Negri Sembilan) in 1884, the Pahang rebellion of 1891-94 and Trengganu in 1927. In 1896 Malaya's first local Military Force, the Malay States Guides, was raised, trained and officered by the Police and it served overseas in the First World War in the defence of Aden against the Turks, being reabsorbed into the Police on its disbandment afterwards.

During the «Emergency» (Communist uprising) of 1948-1960, the greatly expanded Police Force, including a large Special Constabulary, took a leading part in operations against the Communist terrorists, scoring numerous important successes.

In the early days, the immediate task of the various State Police Forces raised in the 70's and 80's of the last century was to keep the «public peace». This was a para-military function carried out largely by mounted patrols of armed Police along the existing system of bridle-paths and across the mining areas of the day. Their duties were mostly concerned with the suppression of debt-slavery and curbing the murderous excesses of the «hulubalan» or feudal retainers of local territorial chiefs.

With the turn of the century and the great influx of Chinese and Indian immigrants, the Police had, in addition to normal Police work, other problems which taxed their resources to the limit.

Up to 1932, the Police had to cope with endemic gang robberies, banditry and kidnappings for ransom, mostly carried out in the tin mining areas by armed Chinese gangs.

The suppression of heavy public gambling organized by wealthy promoters and supported in enormous numbers by all sections of the community, was another particular problem.

Perhaps the worst problem of all was the suppression of Chinese Secret Societies — particularly those of the Triad[3] variety — introduced from their homeland by immigrants from various districts of south China. These, until brought under control, held the whole Chinese community in their grip.

Combatting subversive organizations of all kinds, invariably introduced

---

(3) The «Triad» is the name of one of the largest and best organized criminal groups in Malaya.

into the country by alien immigrants, has been and still is a particular problem for the Malayan Police, the most difficult and intractable of these being international Communism. It was introduced into Malaya in the 1920's via China and is, in Malaya, principally a Chinese movement.

2. *Command Structure*

The Royal Federation of Malaya Police Force is headed by the Commissioner of Police who is responsible to the Minister of Internal Security and, through him, to the Cabinet.

The Commissioner has two Deputy Commissioners. There is one true Deputy Commissioner whose function is to assist and stand in for the Commissioner, with full authority, when the Commissioner of Police is absent from Headquarters. The Commissioner of Police, apart from being often engaged in ministerial discussions, frequently tours the whole country inspecting the Force and the work of the officers and men.

The second Deputy Commissioner of Police is the Director of the Special Branch and it is an indication of the importance placed on Special Branch in the Federation of Malaya that the Director holds the rank of Deputy Commissioner.

The Force is controlled by the Commissioner with the assistance of a Headquarters Staff, which is divided into five Departments, each one of which is commanded by a Senior Assistant Commissioner. The Headquarters staff officers in each Department act on behalf of the Commissioner of Police, but refer to him in all matters of policy and on anything important which the Commissioner may wish to have personal control of. These Departments are as follows:

a. «*A*» *Department* — which deals with all administrative matters as well as Welfare, Control of Personnel, Recruiting, Traffic and other licensing which is the responsibility of Police.

b. «*B*» *Department* — which is responsible for all operations as well as the control of Auxiliary Police, Police Volunteer Reserves (part-time, voluntary Police who are only paid for the hours of duty they perform), the Marine Department, Signals and Communications and the Police Field Force and Federal Reserve Unit. The Police Field Force is the para-military organization of the Police specially trained for jungle operations. It can also be used on an internal security role. The Federal Reserve Unit is the Commissioner's Reserve and can be used anywhere in the Federation; it is specially trained for the maintenance of public order and control.

«B» Department is also responsible for all training and controls the three main training establishments:

(1) The Police Depot, where Recruit and Basic Training, the Basic Training of Officers and re-training Programs are carried out;

(2) The Police College, Kuala Kubu Bharu, which deals with all forms of higher training and Promotion Courses; and

(3) The Police Field Force Training School at Dusun Tua, where normal

policemen undertake conversion courses to fit them for jungle operations.

c. *«C» Department* — This Department deals with all supplies, all armorments, works and buildings, the control of all transport and all matters of finance.

d. *«D» Department* — deals with all matters relating to criminal investigation, the investigation of secret societies and the maintenance of criminal records.

e. *«E» Department* — Special Branch, which is the only intelligence organization in the country and is paramount. Its duties are not only as the Special Branch of the Police Force but it is also the Government counter-intelligence organization. At Department level it is also headed by the Senior Assistant Commissioner who is the staff officer to the Director of Special Branch. «E» Department is also responsible for the Special Training School, which is not controlled, like the others, by «B» Department.

3. *Strength*

The Federation of Malaya Police Force at the moment stands at just over 20,000 men, of which 471 are Gazetted Officers (Captain and over) and 1,085 Inspectors (Lieutenants).

During the Emergency there were over 30,000 regular Policemen and 41,000 Special Constables. Thus, the total Force at that time was 71,000. The Special Constables, Policemen recruited for short-term engagements, were trained to a lower Police standard, the accent being placed on their paramilitary duties.

The Force throughout the country is divided into ten Contingents, each of which is controlled by a Chief Police Officer (C.P.O.). The rank of a C.P.O. varies according to the size and responsibility of the Contingent they command. The major Contingents are commanded by a Senior Assistant Commissioner.

Every Contingent corresponds to a State of the Federation. Each State has its local Government, but the Chief Police Officer is not responsible to the State Government. Nevertheless he is called upon to work in the closest possible co-operation with the State Government, but he takes his orders only from the Commissioner of Police.

Each Circle is controlled by the Officer Superintending Police Circle (O.S.P.C.) and he has a similar departmental staff to Headquarters and Contingent, i.e. «A», «B», «D» and «E» Sections, but «C» Department (Finance, etc.) does not exist below Contingent level. Such financial matters that are necessary are handled at lower levels by «A» Department.

There are 20 such Circles in the Federation of Malaya.

There are 76 Police Districts in the Federation, each under the Command of the Officer-in-Charge Police District (O.C.P.D.).

Districts have only three Departments. The O.C.P.D. is in charge of all operations and has an Assistant O.C.P.D. who handles all Administration. At this level the C.I.D. («D») and

Special Branch («E») are still maintained as Departments.

In some areas (mainly towns) it is necessary to have Sub-Districts, or Divisions, usually controlled by an Inspector. There are nine such Sub-Districts in the Federation.

The lowest command is at Police Stations, or Posts, of which there are 693. At this level the area is policed by Constables on beats and/or patrols, or by a village constable responsible to the Station.

4. *Recruitment*

There are three methods of entry into the police service, i.e.:

a. as a recruit police constable,

b. as a probationary police inspector, and

c. as a probationary assistant superintendent of police. All three methods of entry into the service provide for an avenue of promotion up to the highest ranks of the Force. The minimum educational qualifications for each method of entry into the police service are:

a. Constable — the successful completion of the sixth year of primary education.

b. Probationary Police Inspector — The Oversea School Certificate or the Federation Certificate of Education, and

c. Probationary Assistant Superintendent of Police a degree from a recognized university or the Bar Final Examination.

Constables are appointed by the Commissioner of Police in accordance with the Police Ordinance, 1952. Inspectors are also appointed by the Commissioner of Police under the Police Ordinance; in practice, however, the advice of the Police Force Commission, which is constituted under the Constitution of the Federation of Malaya, is the appointing authority for officers of the rank of Assistant Superintendent of Police and above, except that the Commissioner of Police is appointed by the King.

No member of the Police service may belong to a trade union, since it is a basic principle of the service that its members must not only be free from all forms of political bias but must also be demonstrably free of it. However, for the purposes of enabling police officers to consider and bring to the notice of the Government of the Federation of Malaya all matters affecting their welfare and efficiency, including pay, pension and conditions of service, other than questions of discipline and promotion affecting individuals, a Police association has been established by law. This Association negotiates with the Government of the Federation of Malaya on matters affecting pay and conditions of service through a Police Council.

5. *Training*

The Force possesses modern training facilities at the Police Depot, in Kuala Lumpur and at the Police College in Kuala Kubu Bharu. It also possesses a Special Branch Training School in Kuala Lumpur for the training of personnel for the Special Branch of the

Force. The course includes basic police training for all ranks, promotion courses, police administration, internal security, jungle training and courses connected with such subjects as signals, M.T. and Stores accounting are held.

This Force has afforded training facilities for Police officers from the following countries:
- a. Thailand
- b. Burma
- c. Philippines
- d. North Borneo
- e. Sarawak
- f. Nepal
- g. Bolivia
- h. Nigeria
- i. Singapore
- j. Viet Nam
- k. Cambodia
- l. Laos
- m. Brunei
- n. Indonesia

A high proportion of the gazetted officers of the Force have had higher training overseas, particularly at the Police College, Ryton-on-Dunsmore, England, the Scottish Police College at Tulliallan Castle, Scotland, and at the Metropolitan Police College, Hendon, London. In addition, a number of officers of the technical branches of the Force, i.e. Signals, Transport, Marine and Armaments have had higher technical training overseas. To date there has been only one officer who has attended a Police Course in the United States.

FEDERATION OF MALAYA
POPULATION FIGURES

1957 (National Census)

MALAYA	3,514,008
CHINESE	2,595,000
INDIANS	714,000
OTHERS	133,000
TOTAL	6,957,000

1960 (Estimated)

TOTAL	7,400,000

6. *Police Volunteer Reserve*

Police Volunteer Reserve Units exist in all main towns and in many of the smaller towns throughout the Federation. Members of this Reserve perform beat and patrol duties alongside the Regular Force, usually during after-office hours. They also perform motor transport, signals, telephone operating and enquiry office duties. Their support is most noticeable on occasions of public functions.

The present strength of the Police Volunteer Reserve, at present is as follows:

a. Gazetted Officer	41
b. Superior Officers	103
c. Subordinate Police Officers	289
d. Reserve Police Constables	2,077
Total	2,510

On page 127, Ill. 24, sets forth in outline the Malayan police organization.

7. *Emergency Organization*

The Special Constabulary was that portion of the Police Force recruited for the Emergency. They were recruited from throughout the nation and not necessarily assigned to their places of origin. The enlistment was for a period of three years with a government option to extend the enlistment. Beginning salary was $120 Malaya per month (about $40 US). Initially, they only had an armband for identification but were subsequently uniformed. At first they were employed, trained and directed by the rubber estates, lumber companies and mines.

In 1948, the British brought in a group of some 300 men who came to be known as the «Palestine Sergeants», because a large number of them had seen duty in the occupation days in Palestine, and many were sergeants. Actually, a number were officers and many came from other places than Palestine. The important point was that this group served as a hard core to develop the Special Constabulary,

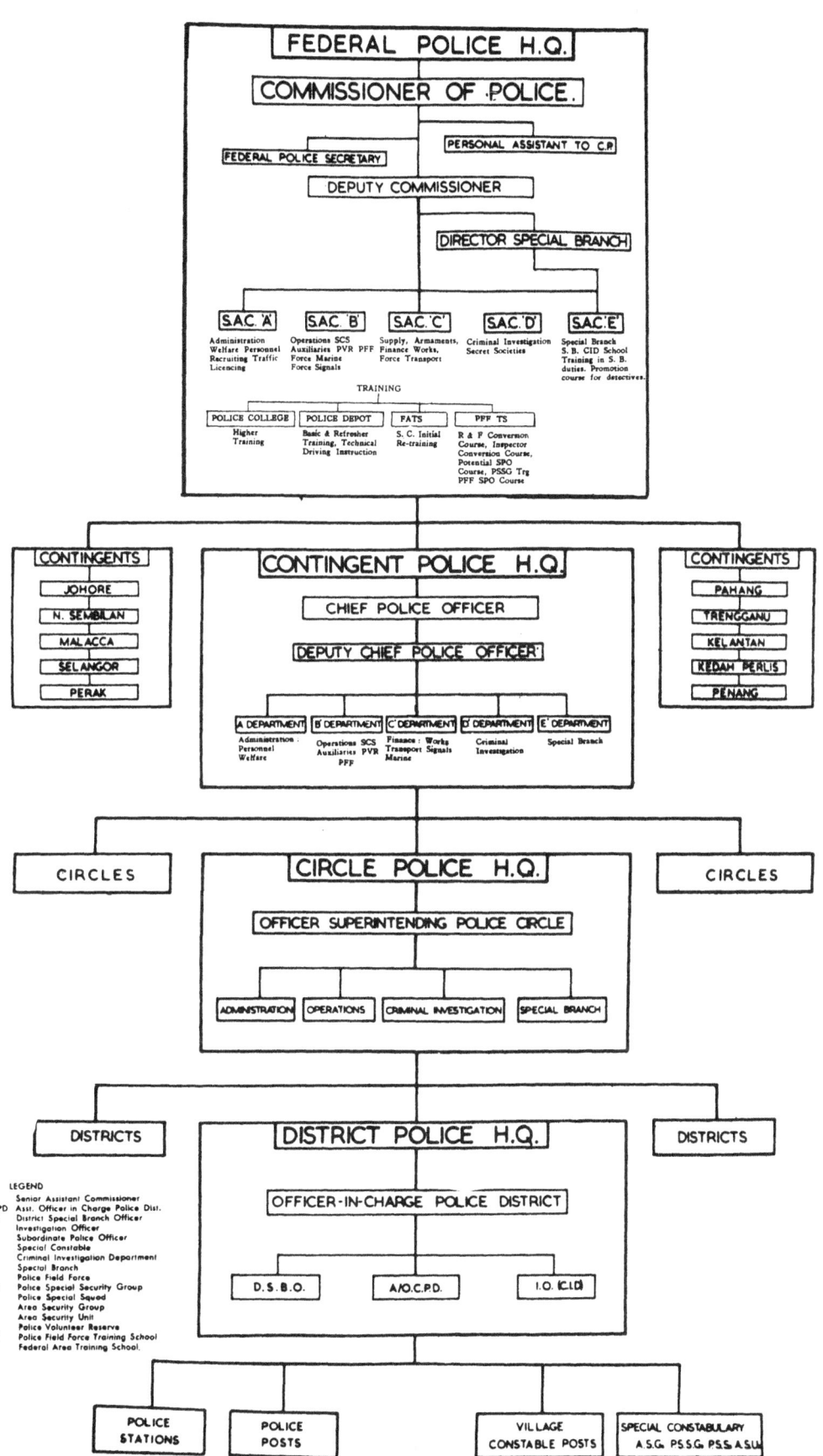

Ill. 24. *Organization chart of the Royal Federation of Malaya Police Force.*

train it and direct it. To get things going, a crash training program of one month was conducted on a local basis, which was gradually changed to state level schools lasting from three to 6 months, depending on the level and experience of the individual being trained. This included conventional police subjects, with considerable emplasis on jungle and para-military training.

As the government gradually took over the operation of the force, they were paid by the Federation. They were completely phased out by 1960, the last 10,000 being in the state of Kedah.

The functions of the Special Constabulary in general terms were:

a. To serve as bodyguards and security protection for the estate and mine managers and their properties.

b. Patrol the estates, operate gate controls and give protection to the rubber tappers, lumbermen and miners.

c. Protect and control food and supply convoys enroute to the estates and mines from the source to the destination.

d. Rural internal security in the New Villages, including resources controls and general policing.

(1) Organization

Each New Village had a Police Special Security Group attached to it, its size depending on the size of the village concerned. At Sintok, a village with a population of 120 people, in November of 1962 there was a full time regular police officer in charge. Under him there was one sergeant, 3 corporals and 30 privates, all full time, paid policemen. They reported to the District Police Officer in Charge for administrative purposes and to the Border Security Commissioner for operations. A picture (Ill. 25) of a squad of these police is shown below.

Ill. 25. *Squad of Special Constables, a basic element of the Malayan Police Special Security Group.*

A reserve group called the Home Guards was recruited on the average basis of one per house in each village. These volunteers were not paid a regular salary, but were paid 28 cents Malaya (about 9 cents US) per hour of actual guard duty. For the most part, the Home Guard performed defensive duties during the hours of darkness when the regular police were on patrol and ambush duty. Some of the Home Guard did actually go out on patrols.

The regular police were armed with Bren guns, carbines, Sterling submachine guns, Mark 5 rifles, lugers and carried hand grenades. Shotguns were the usual Home Guard weapons. Both groups were furnished uniforms free of charge.

The voluntary Home Guard was ultimately used for spot, emergency situations only. Early efforts to use them regularly for police duty resulted in failure. They were almost impossible to discipline, since they were volunteers. Fines were even levied for failure to perform duties properly or for breach of discipline, but this usually drove them to the CT. All were screened by the Special Branch, but, even so, there was many instances where the Home Guard would pretend to be asleep and let the CTs in to raid a village, stealing weapons and food.

C. RESETTLEMENT OF POPULATION

Early in the game it became obvious that resettlement of certain segments of the population was advisable in areas where the population was widely scattered, either in single family units or small groups of families living on the land which they cultivated. In the circumstances it was to all intents and purposes impossible either to prevent constant contact between the terrorists and the people or, and what is rather more important, to provide protection for the people so that they would not be forced by threat of death or injury to assist the terrorists.

It was found by practical experience that the largest feasible new village would have a population of approximately 5,000; however, this was the exception and it was found that a village of some 2 to 3 thousand persons was the ideal both from the point of view of Defense and of Administration.

The establishment of a new village was a task which required careful planning and the closest coordination between all the Government departments concerned if it was to be successful. It was, of course, essential that it should be successful since in any case people are averse to being moved from what they regard as their homes and if they find that they are moved into conditions no better, and possibly worse, than those in which they were living before being moved, they will of course become hostile and Government will have failed to achieve one of the first essentials, to «win their hearts and minds».

Planning to establish a new village, once it has been decided that resettlement of an area is essential, proceeded as follows:

(1) Establish the number of families to be moved, together with their occupations, i.e., cultivators, rubber tappers, and small businessmen.

(2) Select a site for the new village. The site was preferably one which is easily defendable and which is, if possible, within a reasonable distance of the land at present under cultivation by persons to be resettled. If it was not possible to select a site conveniently close to existing cultivated land, then alternative land was selected which was given to the people in lieu of that

from which they have been removed. The new village was, in most cases, readily accessible by the existing road network since the construction of roads is an expensive and lengthy proceeding.

(3) Having selected the site it was marked off into the requisite number of house and shop lots (approximately 1/8th of an acre per house) and sites provided for a School, a Community Centre, Police Station, medical dispensary, playing fields, and roads were constructed to serve the house and shop lots. Arrangements were made to provide piped or well water.

(4) Once this was done the perimeter of the village was surrounded by a double chain-link or barbed wire fence, each fence some 8 feet in height and with approximately 20 yards between the 2 fences. The fences were lit by flood-lights spaced along it and pointing outwards, so that a distance of about 40 yards outside the outer fence was illuminated. All undergrowth and natural cover was cleared for a distance of 50 yards from the outer fence. The same generator which provided current for the perimeter lighting was used to provide a supply of electricity for the villagers. Preferably there was only one entrance to the village and that secured by a stout gate, with a strong point covering it from which protection can be afforded to members of the Security Forces when on Gate Check duties or on opening the gates in the morning.

(5) The Police Station was then constructed at a commanding site in the village best suited for defence and from which Security Forces could be moved most expeditiously to any part of the village.

(6) During the above phases the site of the village and the workmen engaged therein were protected against terrorist attack by Security Forces, if necessary living in temporary accommodations, but well protected by barbed wire and other defenses on the site.

(7) When the above phases were completed, all was ready for the movement of the people from their existing houses into the new village.

The actual move itself again required careful planning with the object of causing the least possible disruption to the lives of the people. In general, it was found desirable that details of who is to move and when be kept secret until the last possible moment to avoid the people moving away on their own to fresh areas and again setting up in isolated groups. However, against this must be set the desirability of permitting the persons to be resettled, bringing with them all their personal property, live-stock, and other necessaries and removing serviceable building material from their existing houses for the construction of their houses in the new village. It was generally found that some 3 to 4 days notice of the move should be given to the people involved and that during this time the area in which they are living must be completely occupied and dominated by Security Forces in strength.

The people were warned that the move would take place on a certain day or on a number of days commencing from a certain day and each householder was told the day on which he would be moved. House-holders were encouraged to remove as much as possible of their existing houses, and transport (usually Police or Military) was provided to lift both the individuals and their property to the new village. To avoid any interference from the terrorists the actual movement was made in well escorted convoys.

If, due to distance, it was impossible for the people destined for resettlement to continue to cultivate their existing land, compensation was paid for standing crops which could not be harvested prior to the move and these crops were then destroyed by Security Forces. Similarly, any buildings or temporary quarters which were not demolished by the persons to be resettled were destroyed by Security Forces so that they could not subsequently be used by the terrorists.

On arrival at the site of the new village, the resettled persons were accommodated, in the first instance, in temporary communal buildings erected by Government prior to their arrival, and arrangements were made for their feeding. The first task of the new villages was to construct their houses and for this assistance was given in the form of building materials, and, where necessary, a degree of professional advice and guidance.

While the villagers were erecting their houses, new land which was provided in lieu of the inaccessible land from which they had been removed was allocated to families.

During the period of resettlement villagers were either paid an allowance for feeding themselves or, alternatively, were provided with food from a communal kitchen. In addition, a grant was made to each family to a maximum of M$500, (about $167 U.S.) and proportionate to the size of the family, to assist them in rehabilitating themselves.

In certain cases the procedure was slightly different in regard to the housing of persons to be resettled in the new village. These local variations were adopted to suit the particular requirements of the area. For example, where the population was already living in close proximity to the site of the new village, they might be given a week to move their house piece by piece into the new village. During this period, of course, the area would be strongly occupied by Security Forces. In other areas where there was plenty of time and distances were perhaps great, houses were actually built for the people to be resettled before they moved into the village. In these cases, of course, the various allowances payable were substantially reduced. The principle adopted was as outlined above, but each State and District War Executive Committee (which were the organizations which planned resettlement) was given reasonable freedom within the overall policy to make local variations to suit individual cases.

Once all the persons concerned had been brought in the new village, the area outside the new village was placed under curfew between the hours of 6 o'clock at night and 7 in the morning;

all villagers were required to be within the perimeter wire of the village during this period and in certain cases a house curfew was sometimes enforced between the hours of 10 PM and 5.30 AM during which all the villagers were required to remain inside their houses.

All the villagers leaving the village were searched by Security Forces at the gate (women being searched only by women) and special booths were set up so that this searching could be done in privacy. The object of the search was to prevent all forms of supplies being taken from the village for the benefit of the terrorists. The village government consisted of a village Committee freely elected by the villagers. There were usually from 9 to 11 family heads, mostly Chinese, and a Chairman. In the early stages these were all appointed by the Resettlement Office. In 1954, Village Councils, elected for a term of from one to three years, began to replace the appointed Committees. These Councils were elected by universal suffrage. They had members designated for such things as sanitation, education and building but there was no police delegate. However, the police attended the Council meetings on an advisory basis, but had no vote.

The Resettlement Officer responsible for a particular village usually attended meetings and had a great deal of power initially. However, as the Council member training programs began to take effect, and the villagers showed their ability to govern themselves and exhibited their loyalty, the control of the Resettlement Officer was gradually diminished and ultimately the villagers even collected taxes. This had a very positive effect in combatting the CT propaganda against the government efforts.

A number of difficulties were experienced initially. Some villages were built in heavy jungle on terrain impossible to defend and had to be abandonned. Commitments were made relative to land distribution and payments of indemnities that could not possibly be carried out. Personnel problems with inexperienced and untrained Resettlement Officers caused many headaches by such action as abuse of power, getting drunk and shooting up a village. However, with time these things were largely eliminated.

Another serious problem involved the resettling of the indigenous peoples, similar to the Montagnards of Viet Nam. This movement was tried, but was a complete failure. They were found to be impossible to resettle into a relatively modern establishment and to adjust to such circumstances so radically different from their own way of life. As a result, most drifted away and the rest became pitiful burdens to themselves with civilization's aliments such as tuberculosis, colds and measles, decimating large numbers.

In the Federation of Malaya some 510 new villages were constructed and approximately 600,000 citizens resettled. Malaya had a total population at that time of 6,500,000 people. The families averaged six in number. When the family had married children these were counted as separate families and given their own piece of land so they could start their own establishment.

The total cost of the actual resettlement was approximately M$115,000,000 (about $38,333,333 U.S.). However, this figure does not take into account the provision of such amenities as Schools, Medical Centers, and Police Stations, which were paid for out of the budgets of Departments concerned. Maintenance of defences of the villages, including the perimeter fence, was paid for from funds allocated to District War Executive Committees. It was found that generally a chain link fence was, although more expensive to erect, infinitely cheaper to maintain than barbed wire fences. The cost of perimeter lighting reached a maximum of approximately M$2,000,000 (about $666,667 U.S.) a year which, as the emergency improved and areas became clear of terrorists (thereby rendering perimeter lighting no longer necessary), has now been reduced to approximately M$150,000 (about $50,000 U.S.) for 1961. It was virtually nothing in 1962, since at that time there were only 5 new villages left, which were located on the Malaya - Thailand border.

Although at first new villages were not popular and great play was made by the terrorists on the «concentration camp» aspect, in general, once the villagers discovered the value of the amenities provided — shools, medical services, water supply, and electricity — they rapidly accepted the situation and it is worth noting that once the emergency was over, there was little inclination on the part of the new villagers to return to their individual and scattered houses.

D. MOVEMENT CONTROLS

Sintok, Keddah State, a town located near the border of Malaya - Thailand in the north, is a New Village still under emergency conditions, but the guerrilla activity is not as severe as formerly. The principal activity of the insurgents is an occasional raid or isolated attack for food and supplies and the goverment's principal mission is running down and capturing or shooting the Communist Terrorists, locally called «CTs». Only 5 new villages remain, all in the border area.

Under these conditions, the controls are somewhat relaxed. Under the more severe conditions, the Identity Cards were collected when the people left the New Villages to prevent the CTs from stealing and destroying them. However, now the people carry their cards all the time.

Certain areas still remain as «Restricted Areas» and certain portions of the jungle and forest near Sintok are currently so designated. The lumbering and mining workers who must go into these Restricted Areas are issued work passes, which are kept at the police post in Sintok, and are issued to the worker daily (see Ill. 26, following). A simple register, which is a bound book, is kept of the time in and out for the work pass for each worker. It also shows the worker's serial number, ID card number and his name.

These Restricted Areas were individually organized for specific areas and even in the daytime passage was

Ill. 26. *Malayan Police issuing daily local passes; note the simple book record of the issue.*

not permitted without a pass or permit. If the restricted areas encompassed farms, workers were escorted to and from the fields at harvest time and all food stuffs were stored in central storage areas. Harvest fields were patrolled at night and flares were frequently fired over known danger spots, accompanied by sweeping machine gun fire.

The Sintok Mining Co., is typical of how the private business operation cooperates in the controlling of movement. The company photographs the workers, makes out the work passes and turns the list of names over to the police. The company maintains its own register, with time in and out and identifying data. During the height of the emergency when the mine was in full operation, the company retained a full time security officer who happened to be a retired Canadian Mounted Policeman.

A substantial portion of the security effort was exerted at the New Village and estate or mine gates where strict control was maintained. All static checkpoints were in fact gates of New Villages which straddled the roads and highways, affording more protection than could be experienced in an isolated point.

Curfews were consistently maintained during the hours of darkness. In highly sensitive areas, curfews were sometimes extended to house curfews, and on occasion, such as when an operation was being conducted in the immediate vicinity, house curfews were enforced in the daytime. These stringent measures only lasted at the most two or three days, but except for an hour or two a day to permit buying of food, were strictly enforced. In some situations where large groups of rubber tappers were known to be sympathetic to the CT, they were let out of the village to tap the trees from 6:00 AM to noon only, and then under constant patrol.

The static checkpoints were operated in all villages and on all roads in the restricted areas. The shifts were four hours each — four on and four off — and each post had a minimum of 3 men for each lane of traffic. Two men did the searching and one man guarded the searchers with a shoulder weapon at the ready. At the height of the emergency, all supply vehicles moved in convoys, eliminating the need for searching them, and no passes were necessary for these. Private vehicles required passes for restricted articles only. Under the usual situation, trucks and vehicles were spot-checked in the conventional manner. Cargo was removed selectively and was not completely unloaded unless suspicious circumstances developed. Sacked goods, such as rice and salt, were probed with a pipe 5 feet long and $1/2$ inch in diameter (1.5 meter by 1.25 cm.) and sharpened at one end. Thus the policeman could tell whether the contents of the sacks were as represented by inspecting the material that ran down the pipe or probe. A solid metal probe, about the size of a pencil and 5 feet long, was used to probe for hidden weapons and similar pieces of hardware. Drivers and cyclists were often caught with sugar and rice concealed in hat bands and in special belts around the waist.

Substantial mobile checkpoint effort was conducted to support the static points. The mobile points were established on a surprise basis and their location was varied. Road blocks were used and official signs and vehicles, which the CTs did not have, were placed to identify the checkpoint as a government one. The CT did not have the capability to establish checkpoints of their own.

Waterways as well as highways were controlled. All boats and fishermen were registered and their area of operation defined and they were required to comply with these limitations. All marine checkpoints were mobile both day and night and were supported by patrols. Boats had searchlights and men were, of course, armed. In one district examined there were 4, thirty-foot boats, with a crew of ten men. There were a number of 15-foot fiber glass outboards, with 2 men each, similarly equipped. They used 18 and 25 horsepower outboard motors and noise was not considered to be an important factor. As a general rule, everything that moved on the waterways was stopped and searched. (Patrols on the high seas will be discussed in a separate section).

Tenant Registration was used to make head-counts in the villages on an organized, irregular basis. This was usually done at night during the curfew and there was no other legitimate movement. There was a minimum of public resentment to this activity.

Fire protection was not a function of the police, but police reported that there was training and that practice drills were held. These were conducted by the Resettlement Officers.

All investigations into resources control were referred to the investigative branch of the regular police force.

There were no special restrictions on trains. All railroad stops were in New Villages or were fenced and guarded with the usual gate controls found elsewhere. Airlines were similarly handled. Buses were searched completely in restricted areas, but there was no control between checkpoints and no passenger manifests were required on any of the above transportation facilities. There were no Suspect Indicees in the terminals, but dossiers on known CTs were maintained at District Police offices.

Resources control measures began as a Food Denial program, aimed primarily at starving out the CTs and making them either surrender or attempt attacks and raids which would bring them into contact with government forces. Likewise, it was believed, and proven to be true, that with the limiting of food supplies to the villagers, any effort on the part of the CTs to take a portion of their food would result in resentment of the CTs by the general public. Party liners and other marginal operators heard the hunger pangs in their stomachs above the call of the Communist propaganda.

However, it was found that «denial» was actually too strong a word;

that in practice it was not physically possible to deny food completely over large areas. This could be done in small, tightly controlled communities, but even there the seepage of from small to large amounts of foodstuffs occurred. Therefore, such a program was realistically aimed at depriving the enemy of as much food as possible on the basis of increasing efficiency of control measures and creating a situation of diminishing returns for the CTs.

As the war progressed, the Food Denial program began to encompass all sorts of critical materials from ammunition to clothing, which the CTs required to support their effort, but the name of the effort continued the same. The «Emergency Regulations Ordinance of 1948», ammended as to 1953, is the basic piece of legislation for this purpose. Pertinent portions are set out in chapter 13.

The basic document in materials control was the «Foodstuffs Movement Permit» which was used not only for foodstuffs but for other materials and hardware as well. It was initially issued by the Food Control Office in the District administrative group, not by the police, whose role was limited to the enforcement of the relevant provisions. As the New Villages spread, Food Control Offices were established at the village level and the permits were issued there as a much greater convenience to the public. The form was prepared in duplicate with one copy given to the driver and one kept in the file.

As an enforcement measure, the permit was presented at all check points where the load was inspected. Patrols along the highway were used to prevent unautorized off-loading in between delivery points. There was no investigative follow-up to determine if the cargo reached its destination, other than a comparison of the documents, an admitted weakness.

Each state printed its own ration card and determined the items which should be rationed and the amounts. Usually they were rice, salt and cooking oil. Samples of the cards are seen in Ills. 27 and 28, following.

Central cooking was a technique used in a few widely separated instances. However, it was expensive in terms of manpower and required a high degree of control. One such operation was conducted in the southeast tip of Johore State, Kota Tinggi Circle, Pengerang District, in 1958 and 1959 where some 30 CTs had been driven. This locality contained no New Villages and was populated largely by fisherman and poultry farmers living scattered out over an area of about 20 miles on a side. The Lebam River formed the northern border making an island of the tip of the peninsula. Heavy jungle covered a substantial portion of the landscape.

One of the first steps was to cut and clear a 100-yard strip along the east coast for access. There were a few existing roads in the western portion. A complete census of the population was conducted, including details of their resources. Central kitchens for cooking rice, which was all stored by the government, were set up every three or four miles under the

Ill. 27. *Sample A of a Restricted Articles Ration Card from Malaya, front and reverse the same; this card covers salt, oil and one other unspecified item.*

Ill. 28. *Sample B of a Restricted Articles Ration Card from Malaya, front and reverse the same; this card covers oil, mee, salt and sugar.*

— 138 —

supervision of a Food Denial officer, and under police protection. Canned goods could be purchased, but were punctured and rationed.

1,000 policemen, including members of the Special Branch, were assigned to the area supported by 2 batallions of soldiers. The results were positive, though expensive, 21 of the original 30 were killed or captured and the last 9 gave themselves up because they were starving.

«Food Lift Operations» were an effective method of enforcement of the Food Denial program. Through the checking of shops and licensed merchants, and from intelligence sources, often there were instances in which a village was suspected of hoarding food stuffs and supplies for the CTs. A «swoop» or raid, usually a joint police and military operation, would be conducted in the early morning hours. Accompanying were public relations teams with public address systems to explain matters to the villagers and to control any panic which might result. All excess food and supplies were removed from the village and confiscated under the laws passed for the purpose.

E. MARINE OPERATIONS HIGH SEAS

The marine operation for the high seas is headed up by an Assistant Superintendent of Police, with offices located in Penang, on the west coast of Malaya. In 1947, there was a marine branch for policing whose principal problem was the Chinese pirates operating in the Straights of Malacca. At that time the CTs began to operate so the emphasis changed. The piracy problem continues until today, although somewhat abated.

The Penang Marine Branch operates from that city to about 80 miles north to Langkawi Island and about the same distance to the south. There is a similar operation at Fort Swetendam, south of Penang.

They use a variety of craft. There are 3 «P» class coastal patrol boats, 75 feet long, with a 14-man crew and a cruising speed of 10 knots. They also have 56-foot launches for somewhat shorter runs, but with the same crew. The boats most likely to be in combat were armoured and all carried Bren guns and shoulder weapons.

The patrols were customarily of 3 to 4 days duration although sometimes they were longer, depending on their ability to refuel enroute. These were conducted both day and night along the shoreline and they stopped and checked all local vessels. Thorough searches were conducted on intelligence or in case of suspicious activity.

The crews were made up of ex-sailors who were given 9 months of police training rather than trying to train policemen to be sailors. The difficulty was that the policemen did not like the long cruises away from home, many were subject to seasickness and simply did not like the day-to-day drudgery of a sailor's life on board a vessel. The group is now performing all customs, immigration and sea rescue work. A number of successful captures of CT smugglers and material were effected, but no details are currently available.

Full radio communication was available between craft, including CW, VHF and Radar, and a Police Signal Center operates out of Penang for the marine network. They have their own shops for line maintenance at each detachment, such as Penang, with major overhauls being done by the Navy yard at Penang.

F. FAMILY CENSUS

A Family Census program, as it is referred to in Viet Nam, was in effect during the Emergency and was called «Tenant Registration». Its purpose was initially a part of the resettlement proceedings to determine the size of the village and the amount of equipment, supplies and personnel to be moved. It was performed by the Resettlement Office rather than the Police and has now been discontinued and forms were no longer available. The police, however, did use Tenant Registration as an investigative tool and as a result of «head counts» in the New Villages they made some interesting captures and supply seizures.

G. NATIONAL IDENTITY CARD PROGRAM

This program was in existance throughout the Emergency. However, in 1960 it became necessary to change the system to a safety-paper card, machine laminated, as a protection against forgery and counterfeiting. The system was an effective control and was essentially conventional. The details are contained in the report by the writer, «The National Identity Card Program — The Federation of Malaya», published Saigon, October, 1961.

H. COORDINATION

There appeared to be and have been throughout the emergency, very close coordination between the Police, the Military and the rest of the civil government. The top coordinating group, located in the capital, Kuala Lumpur, was called the Emergency Operations War Council and was composed of the British Resident Governor General, Chairman, the Prime Minister, the top Police official, the head Military officer of the country and other cabinet level ministers totalling at one time 15 people. This Council met a least once a week, formed national policy, established national plans and coordinated operations on a nationwide basis.

More active committees were formed at the State and District level, which were charged with the actual day-to-day running of the war effort. These committees were called the State (or District) War Executive Councils. The Chairman was the top colonial official in the state or district, the British Resident. He has been replaced recently in the British withdrawal by another member of the committee, the Mentri Besar, or Prime Minister of the state. Other active members were the Chief Police Officer, the Brigadier representing the military, the head of the Special Branch and the heads of all civil departments of the State or District government. The principal difference between the State and District Councils was the level of the executives involved. Once a week the full Council met.

A more informal group consisted of an Operations Sub-Committee which met daily and was, and is still, referred to irreverently as «Morning Prayers». It consisted of the Chief Police Officer, Chairman, the Brigadier, the Special Branch and any other persons whose presence was required. All things were coordinately continously in this fashion and the group was in constant individual contact. One observer stated «They practically lived in each others' pockets».

Morning Prayers were held in a conventional operations rooms with maps and charts showing the current situation kept up to the hour, location of friendly and enemy forces, smuggler routes, local conditions, foods supplies and the myriad of other details required to coordinate counterguerrilla activity.

I. INCIDENTAL INTELLIGENCE

A number of tricks were tried by CT sympathizers to avoid the ration controls. As people were allowed to take only lunches out to the fields, and were given a careful physical search each time they passed the gate, extra sugar was poured in the tea buckets and allowed to settle to the bottom where it could often pass undetected. Bicycle tubes and frames were filled with sugar, rice and similar food stuffs. Strict control was maintained on canned goods in the village stores and markets. Such necessaries as canned milk cans were punctured upon sale so that they would spoil in short order unless consumed within a reasonable time.

Malaya was in a favored position financially. The Korean war brought on a heavy demand for tin and rubber, so that the mine and plantation owners profited mightily during the emergency. Thus, they could afford their own police forces, which they hired and paid for themselves as most major, prosperous industries do everywhere.

Controls and resettlement were not initially popular and were not expected to be. Therefore, an intense and continuing public relations program was conducted. Generally, this was composed of four elements: (1) The public was told in advance what was expected of them, what the ground rules were going to be (2) The people were told the reasons for the imposition of controls or actions of resettlement (3) The need to do these things was blamed on the Communist Terrorists (4) The public was promised that controls would be lifted when the need for them was over. This latter element, lifting of controls, was adherred to strictly.

The Police did, of course, encounter problems in identifying the CTs. In Malaya, however, they often did wear jungle green uniforms, with peaked caps and a red star. They were seldom seen more than 100 yards from the jungle's edge in daylight, and would usually begin firing the minute they saw loyal forces. Often small raid or hold-up groups of two to four would prowl the roads in civilian clothes and the tip-off was shirt worn outside the trousers so as to conceal pistols and grenades carried at the belt.

Currently there are some 500 CTs left of the hard-core, militant group, all believed to be on the northern Malaya-Thailand border. The Malayan Police have a complete dossier on each CT and the problem is now one of hunting the fugitives down. Relatively large forces of men, police and army, are still engaged in tracking these people down, as the thick jungle must be combed literally foot-by-foot. The CT are now living largely like animals in the jungle and searchers must get down on hands and knees for thorough coverage. Some of the guerrillas are captured in filthy borrows, covered over with straw and brush.

The police suffered approximately 3,500 casualties, whereas the CTs casualty number was about 10,000.

The war was financed largely by funds generated within the Federation. However, Britain did furnish some financial assistance, but the amounts and percentages were not available.

A technique to gain public support was P.O. Box 5,000. This was a sealed complaint or suggestion box posted prominently in all villages. A number of good suggestions were received and a surprising amount of intelligence was collected through this means.

Chapter XII
WHAT THE AUTHORS SAY

There has been no so-called «official» police history of the Emergency. However, there is a modest amount of literature on the subject written by persons who were either involved directly in the war, such as policemen and soldiers, or close observers, such as newspaper men. Since these were contemporary historians and to a degree participants, it seems worthwhile to draw on their observations and experiences. However, this is being generally limited to comments and incidents bearing directly on resources control and the police involvement in such a program. The books themselves, of course, should be referred to for more complete treatment. Every effort has been made to avoid quotations out of context and to present both sides of the picture where such was in existence.

«Transformation in Malaya» by J. B. Perry Robinson, published by Secker & Warburg, London, 1956.

Mr. Robinson was a journalist and government official who went to Malaya as Senior Information Officer in 1952. He was engaged in the psychological warfare campaign against the terrorists and was also an official historian.

It took the police quite a while to learn how to operate under the conditions and to gain public support in insurgency situations. Mr. Robinson states:

«Axiomatic as it may appear today, it was not generally understood that it was useless to expect the rural Chinese to cooperate with the Security Forces until the Security Forces were able to protect them.

A visit by a Security Forces patrol

to a squatter⁽³⁾ area was an embarrassing occasion for all concerned. The Army or Police, infuriated by the squatters' stubborn silence, by their not having seen anything of an incident committed right under their noses, by their not having the least idea who put up the Communist posters plastered on their huts, dismissed them all as blasted Reds and were liable to knock them about. The squatters, only wishing for the most part to be left alone and quite possibly with no love for the bandits, knew that to give the smallest item of information to the Security Forces would lead to immediate and savage reprisals from the bandits listening in the jungle.

They (the squatters) were accessories to murder (if not actual murderers) and there is no condoning their malice; but the cardinal element in their situation and the conditioning factor in their behaviour was pressure; from which side was the pressure the greatest?

The need to separate the squatters from the bandits was perceived within the first week of the Emergency. So long as the squatters were there on the jungle fringes — aiding and abetting or passively submitting to the bandits — the Army and Police could not distinguish friend from foe. They could not operate freely in the vital area, the edge of the jungle; not only were the squatters and their vegetable gardens in the way of hostilities, but they betrayed the Security Forces every time; and above all, the bandits had innumerable safe refuges and disguises in the squatter huts and ample supplies of food and money... So long as the bandits stayed in the jungle, they always had interior lines of communications and were always on the «other side of the hill».

The role of the police is commented upon in the following quotations; also observe the comments concerning the continuing internal security and resources control problems lasting long after the New Villages were established.

«In each new village at its establishment a strong Police post was set up from which the perimeter wire was patrolled, the watch-tower or towers with their searchlights manned, and the curfews enforced. The prime purpose of these posts (as of the dusk-to-dawn curfews) was the defense of the new villages rather than the surveillance of their inhabitants...

They (the bandits) have, of course, had no small measure of support from inside the villages. One of the main purposes of resettlement was to detach bandit sympathizers from effective contact with the bandits and every new village, when it was established, probably contained a substantial number of active Min-Yuen (informal local communist party) members and of fellow-travellers who were determined to continue to aid the bandits to the maximum of their ability. A gradually dwindling number of them have continued to do so. The new villages are still today the bandits' main source

---

(3) To get the Vietnamese picture, substitute «hamlet» for «squatters», which in Americanese generally means a village.

of supplies from outside the jungle, with the possible exception of the big towns (notably Kuala Lumpur).

Nevertheless, even the most skeptical policeman in the Special Branch will admit today that the state of mind or heart of the new villages vis-a-vis Government has on the whole steadily improved over the last five years. He will probably aver that the improvement is entirely a question of pressure and that the reason for the improvement is that the pressure of the Security Forces has steadily become greater on the whole than the pressure from the bandits... On the other hand, there are plenty of instances of new villages which, early on, settled down to turning themselves into stable, contented communities. From these villages there may always have been and there may still be parcels of food thrown over the barbed wire at night, or whispers of Security Force movements going out to the bandits by day (probably through quite young children);...»

So it can be readily seen that there is no *one panacea* that will whip the guerrilla and that includes the Police Force and New Villages, or Strategic Hamlets.

Police activity covered a variety of things. Harry Miller in «Menance in Malaya», published by George G. Harrap & Col, Ltd., 182 High Holborn, London, 1954, compiled a number of these activities. Mr. Miller was Chief Correspondent for the «Straits Times» of Singapore for five years and was resident in Kuala Lumpur. He had many close friends amongst the police officials and was able to observe their operations and report on them first-hand. He states:

«Briggs[4] said, «The terrorists must be baffled everywhere in their attempts to dominate the populated areas.» He insisted that they must not be allowed to maintain their supply sources or organize new channels for them.

Although the original terrorist supply and extortion organizations had been disrupted by the resettlement of the squatters, they still had wide spread reserves and they adopted new tactics to get more. They scattered among the remaining squatters, and especially among estate and mine laborers, whom they intimidated into feeding them and aiding them by incidents such as rubber-tree slashing...

As the program developed the terrorists established a system of food dumps planned to maintain them for an indefinite period until they were able to renew and reopen contact with their former helpers in the resettlement areas and in the estates and mines. It was known all over the country that laborers and villagers were obeying the orders of Min-Yuen agents to take from their homes one cigarette-tin of food daily and to give one day's pay per month as protection money to the Communists. They had also been

---

(4) Lieutenant-General Sir Harold Briggs, a veteran of World War II in the Western Desert of Africa and Burma, was Director of Operations for the Federation for eighteen months beginning in March, 1950.

ordered to pass food over the fences around their newly situated homes...

He (Briggs) drew a list of foods that were to be denied the Communists through restricted sale in shops and control in movement. He listed pade, rice, tapioca, cooking-oil, sugar, salt, concentrated food, tinned foods, cooking fats, dried fish, paper, printing materials, drugs, medicines, vermicelli and rice products.

Village small town, resettlement areas and laborers' homes were to become guarded food larders. Any area from which bandits got or could get their food supplies might be declared «food-restricted areas.»

Residents in these areas were bound by law to keep a thirty-five-yard wide belt round their perimeter fence clear of undergrowth and obstacles to make it difficult for terrorists to creep up unobserved by day and night. They were forbidden to take out of their homes any amount of food, however small. All meals were to be eaten in the home. The ban extended to clothing and money. Only essential amounts of each might be carried out of a controlled area.

Shopkeepers had to keep full records of customers and their purchases. The State Government had the power to restrict the number of shops in an area by closing some down.

Except for fresh fish, shell fish, fresh vegetables, fresh fruit, live poultry, and eggs, no food could be moved by road anywhere at night. All transport carrying these foods had to cover their consignments with tarpaulins, which had to be securely roped down. Their drivers could not halt anywhere along the roads except within town or village limits. They could not turn off their direct routes or unload except at their proper destinations.

Theoretically nothing had been left out of these all embracing measures to cut supplies to the bandits. Briggs told the people, «You will now be able to say to the Communist extortionists when they approach you that you are no longer able to bring them food, money or other supplies.» Indeed, this was a device advocated by the Chinese themselves. «Force us by law to stop helping the terrorists and we will do so. Do something to us which will enable us to tell the Communists that we really cannot help them any more, otherwise we shall be punished by you, they said.»

This last statement has a familiar ring from some of the more difficult areas in the delta country of Viet Nam where the people begged to be forced to act and to resettle.

Chapter XIII

THE STATUTES
SUGGESTED STATUTE
RESOURCES CONTROL

1. The chief of a province is authorized, during the period of national emergency, to establish emergency checking procedures as outlined hereinafter when, in his opinion, or upon direction of higher authority, the security requirements in the province merit the establishing of such measures. The Emergency Checking Pro-

cedures shall be declared for specific Restricted Areas, either the Province as a whole, or parts thereof, but in no instance longer than ninety (90) successive calendar days. Renewals may be made any number of times as required.

The purposes of the Emergency Checking Procedures are to define certain Restricted Articles and to provide a method of control of these; to provide a method of control of all transportation units and passengers; to identify all persons moving from place to place and to search all vehicles and persons as required in Restricted Areas.

2. *Restricted Articles*

   a. Any species of animal, whether alive or dead, which is ordinarily used for human food;

   b. Any substance or commodity which is ordinarily used for human food, or in the preparation of human food;

   c. Any substance or commodity, other than vegetable matter, which is ordinarily used for feeding animals, including rice bran;

   d. Paper suitable for use in printing, typewriting or duplicating words or figures or pictorial representation, wax stencils and printing ink and any equipment or machinery suitable for any kind of duplication;

   e. Drugs, medicines and other medical supplies;

   f. Flash lights other than one loaded flash light for bona fide personal use, the onus of proving which shall be upon the bearer, and any electric battery not required for the operation of the particular vehicle;

   g. Canvas or any article made wholly or partly from canvas;

   h. Green or khaki cloth, pliable plastic, or rubberized material;

   i. Clothing and any articles made wholly or partly from the materials listed in sub-paragraph «h», except as normally required for current use of the traveler;

   j. Fire arms of any kind, ammunition and any implements capable of being used as a weapon in quantities more than required for their normal use by aborigines, farmers, etc;

   k. Rope, chain, and wire;

   l. All communications equipment, except single, permanently installed automobile radio receivers;

   m. All fuels, except a normal supply for the vehicle;

   n. Electrical generators and any equipment which may be of use to an insurgent enemy group, except normally installed for the use of the vehicle.

3. *Manifests and Passes*

   a. A shipping Manifest of Restricted Materials shall be prepared in the prescribed form at the office of the District Chief of origin for any shipment to a Restricted Area. It shall be reviewed by a competent official to be designated for the purpose. The driver and helper must present their identity cards which shall be searched against index cards of suspects and fugitives provided him by security officials. Identification in the file or irregularity in the identity papers shall be cause for detention and investigation. The destination and contents of the load shall be shown and the trip shall be approved by the aforementioned official. The manifest shall be produced at each checkpoint or on demand of any competent official. At the destination the Manifest shall be taken to the office of the District Chief where the Manifest shall be countersigned, entered in the Travel Register and filed by the District Chief. Upon arrival of the triplicate copy from the place of origin it shall be compared with the original and any discrepancies investigated. If the shipment does not appear within 12 hours of the estimated time of arrival, an investigation shall be conducted immediately.

b. A Travel Manifest — Commercial, showing the names and identity card numbers of all passengers, shall be prepared for travel to a Restricted Area and approved by a competent official assigned to the transportation terminal for railroads, buses and airplanes. All passengers shall show their identity cards to an official designated at the terminal, who shall search the names against index cards of suspects and fugitives provided him by the Security officials. Identification in the file, or irregularity in the identity papers, shall be cause for detention and investigation. Bus passengers may be required to show their identity papers at any checkpoint.

c. A Travel Permit — Non-Commercial, must be obtained by the driver of any non-commercial vehicle from the office of the nearest District Chief for travel to any Restricted Area. It shall show the names of the driver and passengers and their destination and expected time of arrival. All identity papers shall be checked against the indices of suspects and fugitives as in «b». One copy of the Travel Permit shall be kept by the issuing office, one copy given to the driver, and one copy shall be sent to the District Chief of the traveler's destination. The traveler shall report to the District Chief immediately upon arrival, present his Travel Pass which shall be countersigned, date and time stamped, entered in the Travel Register and returned to the traveler. Upon receipt of the copy of the Travel Permit from the District of origin, it shall be entered in the Travel Register. If the traveler does not appear within 12 hours of the estimated time of arrival, an investigation shall be conducted immediately.

d. A Local Pass shall be issued by the office of the District Chief, to all small, three or four wheel vehicles, with a capacity of six passengers or less, which travel regularly within a single District, or between not more than two Districts in a Restricted Area. All others must apply for the Travel Manifest — Commercial. The Local Pass shall be valid for a single driver for a period of not more than 90 days. The same file checks shall be made as in a. The duplicate will be retained by the District Chief and the original issued to the Driver.

4. Any competent official may, in a Restricted Area:

a. Stop any vehicle, make inquiry

as to its contents, and, if not satisfied, search it;

b. Give the driver any orders considered necessary to insure that any Restricted Article or foodstuff in the vehicle is not used for an unlawful purpose and reaches the place for which it is intended;

c. Detain any Restricted Article if it is likely that it will be used for an unlawful purpose which is not properly supported by a manifest;

d. Detain any Restricted Article if it is suspected that an offense has been or will be committed in respect to it;

e. Search any premises if it is suspected that an offense against these regulations has been committed.

5. No vehicle may, in a Restricted Area:

a. Stop outside the limits of a Municipality or a village other than at a place to which any goods in the vehicle are consigned;

b. Deviate from the normal route;

c. Offload in any place except where the goods are consigned.

6. Goods carried on trains may be searched by Railroad Officers or other competent officials.

7. The Province Chief may prohibit or limit selling by itinerant vendors outside Municipalities or gazetted villages.

8. The Province Chief may prohibit the raising of any foodstuffs, except on such terms as may be specified in any Restricted Area, and, if the owner or occupier refuses or neglects to comply with such an order, he may authorize a person to enter upon the land and destroy any crop and recover expenses from the owner or occupier.

9. The Province Chief may prescribe a curfew for any of the travel indicated herein in Restricted Areas within the limitations of his authority.

10. *Penalties:*

(Herein would be set out a series of violations, **penalties**, and fines.).

THE EMERGENCY REGULATIONS ORDINANCE, 1948.

(F. of M. No. 10 of 1948.)

In exercise of the powers conferred on him by section 4 of the Emergency Regulations Ordinance, 1948, the High Commissioner hereby makes the following Regulations:

PART I

INTRODUCTORY

1. These Regulations may be cited as the Emergency Regulations, 1951, and shall come into force on the first day of October, 1951.

2. In these Regulations, unless the context otherwise requires:

«ammunition» means ammunition for any fire-arm as hereafter defined and includes grenades, bombs and other like missiles, whether capable of use with such a fire-arm or not, and any ammunition containing or designed or adapted to contain any noxious liquid, gas or other thing;

«assessable inhabitant», in relation to any area, means any male who lives in such area and who is or appears to a competent authority, appointed under Regulation 17DA of these Regulations, to be not less than eighteen years of age;

«bank» means any company carrying on the business of bankers in the Federation incorporated by or under any written law in force in the Federation, any company carrying on such business in the Federation under a license issued under the Companies Ordinances, 1940 to 1946, and the Post Office Savings Bank;

«banker's books» include ledgers, day books, cash books, account books, and all other books used in the ordinary business of a bank;

«dependent» means:

(a) wife;

(b) dependent husband;

(c) dependent parents and grandparents;

(d) sons under the age of sixteen years; and

(e) unmarried daughters under the age of eighteen years, and «dependent» used in connection with «husband», «parents» and «grandparents» means wholly or mainly maintained by the wife, son or daughter, or grandson or granddaughter, as the case may be;

«District Officer» includes an Administrative Officer and an Assistant District Officer and, in the State of Perlis, the Commissioner of Lands and Mines;

(Added by L.N. 680/18-12-52).

«document» includes any substance on which is recorded any matter, whether by letters, figures, marks, pictorials or other representations, or by more than one of these means;

«explosive»:

(a) means gunpowder, nitro-glycerine, dynamite, gun-cotton, blasting powder, fulminate of mercury or of other metals, coloured fires and every other substance, whether similar to those above mentioned or not, used or manufactured with a view to produce a practical effect by explosion or a pyrotechnic effect; and

(b) includes fog-signals, fireworks, fuses, rockets, percussion-caps, detonators, cartridges, ammunition of all descriptions and every adaptation, or preparation of an explosive as above defined; and

(c) includes any substance declared to be deemed an explosive by notification under section 4 of the Explosive Enactment of the Federated Malay States;

«fire-arm» means any lethal barrelled weapon of any description from which any shot, bullet or other missile can be discharged, or which can be adapted for the discharge of any such shot, bullet or other missile and any weapon of whatever description designed or adapted for the discharge of any noxious liquid, gas or other thing, and includes any component part of any such weapon as aforesaid;

«harbour» includes the supplying a person with shelter, food, drink, money, clothing, rubber, tin or other valuable commodity, any medicine or drug or other medical supplies, or any material or instrument or part thereof for printing, typewriting or duplicating words or objects in visible form, or means of conveyance, or assisting a person in any way to evade apprehension;

«police officer» includes a special police officer within the meaning of the Essential (Special Constabulary) Regulations, 1948, and a Special Constable appointed under the Special Constables Proclamation;

«road» includes any highway, and any public bridge, and any street, lane, footpath, footway, square, court or passage, whether a thoroughfare or not;

«shop» means any building, stall, structure or other premises, or any part thereof, where any retail trade or business is carried on;

«supplies» includes food, drink, clothing, medicines, drugs or any other stores, instruments, commodities, articles or things whatsoever;

(Substituted by L.N. 680/18-12-52).

«terrorist document» means any document which contains:

(a) any subversive matter; or

(b) any propaganda or matter supporting, propagating or advocating the objects or practices of terrorism; or

(c) any reference to, or account of, any collection of, or any request or demand for, any subscription, contribution or donation, whether in money or in kind, for the benefit directly or indirectly of terrorists; or

(d) any request or demand for supplies for the use of terrorists and includes any document the printing, sale, issue, circulation or possession of which has been prohibited by an order made under Regulation 45 of these Regulations;

(Amended by L.N. 680/18-12-52).

«terrorist» means any person who:

(a) by the use of any fire-arm, explosive or ammunition acts in a manner prejudicial to the public safety or to the maintenance of public order;

(b) incites to violence or counsels disobedience to the law or to any lawful order by the use of any fire-arm, explosive or ammunition;

(c) carries or has in his possession or under his control any fire-arm without lawful authority therefor;

(d) carries or has in his possession or under his control any ammunition or explosive without lawful authority therefor;

(e) demands, collects or receives any supplies for the use of any person who intends, or is about, to act, or has recently acted, in a manner prejudicial to public safety or the maintenance of public order;

and «terrorism» shall have a corresponding meaning;

«unauthorized uniform» means any uniform prohibited by order made under Regulation 6B of these Regulations or under section 2 of the Public Order Ordinance, 1947.

2A. In any Regulation made under the Emergency Regulations Ordinance, 1948, the phrase, or any other phrase to the like intent, «member of Her Majesty's Naval, Military or Air Forces or of any Local Forces established under any written law» shall, unless otherwise expressly provided to the contrary, include only such members who are actually in the service of such forces.

(Reg. added by L.N. 29/2-2-52).

2B. In any Regulation made under the Emergency Regulations Ordinance, 1948, the expression «warrant officer» shall, unless otherwise expressly provided to the contrary, include a «branch officer».

(Reg. added by L.N. 239/15-5-52).

2C. The Chief Police Officer of a State or Settlement and the Officer Superintending a Police Circle shall have and may exercise within the State or Settlement or Police Circle (as the case may be) all the powers which the Officer-in Charge of a Police District has and may exercise within such district under these Regulations and shall be deemed to have had such powers at all times since the coming into force of these Regulations.

(Reg. added by L.N. 680/18-12-52).

3. The provisions of these Regulations shall be in addition to and not in derogation of the provisions of any other written law and, in the event of conflict between any provision of these Regulations and any provision of any other written law, the provisions of these Regulations shall prevail.

PART II
OFFENSES

4. (1) Any person who without lawful excuse, the onus of proving which shall be on such person, carries or has in his possession or under his control:

(a) any fire-arm, without lawful authority therefor; or

(b) any ammunition or explosive without lawful authority therefor, shall be guilty of an offense and shall on conviction be punished with death.

(Amended by L.N. 363/1-7-52).

(2) A person shall be deemed to have lawful authority for the purposes of this Regulation only if he:

(a) is a police officer or a member of Her Majesty's Naval, Military or Air Forces or of any Local Force established under any written law, or any person employed in the Prisons Department of the Federation and in every such case is carrying, or is in possession of, or has under his control such firearm, ammunition or explosive in or in connection with the performance of his duty; or

(b) is a person duly licensed, or authorized without a license, under the provisions of any written law for the time being in force to carry, possess or have under his control such firearm, ammunition or explosive; or

(c) is a person exempted from the provisions of this Regulation by an Officer-in-Charge of a Police district or is a member of any class of persons so exempted by the Commissioner of Police by notification in the * Gazette:

Provided that no person shall be deemed to have lawful authority for the purpose of this Regulation or to be exempt from this Regulation if he

---

* Reg. 4 — Exemption under L.N. 314/49; 539/49.

carries or has in his possession or under his control any such firearm, ammunition or explosive for the purpose of using the same in a manner prejudicial to public safety or the maintenance of public order.

(Substituted by L.N. 363/1-7-52).

(3) A person charged with an offense against this Regulation shall not be granted bail.

4A. Any person who carries or has in his possession or under his control any offensive weapon or any instrument capable of being used as an offensive weapon, not being a fire-arm, in circumstances which raise a reasonable presumption that he has used or intends or is about to use such weapon or instrument for any unlawful purpose, shall be guilty of an offense and shall on conviction be liable to imprisonment of either description for a term not exceeding ten years.

4C. (1) Any person who demands, collects or receives any supplies from any other person in circumstances which raise a reasonable presumption that he intends, or is about, to act, or has recently acted, in a manner prejudicial to public safety or the maintenance of public order, or that the supplies so demanded, collected or received are intended for the use of any person who intends or is about, so to act, or has recently so acted, or for the use of any terrorist, shall be guilty of an offense and shall on conviction be punished with death.

(2) Any person who is found in possession of any supplies for which he cannot satisfactorily account in circumstances which raise a reasonable presumption that such supplies are intended for the use of any person who intends, or is about, to act, or has recently acted, in a manner prejudicial to public safety or the maintenance of public order, or that such supplies are intended for the use of any terrorist, shall be guilty of an offense and shall on conviction be liable to be punished with penal servitude for life.

(3) Any person who provides, whether directly or indirectly, any supplies to any other person in circumstances which raise a reasonable presumption that such other person intends, or is about, to act, or has recently acted, in a manner prejudicial to public safety or the maintenance of public order, or that the supplies so provided are intended for the use of any person who intends or is about, so to act, or has recently so acted, or that such supplies are intended for the use of any terrorist, shall be guilty of an offense and shall on conviction be liable to be punished with penal servitude for life;

Provided that no person shall be convicted of any offense against this paragraph if he proves that prior to being charged with or accused of such offense by a police officer, or a person in authority, he voluntarily gave full information of the offense to a police officer.

(4) In any charge of an offense against any of the provisions of this Regulation it shall not be necessary to specify the person or persons from whom any supplies were demanded, collected or received or to whom any

supplies were provided.

5. (1) Any person who consorts with, or is found in the company of, another person who is carrying or has in his possession, or under his control, any fire-arm, ammunition or explosive in contravention of the provisions of Regulation 4 of these Regulations, in circumstances which raise a reasonable presumption that he intends, or is about, to act, or has recently acted, with such other person in a manner prejudicial to public safety or the maintenance of public order, shall be guilty of an offence and shall on conviction be liable to be punished with death, or with penal servitude for life and whipping.

(1A) Any person who consorts with, or is found in the company of, another person who is carrying or has in his possession, or under his control, any fire-arm, ammunition or explosive in contravention of the provisions of Regulation 4 of these Regulations, in circumstances which raise a reasonable presumption that he knew that such other person was carrying, or had in his possession, or under his control, any such fire-arm, ammunition or explosive, shall be guilty of an offense and shall on conviction be liable to imprisonment for a term not exceeding ten years.

(2) Where, in any prosecution for an offence under this Regulation, it is established to the satisfaction of the Court that the accused person was consorting with or in the company of any person who was carrying, or had in his possession, or under his control, any fire-arm, ammunition or explosive, it shall be presumed, until the contrary is proved, that such last mentioned person was carrying, or had in his possession, or under his control, such fire-arm, ammunition or explosive in contravention of the provisions of Regulation 4 of these Regulations.

6. Any person who, knowing or having reasonable cause to believe that another person is guilty of any offence against any of these Regulations, fails to report the same to a police officer, shall be guilty of an offence and shall, on conviction, be liable to imprisonment for a term not exceeding ten years:

Provided that no person shall be convicted of an offense against this Regulation if he proves that prior to being charged with or accused of such offense by a police officer or a person in authority, he voluntarily gave full information of such other offense to a police officer.

6A. (1) Any person who consorts with any other person whom he knows or has reasonable cause to believe to be a person who intends, or is about, to act, or has acted in a manner prejudicial to public safety or the maintenance of public order, shall be guilty of an offense and shall on conviction be liable to imprisonment for a term not exceeding ten years.

(2) Any person who harbors any other person whom he knows, or has reasonable cause to believe to be a person who intends, or is about, to act, or has recently acted, in a manner prejudicial to public safety or the maintenance of public order, shall be guilty of an offense and shall on conviction be

liable to penal servitude for life:

Provided that, save in respect of the supplying any other person with shelter or assisting any other person to evade apprehension, no person shall be convicted of an offense against this paragraph if he proves that, prior to being charged with or accused of such offence by a police officer or a person in authority, he voluntarily gave full information of the offense to a police officer.

(3) For the purposes of this Regulation, the fact that a person is wearing an unauthorised uniform shall be deemed to constitute reasonable cause to believe that he intends, or is about, to act, or has recently acted, in a manner prejudicial to public safety or the maintenance of public order.

(4) Notwithstanding anything to the contrary contained in any written law, any Chief Police Officer may, on being satisfied that any police officer has absented himself from duty in circumstances which give reasonable cause to believe that he is consorting, or has consorted with, a person who intends, or is about, to act, or has recently acted, in a manner prejudicial to public safety or the maintenance of public order, declare such police officer to be a deserter, and for the purposes of these Regulations such police officer shall be deemed to have ceased to be a police officer from the date upon which he so absented himself.

6B. (1) The High Commissioner may, if he considers it in the public interest so to do, by order prohibit the manufacture, sale, use, display or possession of any flag, banner, badge, emblem, device, uniform or distinctive dress.

(2) Any person contravening any provision of an order made under this Regulation shall be guilty of an offense against these Regulations.

(3) Any article in respect of which an offense has been committed under this Regulation may be seized and destroyed or otherwise dealt with as the High Commissioner may direct, whether or not the identity of the offender is known and whether or not any prosecution has been commenced in respect of the offence.

6C. Any person who is drunk, or who behaves in a disorderly manner while carrying a fire-arm shall be guilty of an offense and shall on conviction be liable to a fine not exceeding five hundred dollars or to imprisonment for a term not exceeding six months, or to both such fine and imprisonment.

6D. (1) Any person who, without lawful excuse, carries or has in his possession or under his control any terrorist document, shall be guilty of an offense and shall on conviction be liable to imprisonment for a term not exceeding ten years.

(2) Every document purporting to be a terrorist document shall be deemed to be a terrorist document until the contrary is proved; and where in any prosecution under this Regulation it is proved that a person was carrying, or had in his possession or under his control a terrorist document, he shall be deemed to have known the nature and contents of such document:

Provided that no person shall be

convicted of an offence against this Regulation if he proves to the satisfaction of the Court:

(i) that he was not aware of the nature or contents of the terrorist document which he was carrying, or had in his possession, or under his control; and

(ii) that he was carrying, or had the terrorist document in his possession or under his control, in such circumstances that at no time did he have reasonable cause to believe or suspect that such document was a terrorist document.

7. Any person who posts or distributes any placard, circular or other document in writing containing any incitement to violence, or counselling disobedience to the law, or to any lawful order or likely to lead to any breach of the peace, shall be guilty of an offense against these Regulations.

8. Any person who by word of mouth, or in writing, or in any newspaper, periodical, book, circular or other printed publication, spreads false reports or makes false statements likely to cause public alarm or despondency, shall be guilty of an offense against these Regulations.

8A. (1) Any person who gives to any member of Her Majesty's Naval, Military or Air Forces, or to any member of any Local Forces established under any written law, or to any public officer, any information orally or in writing which he knows or believes to be false, intending thereby to cause or knowing it to be likely that he will thereby cause such member or officer to use the lawful power of such member or officer to the injury or annoyance of any person, or to do or omit to do anything which such member or officer ought not to do or omit if the true state of facts respecting which such information is given were known to him, shall be guilty of an offense and shall on conviction be liable to imprisonment for a term not exceeding seven years.

(2) Sections 194 and 195 of the Penal Code shall apply to any offence against this Regulation as if it were an offence punishable under the Penal Code.

(Reg. added by L.N. 680/18-12-52).

PART III

JURISDICTION

Not applicable.

PART IV

MISCELLANEOUS PROVISIONS AS TO EVIDENCE AND PROCEDURE

Not applicable.

PART V

DETENTION AND DEPORTATION

Not applicable.

PART VI

ORDERS AFFECTING THE BEHAVIOR, RESIDENCE AND MOVEMENTS OF PERSONS

17DA. (1) The Mentri Besar of a State and the Resident Commissioner of a Settlement may appoint any Magistrate to be a competent authority for the purpose of this Regulation.

(2) (i) In any case where a com-

petent authority has reason to believe that the inhabitants, or any of them, of any area:

(a) have aided and abetted or have consorted with or harbored any person whom they knew or had reasonable cause to believe to be a person who intended, or was about, to act, or had recently acted, in a manner prejudicial to public safety or the maintenance of public order; or

(b) have suppressed or combined to suppress evidence of the commissioner of any offence against Regulations 4, 4A, 4C, 5, 6A or 6D of these Regulations; or

(c) have failed to give information to a police officer of the presence in such area of any person whom they knew or had reasonable cause to believe to be a person who intended, or was about, to act, or had recently acted, in a manner prejudicial to public safety or the maintenance of public order; or

(d) have failed to take reasonable steps to prevent the escape of any person whom they knew or had reasonable cause to believe to be a person who intended, or was about, to act, or had recently acted, in a manner prejudicial to public safety or the maintenance of public order;

he may order that a fine be levied collectively from the assessable inhabitants of such area or any part thereof, or he may order that all or any of the shops in such area shall be closed until such order be revoked, or shall open only during such times and under such conditions as may be specified in the order and he may make both such orders.

(ii) In any case where a competent authority has reason to believe that within any area any person has been murdered or dangerously or fatally wounded by unlawful attack or terrorism, or any property has been destroyed or damaged unlawfully or by terrorism, he may order that a fine be levied collectively from the assessable inhabitants of such area, or any part thereof, or he may order that all or any of the shops in such area shall be closed until such order be revoked, or shall open only during such times and under such conditions as may be specified in the order and he may make both such orders, unless such inhabitants can show that:

(a) they had not an opportunity of preventing the offense or arresting the offender; or

(b) they have used all reasonable means to bring the offender to justice.

(iii) The whole, or, if compensation is awarded in pursuance of paragraph (6) of this Regulation, any balance remaining thereafter, of any fine levied as aforesaid, shall be paid into a special Emergency Fund of the State or Settlement, as the case may be, which shall be applied to such purposes in the State or Settlement as the Mentri or Resident Commissioner may direct.

(3) (i) No order shall be made under paragraph (2) of this Regulation unless an inquiry into the facts and circumstances giving rise to such order has been held by a competent authority.

(ii) A written report of any inquiry and a copy of any order made shall be submitted to the Mentri Besar or to the Resident Commissioner of the State or Settlement in which the area concerned is situated.

(4) The Mentri Besar or the Resident Commissioner, as the case may be, may, at any time after any such order has been made in their absolute discretion, remit the whole of any fine or any part thereof, or may order that any amount which has been paid by any assessable inhabitant shall be repaid to him, or may revoke or vary the conditions of any order closing or restricting the opening of any shops.

(5) (i) In holding an inquiry in pursuance of paragraph (3) of this Regulation, the competent authority shall satisfy himself that the inhabitants of the area are given adequate opportunity of understanding the subject matter of the inquiry and making representations thereon, and, subject thereto, such inquiry shall be conducted in such manner as the competent authority thinks fit.

(ii) The written report mentioned in paragraph (3) of this Regulation shall contain a certificate that the requirements of this paragraph have been complied with.

(6) (i) It shall be lawful for the Mentri Besar of a State or the Resident Commissioner of a Settlement to order that out of a fine levied in pursuance of paragraph (2) of this Regulation, compensation shall be paid to any person who has suffered injury, loss of or damage to his property unlawfully or through terrorism in the area in which the fine was levied.

(ii) Application for compensation shall be made in writing by the person aggrieved or his representative within two months from the date upon which the fine is levied.

(iii) Where the injury, for which compensation is being sought, is a death, a pedentant of the deceased may be deemed to be a person aggrieved.

(iv) No application for compensation shall be granted if it appears that the applicant, or, in the case of a death, the deceased participated in the unlawful acts or terrorism or was blameworthy in connection therewith.

(7) Having considered the written report referred to in paragraph (3) (ii) of this Regulation, and whether or not a competent authority has ordered that a fine be levied under the provisions of paragraph (2) of this Regulation on the inhabitants of any area or part thereof, or that any of the shops in any area shall be closed or that the hours of their opening shall be restricted, the Mentri Besar of the State or the Resident Commissioner of the Settlement in which such area is situated, may (without prejudice to his powers under paragraph (4) of this Regulation) order that the force of police usually quartered in such area shall, for such period as shall be stated in such order, be increased to such extent as he may consider necessary; further, that the cost of such additional police force

shall be borne by the assessable inhabitants of the said area, and, for the purpose of complying with any such order, the Chief Police Officer of the State or Settlement (as the case may be) may recruit the number of police officers necessary or may employ any police officer necessary in addition to the aforesaid force of police.

(Substituted by L.N. 464/19-8-52).

(8) Any fine or cost of additional Police ordered to be paid in pursuance of this Regulation shall be apportioned among the assessable inhabitants of the area by a competent authority in such manner as he may think fit, and, in particular, he may order that each assessable inhabitant shall pay any amount which the competent authority shall specify.

(9) (i) If any assessable inhabitant, who is liable to pay a part of any fine or cost of additional Police, fails to pay that part on demand by a Police Officer, such officer may seize so much of the movable property of such assessable inhabitant, or so much of movable property under the apparent control of such inhabitant, as appears reasonably sufficient when sold to pay such part.

(ii) Any property so seized shall be retained in Police custody for one week from the date of seizure and shall, if the assessable inhabitant pays the part due from him within that period, be thereupon returned to such inhabitant.

(iii) The net proceeds of any property so seized and sold shall be applied first in payment of the expenses incurred in respect of the seizure by the Police and the payment of the fine. The balance, if any, remaining over shall be paid to the State or Settlement Emergency Fund mentioned in paragraph (2) of this Regulation.

(10) A Magistrate or a Justice of the Peace shall be present at and supervise the collection of any fine or cost of additional police, or any seizure of movable property in default of payment of any part thereof, from the assessable inhabitants amongst whom such fine or cost has been apportioned.

(11) Nothing in this Regulation shall be deemed to exempt any person from any penalty, punishment or liability to which he would have been subject if this Regulation had not been made.

(Amended by L.N. 314/3-6-52).

(12) Save as provided in paragraph (4) of this Regulation, an order made by a competent authority under paragraph (2) of this Regulation shall be final and no appeal shall lie from any such order.

(Amended by L.N. 314/3-6-52).

17DB. (Added by L.N. 601/23-10-51 and revoked by L.N. 314/3-6-52).

17E. (1) The Ruler in Council of any Malay State and the High Commissioner in Nominated Council of a Settlement may, if he considers it expedient in the public interest so to do, make, as respects any area in the State or Settlement, as the case may be, an order, hereinafter referred to as an eviction order, directing that any person unlawfully in occupation of land in that area shall leave that area.

(2) An eviction order:

(a) shall prescribe the area to which persons affected by such order shall, unless exempted as hereinafter provided, proceed on leaving any area in compliance with the order; and

(b) may contain such other incidental and supplementary provisions as appear to the Ruler in Council or the High Commissioner in Nominated Council, as the case may be, to be necessary and expedient for the purpose of giving to such order.

(2A) Every person affected by an eviction order shall leave the area mentioned in the order not later than one month from the date upon which such order was brought to his notice or within such longer period (if any) as may be specified in such order.

(2B) The area prescribed under sub-paragraph (a) of paragraph (2) of this Regulation may be within the same State or Settlement or within another State or a Settlement:

Provided that no area within another State or Settlement shall be prescribed as aforesaid, unless the consent of the Mentri Besar of such State or of the Resident Commissioner of such Settlement, as the case may be, shall have been previously obtained.

(3) Any person affected by an eviction order may, at any time before proceeding to the area prescribed under sub-paragraph (a) of paragraph (2) of this Regulation, apply to the authorized officer of the district in which the area, in respect of which the eviction order is made, is situate, for exemption from that part of the eviction order requiring him to proceed to the prescribed area and to be allowed to proceed to another area. The grant of such exemption shall be at the absolute discretion of such officer and the exemption shall be at the absolute discretion of such officer and the exemption shall in no case be granted unless such officer is satisfied that there is another suitable area which such person can occupy, and that such person intends to proceed to such area and remain in occupation thereof. Where any such exemption has been granted, the substituted area shall, for the purposes of this Regulation, be deemed to be the area prescribed in the eviction order.

(4) Any person affected by an eviction order may, before the expiration of the time allowed to such person for leaving the area under paragraph (2A) of this Regulation, give notice to the officer-in-charge of the police station nearest the area referred to in such eviction order that he wishes to return to his country of origin.

(5) Where any person has given such notice, he and his dependants shall leave the Federation within such time as may be specified by order of the Chief Secretary and, until such time, such person and his dependants shall be subject to such restrictions as to residence and to such other conditions as the Chief Secretary may consider desirable to impose, including a condition that such person shall enter into a bond, for the due compliance with the order, of such amount and with such sureties as the Chief Secretary or any

person authorized by him may specify.

(6) The High Commissioner may require any person and his dependents to leave and remain out of the Federation if such person or any of his dependants fail to leave the Federation within the time, or to comply with the restrictions or conditions, specified in an order made by the Chief Secretary under paragraph (5) of this Regulation.

(7) Every person affected by an eviction order (other than a person who has given notice under paragraph (4) of this Regulation) shall proceed to the area specified in such order, or to the area substituted by an authorized officer under paragraph (3) of this Regulation, and shall forthwith take up occupation of such area and shall remain in occupation thereof for a period of not les than two years from the date of taking up such occupation:

Provided that with the permission in writing of the authorized officer of the district in which such area is situate, any such person may, at any time during such period of two years, leave such area. The grant of such permission shall be at the absolute discretion of such officer.

(8) Any person affected by an eviction order who fails:

(a) to leave the area mentioned in such order within the time allowed under paragraph (2A) of this Regulation;

(b) to take up occupation, in accordance with the provisions of paragraph (7) of this Regulation, of the area specified in such order, or of the area substituted by an authorized officer under paragraph (3) of this Regulation; or

(c) to remain in occupation of such area in accordance with the provisions of paragraph (7) of this Regulation;

may be required, by order of the High Commissionner, to leave and remain out of the Federation.

(9) Any person who, under this Regulation, has been required to leave and remain out of the Federation, may:

(a) be detained in custody in such place or places as the Chief Secretary, or any person authorized by him in that behalf, may direct, for such period as may be necessary for the purpose of making arrangements for such person to leave the Federation;

(b) be conducted across the frontier or placed on board a ship by any police officer or officer of the Immigration Department and may be lawfully detained on board so long as such ship is within the territorial waters of the Federation.

(10) No person shall be required to leave and remain out of the Federation under this Regulation if he is:

(a) a Federal citizen; or

(b) a British subject.

(11) Any person required to leave and remain out of the Federation under this Regulation shall, while detained or in the custody of a police officer or officer of the Immigration Department, be deemed to be in lawful custody.

(12) An eviction order shall be in writing signified under the hand of the Clerk to the State Executive Council or

Clerk to the Settlement Nominated Council.

(13) (a) When an eviction order has been made under paragraph (1) of this Regulation and until such order has been expressly revoked by the Ruler in Council or the High Commissioner in Nominated Council, as the case may be, in the same manner as is provided by paragraph (12) of this Regulation:

(i) Any person found in occupation of any land in the area affected by such order at any time after the date of the making of such order, whether such occupation commenced before or after such date, shall, for the purposes of this Regulation, be presumed, until the contrary is proved, to be unlawfully in occupation of such land; and

(ii) Any person found at any time unlawfully in occupation of any land in the area affected by such order, whether such occupation commenced before or after the date of making such order, together with any persons found living with him, may be removed by any police officer from such land to any area prescribed in the eviction order as an area to which persons affected by such order should proceed, or in the case of a person whose occupation appears to such police officer to have commenced after the date of the making of such order to such area aforesaid, or to such other area as the Mentri Besar, if the area affected by such order is in a state, or the Resident Commissioner if the area affected by such order is in a Settlement, may direct: Provided that no person whose occupation commenced before the date of the making of such order shall be removed, without his consent, at any time prior to the expiration of the time allowed under paragraph (2A) of this Regulation;

(b) For the purpose of effecting any removal authorized by sub-paragraph (a) of this paragraph, a police officer may effect an entry into any premises, may use any force reasonably necessary and may detain any person in custody during such removal and for such period as may be necessary for the purpose of making arrangements for such removal;

(c) The provisions of paragraph (7) of this Regulation shall apply to every person removed under the provisions of this paragraph;

(d) Any person who resists or obstructs any police officer in the exercise of his powers under this paragraph, or evades or attemps to evade removal under the provisions of sub-paragraph (a) of this paragraph, shall be guilty of an offense against these Regulations;

(e) A police officer of or above the rank of Corporal may destroy or authorize the destruction of any building or structure erected on any land in the area affected by an eviction order made under paragraph (1) of this Regulation which he has reason to believe to have been erected by any person in unlawful occupation of such land;

(f) The provisions of this paragraph shall be in addition to and not in derogation of the provisions of any other paragraph of this Regulation.

(14) In this Regulation:

«authorized officer» means:

(a) in paragraph (3) of this Regulation an officer authorized by the Ruler in Council of a Malay State or, as the case may be, by the High Commissioner in Nominated Council of a Settlement, making an eviction order to exercise the powers under that paragraph in a particular district or districts; and

(b) in the proviso to paragraph (7) of this Regulation an officer authorized:

(i) where the area prescribed by the eviction order is within the same State or Settlement, by the Ruler in Council of that State or the High Commissioner in Nominated Council of that Settlement; and

(ii) where the area prescribed is within another State or Settlement, by the Mentri Besar of such State or the Resident Commissioner of such Settlement, as the case may be,

to exercise the powers under that paragraph or that proviso, as the case may be, in a particular district or districts.

17EA. (1) In this Regulation and in any order made thereunder, unless the context otherwise requires:

«District Officer» means the District Officer of the district where a food restricted area is situated;

«food prohibited area» means any area declared to be a food prohibited area under paragraph (8) of this Regulation;

«food restricted area» means any area declared to be a food restricted area under paragraph (2) of this Regulation;

«foodstuff» means:

(a) any species of animal, whether alive or dead, which is ordinarily used for human food;

(b) any substance or commodity which is ordinarily used for human food; and

(c) any substance or commodity which is ordinarily used for feeding animals, including rice bran containing more than ten per centum of whole or broken grain rice;

«gazetted village» means any area within a Rural Board area which has been prescribed to be a village for the purposes of the application thereto of specified provision of the Municipal Ordinance;

«good vehicle» means any mechanically propelled road vehicle constructed or adapted for use for the carriage or haulage of goods, or any trailer or vehicle drawn by a mechanically propelled road vehicle;

«home guard» means a person enrolled as a home guard under the Emergency (Home Guard) Regulations, 1951;

«restricted article» means any of the following articles, that is to say, padi, rice, rice products, flour, flour products, tapioca, cereals, oil, sugar, salt, concentrated foods, tinned foods, cooked food, dried fish, paper or any material or instrument or part thereof for printing, typewriting or duplicating words or objects in visible form, drugs, medicines and other medical supplies, torch batteries, cloth and canvas;

(Amended by L.N. 98/26-2-53).

«to sell» includes to offer for sale and to supply, and «sale» shall have a corresponding meaning;

«shop» means any building, stall, structure or other premises or part thereof where any wholesale or retail trade or business in any restricted article is carried on, or where any restricted article is kept or stored for purposes of distribution to wholesalers or retailers.

(2) The Mentri Besar in a State and the Resident Commissioner in a Settlement may, if he considers it in the public interest so to do, by order declare any area in the State or Settlement to be a food restricted area and shall cause the boundaries of any such area to be demarcated or designated in such manner as the Mentri Besar or the Resident Commissioner, as the case may be, thinks fit.

(3) The owner or the person in charge of a shop in a food restricted area shall comply with following provisions, that is to say:

(a) he shall not keep any stock of restricted articles, in his shop or elsewhere, in quantities exceeding those which are necessary for his normal trade or business;

(b) he shall keep a record in such manner and containing such information as the District Officer may direct of the stocks of restricted articles in his possession and of all quantities of all purchases of restricted articles made by him for the purposes of his trade or business;

(c) he shall keep a record in such manner and containing such information as the District Officer may direct of the daily sales of any restricted article;

(d) on demand of any police officer, he shall produce such records for inspection;

(e) he shall not sell by retail any restricted article to any person who is not in possession of a registration card issued to him under the Emergency (Registration Areas) Regulations, 1948, and except on production of such card; and if the owner or person in charge of a shop fails to comply with any of the provisions of this paragraph, he shall be guilty of an offence against these Regulations.

(4) The Mentri Besar in a State and the Resident Commissioner in a Settlement may by order prohibit the owners or persons in charge of all or any shops in a food restricted area from carrying on any business or trade in any restricted article unless such owners or person is in possession of a licence issued for the purpose of this Regulation by, and at the absolute discretion of, the District Officer, except in accordance with any conditions contained in such licence. Any person who fails to comply with such order or with any conditions contained in the licence shall be guilty of an offence against these Regulations.

(5) Save as provided in paragraph (6) of this Regulation, any person who brings into or takes away from any food restricted area any restricted article or any foodstuff whatsoever, whether cooked or otherwise, shall be guilty of an offense and shall, on con-

viction, be liable to a fine not exceeding one thousand dollars or to imprisonment for a term not exceeding three years, or to both such fine and imprisonment.

(6) The provisions of paragraphs (5) and (9) of this Regulation shall not apply to:

(a) any restricted article or foodstuff loaded on any vehicle and consigned to or from a shop in a food restricted area, or in transit through a food restricted area or a food prohibited area;

(b) any article of food in liquid form which may from time to time be approved by the District Officer in respect of all persons or classes of persons entering or leaving a food restricted area or food prohibited area;

(c) any restricted article or foodstuff brought into or removed from a food restricted or a food prohibited area with the permission of the District Officer or any person authorized by him in that behalf. Such permission may be granted either to particular persons or to a class of persons and may contain such conditions and restrictions as the District Officer, or the person authorized by him, may deem fit to impose; and

(d) any footwear or clothing worn on the person or bona fide personal luggage.

(7) *Any police officer, or any member of Her Majesty's Naval, Military or Air Forces or of any Local Forces established under any written law, of or above the rank of sergeant or petty officer (as the case may be), or a home guard or a woman authorized so to do by the Officer-in Charge of the Police district in which such area is situate,* may search any person leaving or entering a food restricted area or found in a food prohibited area:

Provided that no woman shall be searched except by a woman.

(Substituted by L.N. 680/18-12-52).

(8) The Mentri Besar in a State and the Resident Commissioner in a Settlement may, if he considers it in the public interest so to do, by order declare any area which has been declared to be a controlled area in accordance with the provisions of Regulation 17FA of these Regulations (other than the residential part of any such controlled area) in the State or Settlement not being a food restricted area to be a food prohibited area and shall designate the boundaries of any such area.

(9) Save as provided in paragraph (6) of this Regulation, any person who is found in possession of any restricted article of any foodstuff whatsoever, whether cooked or otherwise, within the boundaries of a food prohibited area shall be guilty of an offense, and shall on conviction be liable to a fine not exceeding five thousand dollars or to imprisonment for a term not exceeding five years, or both such fine and imprisonment.

(10) (i) If he considers it expedient so to do, the District Officer of any district may by order direct that any shop shall be closed or that no trade or business in any restricted article

shall be carried on in any shop or that such trade or business shall be carried on only subject to such restrictions or conditions as he may specify.

(ii) In this paragraph «shop» means any building, stall, structure or other premises or part thereof, where any wholesale or retail trade or business is carried on.

(iii) Any person who fails to comply with any such order or with any conditions contained in any such order shall be guilty of an offence against these Regulations.

(11) (i) The Mentri Besar in a State and the Resident Commissioner in a Settlement or any officer appointed by him in writing in that behalf may by order:

(a) declare a ration of rice or of any specified foodstuff in such area and for such period as shall be specified; and

(b) declare the maximum quantity of rice or of any specified foodstuff which may at any time be in the possession of any person other than a trader in rice or any such foodstuff; and

(c) declare the maximum quantities which wholesale and retail shops dealing in rice or any other specified foodstuff may hold.

(ii) When any ration has been declared under sub-paragraph (i) of paragraph (11) of this Regulation it shall be an offense against these Regulations for any person to sell or to deliver any rice or specified foodstuff in excess of the declared ration.

(iii) Any person who contravenes the provisions of sub-paragraphs (i) (b) or (i) (c) of this paragraph shall, on conviction, be liable to a fine not exceeding one thousand dollars or to imprisonment for a term not exceeding one year, or to both such fine and imprisonment.

(12) Any person who between the hours of seven o'clock in the evening and six o'clock of the next following morning transports by any vehicle outside any Municipality, Town Board area, Town Council area or gazetted village any restricted article or any foodstuff or any footwear or clothing shall be guilty of an offense against these Regulations:

(Amended by L.N. 680/18-12-52).

Provided that the provisions of this paragraph shall not apply to fresh meat, fresh fish, shell fish, prawns, crabs, fresh vegetables, fresh fruit, live poultry or eggs, or to footwear or clothing when worn on the person or conveyed as bona fide personal baggage.

(13) The District Officer or an Assistant Controller of Supplies may by order prohibit absolutely or except on such conditions and by any means of transport, public or otherwise, and during such hours as he shall specify, the movement of any restricted article or of any foodstuff on any public or private road and river, stream, channel or other waterway whatsoever, or on or within any territorial waters within his jurisdiction.

(Amended by L.N. 680/18-12-52).

(14) When any restricted articles are being transported by road on any

goods vehicle between the hours of six o'clock in the morning and seven o'clock in the evening, such articles shall be covered by a tarpaulin which shall be securely fastened down.

(15) The Mentri Besar in a State and the Resident Commissioner in a Settlement or any officer appointed by him in writing in that behalf may by order require that the drivers of all vehicles transporting any restricted article or any foodstuff on such roads as shall be specified in such order shall carry a manifest in such form as he may prescribe, showing the nature and quantity of such restricted articles or foodstuffs and their destination.

(16) *Any police officer* and *any home guard authorized by the Officer-in-Charge of the Police district may:*

(a) stop any vehicle and require the driver or other person in charge thereof to declare whether any restricted article or any foodstuff is being carried therein, and to give such information as such officer or guard may consider necessary, and, if not satisfied with any declaration made in answer to such request, search such vehicle;

(b) require the driver or the person in charge of such vehicle in which any restricted article or any foodstuff is being carried to comply with such directions as such officer or guard may consider necessary to ensure that such article is not used for an unlawful purpose or that such article reaches the place for which it is intended;

(c) detain any restricted article or any foodstuff in any such vehicle for such time as may be necessary to ensure that such article is not used for an unlawful purpose;

(d) seize any restricted article or any foodstuff in respect of which he suspects that an offense under this Regulation has been committed or was attempted or intended to be committed.

(17) Where any restricted article or article of foodstuff has been seized under the provisions of paragraph (16) of this Regulation, then:

(a) if, within four weeks of such seizure, no proceedings are instituted against any person for an offense in relation to such restricted article or other foodstuff they shall be restored to the person from whom they were seized if he can be found and, if not, shall be disposed of as may be directed by a Magistrate;

(b) if, within four weeks of such seizure, such proceedings are instituted against any person, such restricted article or other foodstuff may be forfeited or otherwise disposed of in such manner as the Court may direct:

Provided that if such restricted article or other foodstuff is of a perishable nature and likely to decay it may be disposed of forthwith by the officer who has seized them, and any proceeds of such sale shall be dealth with in the manner prescribed in this Regulation for the disposal of a restricted article or other foodstuff.

(18) Any person who, in answer to any request made in pursuance of paragraph (16) of this Regulation, makes any declaration or gives any information which is false, or is not in possession of a lorry manifest where

such manifest has been ordered, in accordance with the provisions of paragraph (15) of this Regulation, shall be guilty of an offense against these Regulations, and if the false declaration is with respect to any restricted article carried in any vehicle, such article and such vehicle shall be liable to seizure and shall, on conviction of such person, in addition to any other penalty, be forfeited whether or not such person is or is not the owner thereof.

(19) The driver or person in charge of any vehicle carrying any restricted article or foodstuff, who, unless obliged by something over which he has no control or unless he is required so to do by a police officer or a home guard:

(a) stops the vehicle outside the limits of a municipality, a town board, a local council area or a gazetted village other than at a place to which any goods in the vehicle have been consigned or at which they are intended to be delivered; or

(b) deviates from the route normally followed in reaching the place to which any goods in the vehicle have been consigned or at which they are intended to be delivered; or

(c) unloads any restricted article or foodstuff or permits any such article or foodstuff to be deposited at any place other than the place to which it has been consigned or at which it was intended to be delivered,

shall be guilty of an offense against these Regulations.

(20) Any police officer, and any Guard, Under-Guard or Ticket Collector appointed and employed under the provisions of sub-section (3) of section 3 of the Railway Ordinance, 1948, may:

(a) open and examine any parcel or package in the possession of any passenger on any train if he has reason to believe that such parcel or package contains any restricted article which he suspects is intended to be made available to any person who intends, or is about, to act or has recently acted, in a manner prejudicial to the public safety or the maintenance of public order, and if on examination he finds that such parcel or package contains any restricted article he may detain such parcel or package until such passenger reaches his destination; and

(b) without warrant, arrest any passenger on a train who throws or is about to throw from the train any package or parcel which he suspects contains any restricted article.

(21) (i) The District Officer of any district may:

(a) prohibit trading or selling by itinerant vendors in any place in his district outside the limits of a municipality, a town board, a local council area or a gazetted village;

(b) restrict trading or selling by itinerant vendors outside the limits of a municipality, a town board, a local council area or a gazetted village to such places as he may think fit;

(c) prohibit the sale of any article by itinerant vendors in any part of his district outside the limits of a municipality, a town board, a local council area or a gazetted village.

(ii) Any person who contravenes any prohibition or restriction imposed under sub-paragraph (i) of this paragraph shall be guilty of an offense against these Regulations.

(Amended by L.N. 654/22-11-51, L.N. 196/17-4-52 and Reg. substituted by L.N. 513/11-9-52).

17F. (1) The Mentri Besar in any State and the Resident Commissioner in a Settlement may, if he considers it in the public interest so to do, by order under his hand, direct that any person shall:

(a) within such period as may be specified in the order, move from the area in the State or Settlement where he is residing to such other area as may be specified in the order; or

(b) not move outside the limits of any area specified in the order,

and such order shall also apply to such dependants normally residing with the person in respect of whom the order is made as are specified therein:

Provided that no order directing that a person shall reside in another State or Settlement shall be made without the concurrence of the Mentri Besar or Resident Commissioner of such State or Settlement.

(2) Any order made under this Regulation shall be effective for such period as may be specified in the order and may contain such conditions, regarding reporting to the Police or otherwise, as the Mentri Besar, or Resident Commissioner, as the case may be, may deem expedient.

(3) So long as any order made under this Regulation is effective no person affected thereby shall leave the area to which he has been ordered to move or remain in, as the case may be, without the written permission of the Officer-in-Charge of the Police District of such area, and any such written permission may contain such conditions as the Officer giving the same may deem expedient.

(4) A person against whom an order under this Regulation has been made may be paid such subsistence allowance, (if any) for himself and any dependants affected by the order, as to the Mentri Besar or Resident Commissioner, as the case may be, may seem just.

(5) Any person who fails to comply with an order made under this Regulation or who contravenes any condition contained in such order or any condition contained in a written permission granted under paragraph (3) of this Regulation, shall be guilty of an offense and on conviction shall be liable to a fine not exceeding one thousand dollars or to imprisonment not exceeding one year or to both such fine and imprisonment.

17FA. (1) The Mentri Besar in a Malay State and the Resident Commissioner in a Settlement may, if he considers it expedient in the public interest so to do, make an order, which shall be published in the Gazette, declaring any area within the State or Settlement to be a controlled area; and in the same or any subsequent order may declare any specified part of such controlled area to be a residential part.

(2) Every such order shall declare:

(a) that after the expiration of a period to be specified in the order (which shall not be less than seven days from the date thereof) and subject to any exemption for which provision may be made by the same or by a subsequent order and to any conditions upon which such exemption may be granted, no person shall reside or continue to reside in any part of a controlled area other than a residential part;

(b) that between such hours or at such times as may be specified in the order and subject to any exemption for which provision may be made by the same or by a subsequent order and to any conditions upon which such exemption may be granted, no person shall be in any part of the controlled area other than a residential part.

(Amended by L.N. 98/26-2-53).

(3) Any person who contravenes the provisions of an order made under this Regulation shall be guilty of an offense against these Regulations.

(4) This Regulation shall not apply to:

(a) members of the Federal Executive or Legislative Councils;

(b) members of any State Executive Council or Council of State;

(c) members of any Settlement Nominated Council or Settlement Council;

(d) any police officer or any member of Her Majesty's Naval, Military or Air Forces or any Local Forces established under any written law;

(e) any person or class of persons exempted from the provisions of this Regulation by the Officer-in-Charge of the Police District.

(Added by L.N. 98/26-2-53).

18. (1) If, as respects any place or premises, it appears to a Chief Police Officer to be necessary or expedient in the interests of public safety or order, or for the maintenance of supplies or services essential to the life of the community, that special precautions should be taken to prevent the entry of unauthorized persons, he may by order declare such place or premises to be a protected place for the purposes of these Regulations, and so long as the order is in force, no person shall, subject to any exemptions for which provision may be made in the order, be in that place or those premises without the permission of such authority or person as may be specified in the order.

Any place or premises in relation to which an order made under this Regulation is in force is hereinafter referred to as a «protected place».

(2) Where, in pursuance of this Regulation, any person is granted permission to be in a protected place, that person shall, while acting under such permission, comply with such directions for regulating his conduct as may be given by the Chief Police Officer or by the authority or person granting the permission.

(3) Any police officer or any person authorized in that behalf by the occupier of the premises may search any person entering or seeking to enter, or being in, a protected place, and may

detain any such person for the purpose of searching him.

(4) If any person is in a protected place in contravention of this Regulation, or while in such a place, fails to comply with any directions given under this Regulation, then, without prejudice to any proceedings which may be taken against him, he may be removed from the place by any police officer or any person authorized in that behalf by the occupier of the premises.

(5) Any person who is in a protected place in contravention of this Regulation, or who on being challenged by a police officer, wilfully fails to stop or who unlawfully refuses to submit to search, shall be guilty of an offense against these Regulations.

(Substituted by L.N. 239/15-5-52).

(6) It shall be lawful for the Chief Secretary to take or cause to be taken such steps as he may deem necessary for the protection of any protected place, and such steps may extend to the taking of defensive measures which involve or may involve danger to the life or any person entering or attempting to enter the protected place. Where any measures involving such danger as aforesaid are adopted, the Chief Police Officer of the State or Settlement in which the protected place is situate shall cause such precautions to be taken, including the prominent display of warning notices, as he deems reasonably necessary to prevent inadvertent or accidental entry into any such dangerous areas, and, where such precautions have been duly taken, no person shall be entitled to compensation or damages in respect of injury received or death caused as a result of any unauthorized entry into any such protected place or dangerous area.

(7) For the purposes of this Regulation «police officer» shall include:

(a) any member of Her Majesty's Naval, Military or Air Forces or of any Local Forces established under any written law;

(b) any prison officer and any officer employed in any place of detention specified in an order made under Regulation 17 of these Regulations;

(c) any other person performing the duties of guard or watchman in a protected place the appointment of whom has been either specially or generally authorized by a Chief Police Officer.

19. (1) If, as respects any area, it appears to a Chief Police Officer to be necessary or expedient that special precautions should be taken to prevent malicious injury to persons or property, he may, by order, declare such area to be a special area for the purposes of these Regulations. Any area in relation to which an order made under this Regulations is in force is hereinafter referred to as a «special area».

(2) It shall be the duty of any person in a special area to stop and submit to search by an officer when called upon so to do, and if any such person fails to stop when challenged or called upon to stop by an officer, he shall be guilty of an offense against these Regulations and may be arrested by such officer without warrant.

(Amended by L.N. 239/15-5-52).

(3) For the purposes of this Regulation «officer» means any police officer or any member of Her Majesty's Naval, Military or Air Forces or of any Local Forces established under any written law.

19A. (1) The Mentri Besar in any Malay State and the Resident Commissioner in any Settlement, if he considers it necessary or expedient in the public interest so to do, may, by order to be published in the Gazette, declare any area within the State or Settlement to be a danger area.

(2) The limits and extent of every danger area shall be demarcated at the site by such means as will, in the opinion of the Mentri Besar or Resident Commissioner, as the case may be, make apparent to persons in or about the area concerned that such area has been declared a danger area.

(3) No person shall enter or remain in a danger area and any person who fails to comply with the provisions of this paragraph shall be guilty of an offense against these Regulations:

Provided that the provisions of this paragraph shall not apply to members of the security forces in the performance of their duty or to any person accompanied by such member.

(4) Any member of the security forces may within a danger area take such measures, including means dangerous or fatal to human life, as he considers necessary to ensure that no person prohibited from entering or remaining in a danger area shall enter or remain in such area.

(Amended by L.N. 98/26-2-53).

(5) No claim of any kind shall accrue to, or in respect of any injury sustained by, any person as a result of his having entered or remained in a danger area in contravention of the provisions of paragraph (3) of this Regulation:

Provided that the provisions of this paragraph shall not preclude the compensation authority provided by the Emergency (Civilian Injuries Compensation) Regulations, 1949, from awarding compensation under such Regulations, if, in the particular circumstances under which a person sustaining the injury, entered or remained in a danger area, such authority considers it equitable to award such compensation.

(6) Where any land, building or other immoveable property is within a danger area, a claim for compensation in respect of such land, building or other immoveable property may be made in the manner provided by Regulation 53 of these Regulations.

(7) In this Regulation «security forces» includes the Police Force, persons commissioned or appointed under the Essential (Special Constabulary) Regulations, 1948, and the Emergency (Auxiliary Police) Regulations, 1948, Her Majesty's Naval, Military and Air Forces and any Local Forces established under any written law in force in the Federation.

(Reg. added by L.N. 29/2-2-52).

19B. (1) The Mentri Besar in a State or the Resident Commissioner in a Settlement may, by notification in the Gazette, declare any fence or barrier surrounding any area that may be defined or specified in such notification to be a perimeter fence for the purpose of this Regulation.

(2) Where any such area is surrounded by two or more fences or barriers separated from each other by intervals, all such fences and barriers, together with the land lying between them, shall be deemed to be one fence for the purpose of this Regulation.

(3) When any fence or barrier has been declared a perimeter fence under this Regulation and such declaration has not been cancelled, such perimeter fence shall for the purposes of this Regulation be deemed to continue to exist notwithstanding any physical gap or defect therein, whether arising from injury to or lack of repair of such fence or otherwise.

(4) The Mentri Besar or Resident Commissioner, as the case may be, shall cause to be provided in any perimeter fence one or more gates or entrances, hereinafter referred to as «entry points», to enable persons to pass in and out of the area concerned. Such entry points shall be deemed for the purposes of this Regulation to form part of the perimeter fence.

(5) Any person who crosses or attempts to cross, or passes or attempts to pass, any article over, through or under any perimeter fence, except as provided in paragraph (7) of this Regulation, or who damages or attempts to damage or tamper with any such fence, or any part thereof, or any gate or movable barrier at any entry point, shall be guilty of an offense against these Regulations.

(6) The Mentri Besar or the Resident Commissioner, as the case may be, may cause to be taken such steps as he may deem necessary to prevent any person crossing any such perimeter fence or passing any article over, through or under such fence and such steps may extend to the taking of defensive measures which involve or may involve danger to the life of any such person, provided, that where any such measures are taken in a place not on, under or within the perimeter fence itself, such precautions shall be taken, including the prominent display of warning notices, as may be reasonably necessary to prevent inadvertent or accidental entry into any such place.

(7) Without prejudice to the provisions of any other written law or any order made thereunder, any person may enter or leave or may convey any article into or from any area surrounded by a perimeter fence through any entry point therein at a time when such entry point is opened by order of the Officer-in-Charge of the Police District in which such area is situated.

(8) In addition to any other powers conferred upon him by these Regulations or under any written law, any Police Officer, or any member of Her Majesty's Armed Forces, or of any Local Forces established under any written law, or any other person directed by the Chief Police Officer of the State or Settlement in which such perimeter fence is situated to guard such perimeter fence, may arrest without warrant any person committing an offense against this Regulation.

(9) No compensation or damages shall be payable in respect of any injury received or death caused as a result of any defensive measure authorized under paragraph (5) of this Regulation, unless the Chief Secretary shall certify that such compensation or damages in the circumstances of the particular case is just and equitable.

(10) Nothing in paragraph (5) of this Regulation shall apply to any police officer, member of Her Majesty's Armed Forces, or of any Local Forces established under any written law, acting in the course of duty or to any other person authorized on that behalf by the Officer-in-Charge of the Police District in which the area is situated, or by any other police officer empowered by the Officer-in-Charge of the Police District.

(11) The provisions of paragraph (6) of Regulation 40 of these Regulations shall apply to any area surrounded by a perimeter fence as if such area had been declared a «Food Restricted Area» under Regulation 17EA of these Regulations. For the purpose of any clearance order made under such paragraph, the outer boundary of such fence shall be deemed to be the perimeter of the area:

Provided that any such clearance order may also be made in respect of any land lying within such area within a distance of fifteen yards from the inner boundary of such perimeter fence. (Reg. added by L.N. 239/15-5-52).

20. (1) Every person within any police district or part thereof which may be designated by order by the Officer-in-Charge of the Police District shall remain within doors, or within such area as may be defined in the order, between such hours as may be specified in the order unless in possession of a written permit in that behalf issued by a police officer of or above the rank of Sub-Inspector.

(Amended by L.N. 106/6-3-52).

(2) This Regulation shall not apply to:

(a) members of the Federal Executive or Legislative Councils;

(b) members of any State Executive Council or Council of State;

(c) members of any Settlement Nominated Council or Settlement Council;

(d) any police officer or any member of Her Majesty's Naval, Military or Air Forces or of any Local Forces established under any written law when on duty;

(e) any person or class of persons exempted from the provisions of this Regulation by the Officer-in-Charge of the Police District.

(Amended by L.N. 680/18-12-52).

21. The Officer-in-Charge of a Police District may, by order in writing, exclude any person or persons from the police district under his charge or from any part thereof.

22. (1) Any meeting or assembly of five or more persons in any place whatsoever may be ordered to disperse by any police officer of or above the rank of sergeant.

(2) Any such police officer may use such force as may be necessary to

disperse any such assembly.

PART VII
ARREST AND SEARCH

23. Any police officer may without warrant arrest any person suspected of the commission of an offence against these Regulations, or of being a person ordered to be detained under Regulation 17 of these Regulations.

24. (1) Any police officer may without warrant arrest any person in respect of whom he has reason to believe that there are grounds which would justify his detention under Regulation 17 of these Regulations. Any such person may be detained for a period not exceeding twenty-eight days pending a decision as to whether an order for his detention under the said Regulation 17 should be made.

(2) Any person detained under the powers conferred by this Regulation shall be deemed to be in lawful custody and may be detained in any prison, or in any police station, or in any other similar place authorized generally or specially by the Chief Secretary.

25. (1) If any person, upon being questioned by a police officer, fails to satisfy the police officer as to his identity, or as to the purposes for which he is in the place where he is found, the police officer may, if he suspects that such person intends, or is about, to act, or has recently acted, in any manner prejudicial to the public safety or the maintenance of public order, arrest him and detain him pending inquiries.

(2) No person shall be detained under the powers conferred by this Regulation for a period exceeding twenty-four hours, except with the authority of the Officer-in-Charge of the Police District concerned or, subject as hereinafter provided, for a period of forty-eight hours in all:

Provided that if such an Officer-in-Charge of a Police District is satisfied that the necessary inquiries cannot be completed within the period of forty-eight hours, he may authorize the further detention of the person detained for an additional period not exceeding fourteen days but shall, on giving any such authorization, forthwith report the circumstances to the Chief Police Officer of the State or Settlement concerned.

(3) Any person detained under the powers conferred by this Regulation shall be deemed to be in lawful custody and may be detained in any prison, or in any police station or in any other similar place authorized generally or specially by the Chief Secretary.

26. Any document which purports to be a warrant or an order made in the Colony under any Regulation or other written law in force in the Colony and similar or equivalent to Regulation 17 of these Regulations and which has been received from any police officer or other Government officer of the Colony, shall be enforceable as if it were on order which had been duly made under Regulation 17 of these Regulations; and if the person named in such order enters or is within the Federation such order may be enforced acordingly by arrest and detention under these Regulations.

27. The powers conferred upon police

officers by Regulation 29 of these Regulations may be exercised by any member of Her Majesty's Naval, Military or Air Forces, or of any Local Forces established under any written law, of or above the rank of warrant officer, and the powers conferred upon police officers by Regulation 23, 24 (1), 25 (1) and 30 (1) of these Regulations may be exercised by any member of Her Majesty's Naval, Military or Air Forces, or of any Local Forces established under any written law, or any other person performing the duties of guard or watchman in a protected place or generally authorized by a Chief Police Officer.

(Substituted by L.N. 464/19-8-52).

27A. The powers conferred by Regulation 30A may be exercised by any member of Her Majesty's Naval, Military or Air Forces, or of any Local Forces established under any written law, when on duty; and, where any authority is required for the exercise of such powers, such authority may be given by any member of such forces of or above the rank of warrant officer.

(Reg. added by L.N. 239/15-5-52).

28. (1) Notwithstanding anything to the contrary contained in any written law, it shall be lawful for any officer in order:

(a) to effect the arrest of any person whom he has, in all the circumstances of the case, reasonable grounds for suspecting to have committed an offense against Regulations 4, 5, 6A, 18, 19 or 19A; or

(b) to overcome forcible resistance offered by any person to such arrest; or

(c) to prevent the escape from arrest or the rescue of any person arrested as aforesaid,

to use such force as, in the circumstances of the case, may be reasonably necessary, which force may extend to the use of lethal weapons.

(Amended by L.N. 239/15-5-52).

(2) Every person arrested for any of the offenses mentioned in paragraph (1) of this Regulation shall, as soon as possible after his arrest, be clearly warned by an officer of his liability to be shot at if he endeavours to escape from custody.

(3) For the purposes of this Regulation «officer» means any police officer or any member of Her Majesty's Naval, Military or Air Forces or of any Local Forces, including the Home Guard, established under any written law, and includes any other person performing the duties of guard or watchman in a protected place the appointment of whom has been either specially or generally authorized by a Chief Police Officer.

(4) Nothing in this Regulation contained shall derogate from the right of Private Defense contained in sections 96 to 106, inclusive, of the Penal Code.

(5) Any act or thing done before the coming into force of this Regulation which would have been lawfully done if this Regulation had been in force, shall be deemed to have been lawfully done under this Regulation.

(Amended by L.N. 239/15-5-52).

Power of search

29. (1) Any police officer of or above the rank of Sub-Inspector may without warrant and with or without assistance:

(a) enter and search any premises;

(b) stop and search any vehicle or individual, whether in a public place or not,

if he suspects that any evidence of the commission of an offense is likely to be found on such premises or individual or in such vehicle and may seize any evidence so found.

(Amended by L.N. 122/20-3-52).

(2) No woman shall be searched under this Regulation except by a woman.

Power of search for and seizure of offensive weapon

30. (1) Any police officer may without warrant:

(a) enter and search any premises;

(b) stop and search any vessel, vehicle or individual, whether in a public place or not,

if he suspects that any offensive weapon of any nature whatsoever, or anything which can be adapted or used as an offensive weapon, is likely to be found on such premises or individual or in such vessel or vehicle, and may seize any weapon or thing so found.

(2) No woman shall be searched under this Regulation except by a woman.

Power to board and search vessels

30A. (1) Without prejudice to the provisions of any other written law, any police officer, any officer of the Customs Department or any officer of the Immigration Department may, when on duty and on the authority of a police officer not below the rank of Inspector, or of an officer of the Customs Department not below the rank of Junior Customs Officer or of an officer of the Immigration Department not below the rank of Deputy Assistant Controller of Immigration, as the case may be, stop, board and search any vessel not being or having the status of a ship of war and may remain on board so long as such vessel remains within the waters of the Federation.

(2) Any police officer, any officer of the Customs Department or any officer of the Immigration Department searching a vessel under the provisions of paragraph (1) of this regulation may seize any evidence found therein of the commission of any offense under the provisions of any written law for the time being in force.

(3) The master or person in charge of a vessel who fails to stop such vessel when required so to do under this Regulation and any person resisting or hindering or in any way obstructing any police officer or officer of the Customs Department or of the Immigration Department searching a vessel or seizing any evidence under this regulation shall be guilty of an offence against these Regulations.

(Reg. added by L.N. 122/20-3-52).

PART VIII

POWERS OF SEIZURE AND TAKING POSSESSION OF PROPERTY

31. (1) Without prejudice to the pro-

visions of Regulation 36 of these Regulations, any police officer of or above the rank of sergeant and any member of Her Majesty's Naval, Military or Air Forces, or of any Local Forces established under any written law, of or above the rank of Warrant Officer or any member of any Local Forces established under any written law authorized in writing in that behalf by the Mentri Besar of a State or the Resident Commissioner of a Settlement may seize any rice or any other article of food which by reason of its quantity or its situation is or is likely to or may become available to any persons who intend, or are about, to act, or have recently acted, in a manner prejudicial to public safety or the maintenance of public order.

(Amended by L.N. 98/26-2-53).

(2) Any such police officer or member of such Forces as aforesaid may without warrant:

(a) enter and search any premises;

(b) stop and search any vessel, vehicle or individual, whether in a public place or not,

if he suspects that any rice or other food liable to seizure under this Regulation is likely to be found on such premises or individual or in such vessel or vehicle.

(3) Any rice or other food seized under this Regulation shall be delivered to a District Officer who may either retain possession thereof and pay compensation therefor or may make such arrangements as he may think fit for the return of such rice or other food to the person from whom the same was seized in such quantities at such intervals and over such period as he may deem expedient:

Provided that where a District Officer is satisfied that any rice or other food delivered to him under this paragraph was in the possession of or was intended for the use of any persons who intend, or are about, to act, or have recently acted in a manner prejudicial to public safety or the maintenance of public order, he may order such rice or other food to be forfeited and in such case no compensation shall be payable in respect thereof.

(4) In the event of any dispute as to the amount of compensation payable in respect of any rice or other food retained under paragraph (3) of this Regulation, such compensation shall be assessed in the manner provided in Regulation 53 of these Regulations.

(5) Any person aggrieved by an order of a District Officer under the proviso to paragraph (3) of this Regulation may appeal to the Mentri Besar of the State or Resident Commissioner of the Settlement, as the case may be, whose decision shall be final.

32. (1) Without prejudice to the provisions of Regulation 35 of these Regulations, any police officer of or above the rank of sergeant, or any member of Her Majesty's Naval, Military or Air Forces, or of any Local Forces established under any written law, of or above the rank of Warrant Officer, may seize and occupy any building or other structure, whether permanent or temporary, and any land pertaining thereto, which he has

reasonable cause to believe:

(a) belongs to or has been used by any person or persons who intend, or are about, to act or have recently acted, in a manner prejudicial to public safety or the maintenance of public order; or

(b) belongs to or is occupied by any person who is harbouring or has harboured or whose servant or agent by whom he is in occupation is harbouring or has harboured any person or persons who intend, or are about, to act or have recently acted, in a manner prejudicial to public safety or the maintenance of public order.

(2) Every seizure under this Regulation shall be reported as soon as practicable to the Mentri Besar or Resident Commissioner, as the case may be, of the State or Settlement in which such building or structure is situate, and such Mentri Besar or Resident Commissioner may, if satisfied that such building or structure belongs to or has been used by any such person or persons as are mentioned in paragraph (1) of this Regulation, by order direct the forfeiture of such building or structure together with any land pertaining thereto, and in such case no compensation shall be payable in respect thereof:

Provided that the Mentri Besar or Resident Commissioner, as the case may be, shall waive or remit subject to such conditions as he may think fit to impose the forfeiture of such building or structure and the land pertaining thereto if the owner thereof satisfies the Mentri Besar or Resident Commissioner, as the case may be, that the building or structure was used by persons who intend, or are about, to act, or have recently acted, in a manner prejudicial to the public safety and the maintenance of public order, or that such persons were being or had been harboured by his servant or agent, as the case may be, without his knowledge or consent and that he exercised all due diligence to prevent such building or structure being so used or the harbouring of such persons, as the case may be.

(3) For the purposes of paragraph (2) of this Regulation land pertaining to a building or structure means the land on which such building or structure stands together with such land adjacent thereto as, in the opinion of the Mentri Besar or Resident Commissioner concerned, is used or enjoyed in connection with the occupation of the building or structure. Where a part only of the land comprised in one document of title is forfeited under the provisions of this Regulation, the order of forfeiture shall define as far as is practicable the limits of the part so forfeited and, the approximate area thereof.

(4) Where under paragraph (2) of this Regulation any land comprised in any document of title is forfeited in any State, then:

(a) a copy of the order of forfeiture shall be served on the proper registering authority and an entry to the effect that the land has been forfeited shall be made by the proper registering authority upon the register document of title relating to such land; and

(b) the person in whose possession the issue document of title may be shall deliver up the same on demand to the proper registering authority for cancellation; and

(c) upon the cancellation of the existing document of title, a new document of title for any unforfeited part or parts of the land comprised in the cancelled document of title shall, upon payment of any necessary survey and other fees by the proprietor, be prepared and registered and the new issue document of title in respect of such unforfeited part or parts shall be issued to the person entitled thereto.

(5) Where under paragraph (2) of this Regulation any land is forfeited in any Settlement the Registrar of Deeds of the Settlement in which such land is situate shall make an entry in the books of the Registry that such land has vested in the Crown.

PART IX

POWERS OF CONTROL

39. (1) Any Officer in Charge of a Police District or any person duly authorized by any such Officer may by order, or by giving directions, or in any other manner, regulate, restrict, control or prohibit the use of any road or water-way by any person or any vehicle or close any road or water-way.

(2) Any Officer in Charge of a Police District may, by the issue of permits to which conditions may be attached or in any other manner, regulate, restrict, control or prohibit the travelling by any person in any train, motor car, motor bus or vehicle of any description, and may similarly regulate, restrict, control or prohibit the travelling by any person in any vessel.

CHAPTER XIV

THE PLANNING PROCESS

The first three portions of this manual have been explanatory as to the subject matter to be learned. In this, the last chapter, the material that the student has learned will be applied in order to learn how to prepare a plan of action to accomplish the objectives desired. In other words, students will now learn how to assign the various forces their duties so that a resources control plan of action will give workable field operations. In a sense, the preparing of the plan will be the final examination, the determination of whether the student is capable of putting into use, that which has been presented about forces and their duties.

What is planning ? « Municipal Police Administration » states that, « Planning may be considered the heart of administration. Without it the objectives of any organization cannot be achieved effectively and efficiently. Planning precedes and accompanies the twin tasks of operation and management. Failure to plan invariably results in the resources of the department not being used to their best advantage. Planning is the process of developing a method, procedure, or arrangement of parts intended to facilitate the achievement of a defined objective ».[1]

---

(1) By the International City Managers' Assn., 5th Ed., 1961, printed by Cushing-Malloy, Inc., Ann Arbor, Mich.

The plans are developed by the staff officers, those officers charged with the responsibility of supervising, for the Province Police Chief, the paper document when it goes into action as an order; in this case the order establishing a resources control program for a province. The plan should be complete with the staff officer developing all of the pertinent material by study and research. It should be complete when it is presented to the chief or superior so that he is in a position to approve or disaprove based on what he has on the paper in front of him.

The first step in preparing a plan is to prepare a staff study. This document is the basis for making plans and must have the approval of higher authority before work on the actual operational plan can begin. In order that later plans and orders are workable, the study should be agreed to by prospective participants. This assuming of future workability is called staff coordination.

The U.S. Army has developed a format which is generally conceded to be one of the best administrative approaches and is as follows with explanations:

FORM AND CONTENT OF A
COMPLETED STAFF STUDY[2]

File No........ Department ....
Division .... Date ....
SUBJECT: Sufficient information for identification.

A key statement from paragraph #1 is usually sufficient.

1. PROBLEM. A concise statement of the problem in form of a mission or objective. Frequently noted as an argument or statement of fact rather than as a problem, which is in error. A single subject is correct.

2. ASSUMPTIONS. Any assumptions necessary for a logical discussion of the problem which cannot be accepted and considered as facts. Omit this paragraph if not needed. Frequently confused with facts.

3. FACTS BEARING ON THE PROBLEM. Essential facts, in logical sequence, which must be considered. Facts must be undeniable and pertinent.

4. DISCUSSION. A careful analysis of the essential facts and assumptions, presenting considerations, pro and con, to arrive logically at sound conclusions. Keep discussion brief. They must be pertinent, objective, and adequately support the conclusions.

5. CONCLUSIONS. Statement of the results derived from a reasoned judgment of the essential facts. Do not include alternate lines of action.

6. ACTION RECOMMENDED. Complete, concise and clear cut statement of action recommended presented in such form that all remaining for the Chief to do is to indicate his approval or disapproval.

(signature)
Initiating Staff Officer

ANNEXES. List those accompanying the study.

---

[2] From Form 16, Staff Officers' Manual (FM 101-5) U.S. Dept. of the Army adapted by «Municipal Police Administration», op. cit. page 22.

CONCURRENCES. Each staff officer concerned indicates his concurrence by name, rank and official position title. (Note that this act of coordination is what makes the study an agreement of parties concerned).

NONCONCURRENCES. Each officer concerned indicates his nonconcurrences by name, rank, and official position title. Reasons for nonconcurrence stated briefly on separate memorandum attached as additional annex.

CONSIDERATION OF NONCONCURRENCES. The author of the staff study states the result of his consideration of any nonconcurrences. If his consideration shows that the nonconcurrence cannot be supported, the reasons therefore will be stated. The author will sign or initial this consideration of nonconcurrence.

ANNEXES ADDED. List the annexes containing concurrences.

ACTION BY APPROVING AUTHORITY. (Heading not necessary).

Date

Approved (Disapproved) including (excluding) exceptions.

Signature

There is a variety of types of plans presented by various authors on the subject of planning, but for the purpose of resources control planning, only one will be considered, the Operations Plan. An operation plan is a detailed statement of the course of action to be followed in an operation extending over considerable space and time and usually based on stated assumptions. It always includes an assignment of duties (tasks) to certain responsible officials and it announces the forces that will be under these officials. It is employed by higher echelons of command to permit subordinate commanders to prepare their supporting plans and orders. An operation plan may be put into effect at prescribed time or on order and then becomes an Operation Order.[3]

An Operation Order is usually a formal order issued orally or in writing by a commander to subordinate commanders for the purpose of effecting the coordinated execution of a planned operation in the field, and upon being issued becomes a General Order as discussed in Chapter IV, «Rural Police; Function and Administration».

The Quang Ngai Plan which follows, is a draft of an action Operations Plan prepared for the province of that name. It should be studied and used as the basis for map exercises to be conducted in the courses of instruction. It is not perfect in its composition, but does serve as an excellent guide for the student. Note that before this «plan» would go into effect it must be made an «order» and the subordinates must have time to issue their «orders».

March 1963

SUBJECT: *Plan for Resources Control — Quang Ngai Province*

1. Problem:

   An effective program designed to

---

[3] From US Marine Corps Manual «Staff Organization and Functions», MCS 1-10e, 1955.

control the movement of population and material is essential to the suppression of Vietnamese Communist activities within II Corps Tactical Zone. Food, clothing, medical supplies and munitions are examples of the most critical items needed for continued guerrilla operations. The insurgents are generally conceded to have three principal sources of supply:

A. Supplies, especially technical equipment, brought into the country from so-called «safe-havens» over overland routes, or by sea.

B. Supplies produced by the insurgents themselves in relatively insecure and accessible areas within the country. This source is generally restricted to food stuffs and food products and is limited at best.

C. Supplies gathered from the economy. These include weapons and equipment captured from military and paramilitary units, food and equipment procured from the population through sympathy, persuasion, extortion or intimidation and supplies procured outright in normal market areas by insurgent agents and emissaries.

2. Discussion:

A. Rigid controls on the movement of population and materials are emergency measures in time of war, created to meet an existing problem and intended for termination at the conclusion of the emergency. Controls encompass such actions as manifesting supplies for movement, personnel identification and pass control, curfews, control of crop distribution and utilization and implementation of appropriate legislation and directives through careful and impartial enforcement.

B. Studies of the campaigns against the Communist guerrillas on the Malaya peninsula, and in the Phillipine Islands have demonstrated that controls of this type can be extremely successful in making the guerrilla's position particularly untenable and can be a major factor contributing to final victory. In Malaya, as in Vietnam, controls were not initially popular, but an effective civic action and public relations program coupled with the controls was successful in placing the onus of responsibility with the Communist and winning popular support.

C. Briefly, operations are conducted in the following manner:

(1) Static checkpoints are established on the main axes of communications, both land and water, over which population and materials can move toward Viet Cong controlled areas. These checkpoints enforce controls on movement of critical resources, check ID cards, manifests, etc. They search persons and vehicles on a selected basis, detain suspects, confiscate contraband, etc.

(2) Mobile teams are formed with the capacity of operating checkpoints at new and different locations on a random basis or upon intelligence indicating VC utilization of certain routes. These checkpoints are operated in the same manner as the fixed checkpoints, but they are moved around from time to time and serve to keep the enemy off balance.

(3) Other mobile teams are utilized to conduct operations against the known movement of material by conducting small, limited ambushes and informal checkpoints deep in VC territory along secondary trails. In addition, these teams can assist in conducting hamlet operations, in which hamlets are sealed off and search for suspects and caches of food and unauthorized weapons.

(4) Utilization of the junk fleet to seal off the coast line of the Province in which the program is implemented, to deny Communist infiltration of supplies and resources by sea.

(5) Establishment of headquarters at Province and District levels. The overall control of the operation rests with the Chief of the National Police Province. The Province Police headquarters plans operations, performs investigations and gathers intelligence under his supervision. Very close liaison is established between this headquarters and the military forces operating in the area. The value of military intelligence to this program, and the value of information gathered at the checkpoints and by the mobile teams and other operatives to the military, is inestimable.

D. Enforceable National legislation and decrees are presently in effect dealing with the control of the movement of resources within South Viet Nam. A summary of this legislation is included as Annex A.

(1) Legislation is useless without effective enforcement. At present, although a great number of checkpoints do exist within South Viet Nam, no real progress is being made. Many factors influence this:

(a) Currently, checkpoints are operated by a variety of headquarters and organizations — i.e. ARVN, Province. Sector, District, etc. and are manned by a variety of personnel — i.e. Military Police, Infantry, Armor, Civil Guard, Self Defense Corps, Civilian Irregular Defense Forces and in one case, Republican Youth.

(b) Personnel manning checkpoints are not trained in the techniques useful to successful operation of a resources control program. Training should include such specifically police-type material as search and seizure, apprehension techniques, handling of prisoners and a thorough background in the principles of the laws they are enforcing. Personnel manning checkpoints and conducting control operations must have a good knowledge of these laws, their own powers and the limits of their jurisdiction. Finally, all personnel must be trained in the public relations aspects of the program they are conducting.

(c) No real connection exists between checkpoints and local organizations operating them. Often a number of different organizations operate checkpoints in the same vicinity. Thus no coordinated planning is feasible and a very valuable source of natural intelligence at the «grass roots» level goes untapped.

(2) The most effective method of welding a workable program of resources control appears to rest in the

assignment of forces tailored to the needs of the problem and adequately trained in the techniques necessary for solving it.

E. An attempt was made during the Autumn of 1962 in Phu Yen Province to implement an effective program of resources control through the creation of just such an organization. The United States Operations Mission, in cooperation with military advisors from II Corps and Province officials, recruited and trained a civilian force designed to operate a series of checkpoints throughout the province and to conduct operations in the manner described. In Phu Yen Province, a civilian police-oriented program was ideally suited since the Clear and Hold Operation had progressed to the point where military forces were contemplating a gradual cutback in strength in the area.

(1) Training of the force, which numbered 200 men, was sponsored, financed and conducted by USOM. The Minister of the Interior, the Province Chief and the Commanding General, II CTZ were in accord on the necessity of such a program.

(2) At the conclusion of the training course, USOM submitted to the Minister of the Interior, the final budget for the operation. USOM could not assure continued US financial support for the program beyond an initial period, and consequently, operations were postponed until fiscal planning and coordination could be completed.

(3) Since that time, a number of significant developments have occured.

The directorate of the National Police have agreed to assume administrative control of civilians utilized in resources control operations and to give them a semi-police status as security guards. In addition, USOM and the Minister of the Interior have agreed on the expenditure of 2,500,000$00 VN for Calendar Year 1963 for the implementation of the program in Phu Yen alone. At the present time, a new Province administration is in office, and although preliminary discussions have been held, effective implementation of the program is delayed pending the receipt by the Province Chief of the full endorsement of the Minister of the Interior.

F. A temporary delay in Phu Yen Province, due to administrative and fiscal coordination, should not hamper programs in other provinces. The urgent need for an effective program of resources control goes unchallenged. Particularly critical is Quang Ngai Province. In this strategic area, Vietnamese Communist rebels in considerable numbers, maintain strongholds in the mountains of the interior. The great majority of the population inhabits the coastal plain where the major market areas and the most fertile soil is found. The connection between the two areas in Quang Ngai consists of a series of long, east-west valleys through which a number of land and water arteries of communications pass. In all, there are six (6) major axes of communication between the fertile coastal plain and the inland areas dominated by the Viet Cong. Ill. 29, chart entiled Annex B, page 185, shows these axes.

(1) Because of the long trek across

QUANG-NGAI PROVINCE

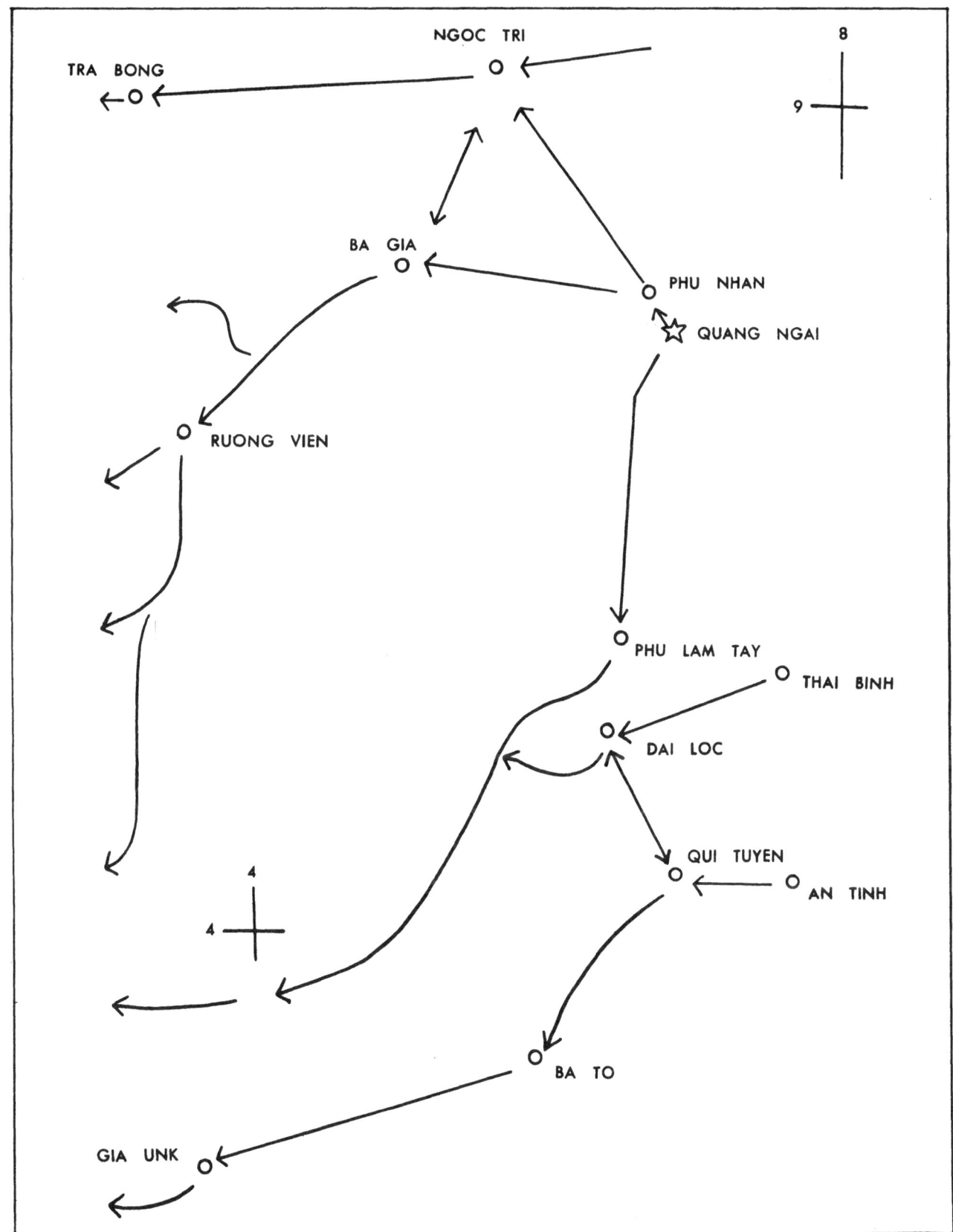

Ill. 29. *Annex B (General Description of East-West Axes of Communications)*

the mountains, it is impractical for the insurgents to bring any but the most technical equipment into the country from this source. While the seacoast in certain areas provides relative access, the cargo carrying capacity of small vessels is limited, the journey long and the risk great. The majority of the insurgents supplies and equipment must be procured inside of the country, unless they are to dissipate a large portion of their strength by maintaining a long supply line. See Exhibit No. 1 a map of the Quang Ngai province (see page 187).

(2) The inhospitable condition of the mountain areas coupled with increased activity by Vietnamese armed forces makes it very difficult to produce their own supplies in great quantities. Safe to say that as military operations increase in the area, the feasability of such production will diminish. Thus, particularly in Quang-Ngai, the rebels must depend on the economy of the Province for their subsistence and as military operations develop and more areas come under the control of the Government of Vietnam, this condition will increase.

(3) The Communist rebels, then, in Quang Ngai, are particularly vulnerable to an effective resources control program. Such a program, by denying them the use of the principal roads and rivers of the province, will shut off access to the major market towns of the coastal region. Mobile checkpoints will serve to confuse and divert enemy resources and to keep the Viet Cong off balance. With the increase in military activity and the progress of the Strategic Hamlet Program, a resources control program can effectively turn off the faucet of resources available to the enemy, dwindle morale and conceiveably cause major defections among his ranks.

G. A number of examples of the value of checkpoint operations is included as Annex C.

(1) A completed operational plan for a Resources Control Program is proposed as Annex D.

(2) Logistical and Administrative Details appear in Annex E.

3. Conclusions:

A. Control of population and material movement is an effective and necessary tool in combating guerrilla operations.

B. There is a serious need for a resources control program, particularly in Quang Ngai.

C. In Phu Yen Province, some funds have been allocated and personnel have been trained. Operations could begin when adequate administrative and fiscal coordination is effected.

D. In Quang Ngai Province, a successful resources control program can be implemented but will, in the civil authority stage, require additional police forces for the duration of the emergency.

4. Recommendations:

A. That the necessary personnel be recruited and trained for the program and that the civil authority then execute the plan outlined in Annex D.

B. That until such time as Re-

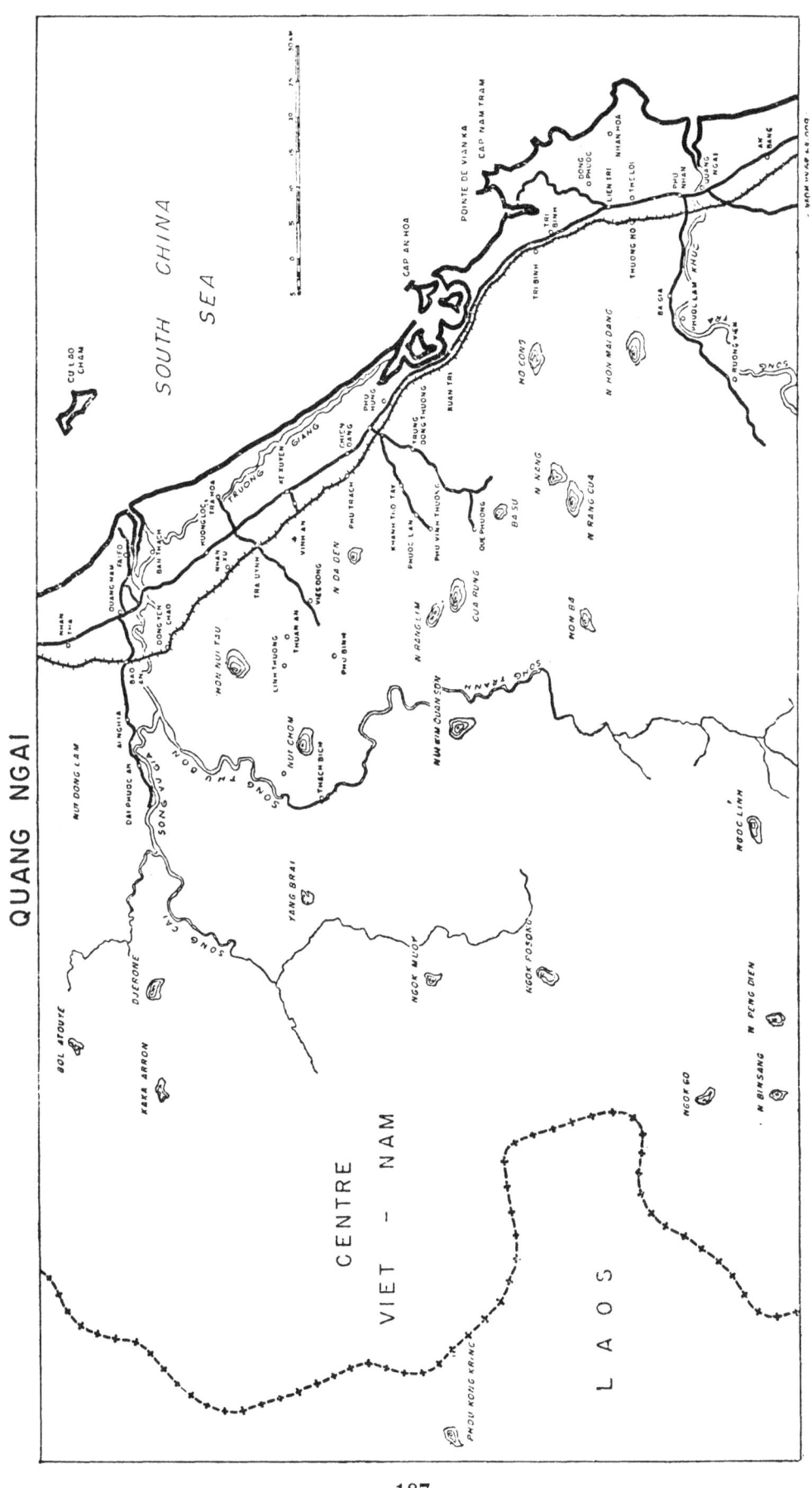

Exhibit 1

commendation A is implemented the military, civil authority, initially utilize military, para-military and existing police forces to execute the program.

ANNEXES:

A — Summary of National Legislation effecting Population and Material Movement Controls.

B — East-West Axes of Communication, Quang Ngai Province.

C — Some examples of the effectiveness of Checkpoint operations.

D — Operations Plan for Resources Control.

E — Administrative and Logistical Details.

ANNEX A: (Summary of National Legislation Effecting Population and Material Movement Controls)

1. References:
    a. Decree No. 1234/BNV-HC-ND
    b. Communique No. 5825/BNV-HC-12
    c. Communique No. 5838/KX-KT-1
    d. Communique No. 6175/HC-Ktt
    e. Order No. 146/PTT/NV
    f. Pertinent directives establishing:
        (1) National ID Card Program
        (2) Family Census Program

2. Critical Materials:

    a. References above specify items which are considered of strategic importance. These items cover a wide range of materials useful to the war-making potential of the insurgents and include:

    (1) All firearms, ammunition, explosives, gun powder, pyrotechnics and parts thereof and elements of manufacture.

    (2) A large number of chemicals, including all nitrates, chlorates, perchlorates, centralite, ether, magnesium, aluminum powder, barium in certain forms, chlorine liquid oxygen, sulpher, and a number of acids which can be compounded into explosives.

    (3) Printing press, type and ink; hydrochloric acid, and other items useful in preparing written propaganda.

    (4) Generators and other electrical and conductive materials.

    (5) Radio sets, binoculars, typewriters, stencils and reproducing machines.

    (6) Cameras, film and projectors.

    (7) Public address systems and tape recorders.

    (8) Pumps

    (9) Boat propelling machines and all kinds of motors.

    (10) Fuels and lubricants

    (11) All antibiotics, medical and surgical implements.

    b. Controls:

    (1) Commodities in stock: shopkeepers and owners are required to:
        (a) Make monthly statements as to strategic materials on hand
        (b) Keep registers with accurate records of transactions.

(2) Movement of strategic materials requires acquisition of a permit from district authorities. A copy of the permit accompanies the bearer and one is forwarded to his destination.

(3) All strategic commodities require:

(a) Records of purchase

(b) Records of authorization for transport

(c) Records of ownership and transfer

(d) Records of consumption

3. Food Products:

a. Specific authority for control of food products appears to be left to the discretion of the Province Chief. Generally, it appears that the Province Chief has the authority to declare certain villages and/or areas as insecure and to limit the amount of foodstuffs which may be kept there, restrict movement of food, etc.

b. For example, in Phu Yen Province, forty nine hamlets were declared insecure and the amount of paddy authorized to be kept by inhabitants of these hamlets was established as 20 kilos (30 days supply) per person. Appropriate restrictions were also placed on movement of foodstuffs.

4. Population Control

a. Very little need be said about the National Identity Card Program. Its progress is well known. As of 28 February 1963, 6,200,000 identity cards had been processed, with a remaining 1,300,000 cards to be processed. As this program nears completion, the value of checkpoints increases.

b. The National Family Census Program is under way. As the family census becomes completed in an area, the opportunity for periodic population checks in the hamlets should not be overlooked.

ANNEX B: (is an illustration)

ANNEX C: (One example of the Effectiveness of Checkpoint Operations)

1. A permanent checkpoint is being operated at the Northern edge of Cantho, Phong Dinh Province, by the National Police.

2. During the recent months of operation, four persons were apprehended as in possession of the contraband.

Two of the men were known Viet Cong. All were captured as a result of routine searches of buses.

ANNEX D: (Operations Plan)

NOTE: This is tentative and subject to alteration in detail

1. Situation

(1) Appendix 1, Intelligence (not illustrated but would accompany a real operations plan)

(2) Appendix 2, Organizational Chart.

(3) Appendix 3, Functional Chart.

(4) Appendix 4, Utilization of Personnel.

2. Mission: The special constabulary unit enforces the controls over movement of population and resources into and within Quang Ngai Province to deny local support to insurgent forces.

3. Execution:

a. Concept of the Operation: The special constabulary units at Province and District level within Quang Ngai Province; organizes, plans and implements a series of static checkpoints throughout the Province to enforce appropriate legislation dealing with movement of resources and curtail flow of critical materials from GVN to VC control, mobile team is formed which conducts checkpoint operations at unannounced locations on a random basis; initiates raids and ambushes based on intelligence; conducts operations related to rural internal security on order; security for checkpoints responsibility of sub-sector military commander; overall operational control under the Province Chief of the National Police.

b. Headquarters Unit (Province):

(1) Plans and supervises resources control activities throughout the Province.

(2) Administers details, prepares receipts and reports of investigations, and other reports.

(3) Supervises investigative activities of District Units conducts investigations in support of District Units.

(4) Conducts a Public Relations Program.[1]

(5) Gathers information and coordinates with the Military Intelligence.

c. Mobile Team

(1) Operates checkpoint, complete with organic security, on a random basis or based on intelligence.

(2) Conducts limited raids and ambushes along secondary roads and trails.

(3) Conducts extensive reconnaissance and patrol activity.

(4) Conducts operations related to rural internal security on order.

d. District Headquarters Unit:

(1) Supervises checkpoints within the District.

(2) Prepares necessary reports of investigations and activities.

(3) Investigates all complaint reports and forwards to higher authority. Follows through on all confiscated items.

(4) Evacuates prisoners from checkpoints to district headquarters. Evacuates confiscated contraband to district headquarters.

e. Checkpoints:

(1) Conducts spot-check of papers, manifests, identifications, etc., of all persons and vehicles.

(2) Conducts detailed and complete search of selected persons and vehicles on a random basis, a ratio to be established through experience.

(3) Confiscates contraband and detains suspicious persons.

(4) Receipts for all confiscated property.

(5) Gathers information within capability.

f. Training: Appendix 4.

g. Security: Sub-sector commander responsible for furnishing adequate

---

[1] See annex for details of Public Relations program.

security for checkpoint operation.

h. Coastline Operations: Activities of resources control are closely coordinated with Junk Fleet Operations to insure adequate resources control of coastal areas.

i. Appendix 6, Location of Fixed Checkpoints.

j. Appendix 7, Operations overlay.

k. Coordinating Instructions:

(1) Overall control under the direction of the Province Chief of National Police.

(2) Close coordination between resources control and military operations planning.

(3) Police coordination for operational and intelligence purposes.

(4) Close coordination between resources control headquarters and junk fleet.

(5) Plans are initiated for orderly phasing out of Military personnel and take-over by the Civil Authority.

4. Administration and Logistics:

ANNEX E: (Admin and Logistical Details)

APPENDICES:

1 — Intelligence (not furnished but would accompany a real operations plan)
2 — Organization Chart
3 — Functional Chart
4 — Utilization of Personnel
5 — Training, Phase I
6 — Location of Fixed Checkpoints
7 — Operationss Overlay

Appendix 4 (Training) to Annex C

1. General

Prior to the initiation of an effective resources control program, all personnel participating in it must be thoroughly trained. This is particularly necessary since personnel will be dealing exclusively with the general public.

2. Training will be conducted in two (2) phases:

a. The first phase, of four weeks duration, will consist of a class of specially selected leaders and key personnel from both and will be geared to training the class as instructors for the remainder of the force:

(1) Specially trained personnel are available from the directorate of the National Police to conduct this course.

(2) These personnel may be secured by a request to the Director General of the National Police, Saigon.

(3) Arrangement for perdiem of instructors and assistance in other miscellaneous training cost for this phase can be made with the United States Operations Mission.

b. Phase two of the training would be of from two to four weeks duration:

(1) Second phase would be conducted by instructors trained in the first phase.

(2) Costs would be minimal since existing facilities could be utilized.

c. Program of Instruction.

For purposes of general information, the proposed program of instruction for Phase I is attached as Tab. A.

TAB. A

(Program of Instruction, Phase I)

to Appendix 4 (TNG) to Annex D

Note Taking and Report Writing	8 hours
Techniques of Instruction	28 hours
Vietnamese Criminal Law	8 hours
Authority and Jurisdiction	2 hours
Preservation of Evidence	4 hours
Handling of Prisoners	4 hours
Surveillance and Arrest	4 hours
Police Intelligence and Investigation	8 hours
Internal Security	4 hours
Narcotics and Anti-biotics	2 hours
Physical Descriptions	2 hours
Passes and Manifests	12 hours
Checkpoint Operations	12 hours
Search Techniques	8 hours
Raids and Ambushes	8 hours
Police Reports	16 hours
Public Relations and Psywar	16 hours
Program Analysis	16 hours
Review	10 hours
Graduation	4 hours
	176 hours

(Based on 44 hour week)

This is a preliminary schedule, subject to modification.

Appendix 6 (Location of Fixed Checkpoints) to Annex D.

1. Exact location of fixed checkpoints will be subject to close analysis and may vary slightly from figures given here.

2. Following checkpoints are proposed (Ref. Map, Quang Ngai, 1,250,000):

a. BS 5896 Highway No. 1 near Tri Binh

b. BS 4387 Vicinity of Nhan Hoa

c. BS 4678 Vicinity of Ba Gia

d. BS 6476 Highway No. 1 north of Quang Ngai

e. BS 6473 Highway No. 1 south of Quang Ngai

f. BS 5074 South of river, near An Phu

g. BS 5074 On the river, boat equipped

h. BS 5865 Between An Hoa and An Dinh

i. BS 6156 South of Phu Lam Tay

j. BS 6156 On the Song Ve River, boat equipped

k. BS 6150 At Dai Loc

l. BS 7243 West of An Tinh

m. BS 9322 Near La Van

ANNEX E: (Administrative and Logistical Details)

1. General

a. Administrative and Logistical Support Program is through normal police channels.

b. Special constabulary unit draws supplies and equipment through normal channels.

2. Items required for operation of program are available in normal supply channels. Normal requisitioning procedures apply.

3. Services: Engineer, construction and services in connection with the program provided by province public

works office.

4. Equipment: Appendix 1 (Majority of equipment in this Appendix on hand with units).

5. Personnel: Appendix 2.

Appendix 1 (Equipment) to Annex E

Note: Request purchase authority, justify in accordance with procedure to the province for funding under emergency financial support.

A. Weapons
B. Vehicles
C. (Flashlights only from Strategic Hamlet supplies)
   a. Headquarters
   b. Mobile Teams
   c. Checkpoints
   d. District Hqs × 6 (with change)
D. General supply items (request purchase, etc.)
   I. Headquarters
      (1) Typewriter, short carriage
      (2) Typewriter, long carriage
      (3) Desk, Field, 4 drawers
      (4) Table, Folding
      (5) Chair, Folding
      (6) Safe, field
      (7) Can, gasoline, 5 gals
      (8) Nozzle, gas
      (9) Spade
      (10) Mimeograph Machine
   II. Mobile Force
      (1) Can, gasoline
      (2) Nozzle, gasoline
      (3) Spade
      (4) Ax
      (5) Pick
   III. Checkpoints (x13)
      (1) Typewriter, short carriage
      (2) Table, folding
      (3) Chair, folding
      (4) Can, gasoline, 5 gals
      (5) Nozzle, gas
      (6) Spade
   IV. District Headquarters (x6)
      (1) Typewriter, short carriage
      (2) Desk, field, 4 drawer
      (3) Table, folding
      (4) Chair, folding
      (5) Can, gasoline, 5 gals
      (6) Nozzle, gas
E. Signal Equipment

I. Exact requirements for signal equipment will have to be determined on the ground.

II. Estimated amount of signal equipment:

(1) Communications between Headquarters and District Headquarters:

(a) Radio: Existing TR-20 Nets can be utilized;

(b) Wire: Existing ARVN circuits can be utilized.

(2) Communications between Headquarters and mobile units:

(a) Radio communication only;

(b) Mobile STD equipment can be effectively utilized.

(3) Communication between district and checkpoints:

(a) Wire will suffice for most checkpoints;

(b) Some additional wire will have to be installed;

(c) Some checkpoints will require radio communications which should be arranged with the province representation of CTD.

III. One (1) loudspeaker apparatus for Public Relations section.

APPENDIX No. 1
THE REORGANIZATION OF THE NATIONAL POLICE

THE PRESIDENT OF THE REPUBLIC

Considering Decree No. 124-TTP of May 28, 1961 fixing the composition of the government;

Considering Ordinance No. 9 of July 14, 1950 modifying ordinance No. 16 of June 1, 1960 stipulating general statutes for public servants;

Considering Ordinance No. 175-NV of May 23, 1955 fixing wages and allowances in nature and in cash for public servants and employees;

Considering arretes in force fixing statutes and organization of the Police and Surete;

DECREES:

ARTICLE 1 — There is hereby integrated all the (present) National Police and Surete services, Municipal Police of Saigon, the Municipal Police of the provincial chief town, and Rural Police of Southern Vietnam, into one single organization called the «National Police», having jurisdiction all over the territory of the Republic of Viet Nam. Police wages, allowances, uniforms and badges of the National Police shall be standardized.

ARTICLE 2 — The National Police shall include the following responsibilities:

   a. Special Police
   b. Judicial Police
   c. Uniform and Traffic Police
   d. Administrative Police
   e. Combat Police
   f. Scientific Police
   g. Immigration Control
   h. In-service and Technical Training.

1. *The Special Police*

Responsible for prevention and detection of all activities prejudicial to National Security and for bringing the offenders to competent authorities for action.

2. *The Judicial Police*

Responsible for assisting the judicial agencies in searching, ascertaining and investigating all high, heavy and petty offenses, for bringing subjects, evidence and records to the Public Prosecutor qualified for prosecution. It also carries out all operations as may be assigned by the Courts of Justice according to laws in force.

3. *Uniform and Traffic Police*

Responsible for maintaining order and regulating daily traffic in public places; carrying out local police and administrative regulations.

4. *Administrative Police*

Responsible for controlling activities and events which might bear influence over public peace and order such as civilian associations and missions, use and storage of weapons and ammunitions, radio receivers and transmitters, entry and exit activities of the Vietnamese, and for making administrative investigation of legal entities.

5. *Combat Police*

Responsible for supporting intelligence activities, police operations, for destruction of armed terrorist activities or isolated cases of sabotage by the enemy. It is also responsible for supporting local police units.

6. *Scientific Police*

Responsible for making analysis, comparison, and examination of physical evidence or traces and marks collected at the scenes of the crime upon request or assignment of the responsible authorities.

7. *Immigration Control*

Responsible for controlling the number of foreign nationals residing on the territory of the Republic of Viet Nam, their backgrounds and their movements; for issuing entry and exit visas and making administrative investigations concerning these foreign residents.

8. *In-service and technical training*

Responsible for giving technical and special training to the police personnel.

ARTICLE 3 — The organization of the National Police includes, from top to bottom, the following commands:

At Central level: *Directorate General of Police*

At Region and Municipal level: *Regional Directorate and Municipal Directorate*

At Province, City and Precinct level: *Provincial Police, City Police and Precinct Police*

At provincial district and Sector in Saigon: *District Police*

At Village level: *Village Police*

CHAPTER I

SECTION I

The Directorate General of Police

ARTICLE 4 — The Directorate General of Police, headed by a Director General assisted by a Deputy Director General, is composed of many services and bureaus.

According to their operational natures, these services and bureaus are grouped into 3 blocks:

— The Police Operations block
— The Administrative block
— The Special Police block

Each block is supervised by an Assistant Director directly responsible to the Director General and Deputy Director General.

ARTICLE 5 — The «Police Operations» block includes the following Services and Bureaus of purely operational nature:

1. Judicial Police service
2. Immigration service
3. Administrative Police service
4. Combat Police service
5. Uniform and Traffic Police service
6. Headquarters Security Bureau

ARTICLE 6 — The «Administration» Block shall include the following

Services and Bureaus of managerial and support nature:

1. Personnel Service
2. Budget and Accounting Service
3. Supply and Logistics Service
4. Laboratory Service
5. Records and Identification Service
6. Legal Bureau
7. Training Bureau

ARTICLE 7 — The «Special Police» Block shall include following services and bureaus whose operations are of pacification nature:

1. Operation Service
2. Plan Service
3. Administrative Bureau
4. Operations Coordinating Bureau

ARTICLE 8 — The following elements are directly responsible to the Director General and Deputy Director General:

— The Private Office
— The Secretariat
— The Special Bureau
— The Telecommunication Bureau
— The Central Technical Bureau
— The Inspection Team

SECTION II

Services and Bureaus of the Police Operations Block

I. THE JUDICIAL POLICE SERVICE

ARTICLE 9 — The Judicial Police service, headed by a Chief of Service, is responsible for:

— Supervising and controlling judicial operations of Regional Directorates and provincial police for the purpose of standardizing judicial regulations and procedures.

— Developing statistics and charts of crimes; and studying prevention and repression measures.

— Acting in the capacity of Judicial Police officers representing the Public Prosecutor regarding crimes which concern several regions, provinces, areas, at one time, or of an international nature. This Service acts also on specific judicial missions assigned by the Superiors.

— Assigning investigators to support local units in their completion of important judicial investigations.

ARTICLE 10 — The Judicial Police Service has 2 bureaus:

1. The Criminal Bureau
2. The Control - Research Bureau

The Chief of the Criminal Bureau is a sworn-in-officer, qualified as a Judicial Police officer. He is assisted by a number of sworn-in-officers.

II. THE ADMINISTRATIVE POLICE SERVICE

ARTICLE 11 — The Administrative Police Service headed by a Chief of Service is responsible for:

— Supervising and controlling the operations at Regional Directorates and provincial police regarding control of weapons, associations, unions, released or confined prisoners, motorized vehicles, radio receivers and transmitters, hotels and rented apartments. It issues passports and exit visas to the Vietnamese.

— Making studies and suggestions for changes of administrative regulations in view of a more appropriate application of these regulations.

ARTICLE 12 — The Administrative Police Service has 3 Bureaus:

1. The Administrative Investigation Bureau
2. The Passport Bureau
3. The Control and Research Bureau

III. THE IMMIGRATION SERVICE

ARTICLE 13 — The Immigration Service, headed by a Chief of Service, is responsible for:

— Controlling and maintaining a census of foreigners applying for residence in Viet Nam, making official reports for prosecution of illegal residents.

— Receiving application for entry of foreigners, submitting the applications and files to the Ministry, and issuing visas after approval is given by the Minister.

— Investigating foreigners who apply for Vietnamese citizenship.

— Conducting administrative investigations of foreign residents.

— Controlling passengers and commodities at Saigon Airport and Harbour.

ARTICLE 14 — The Immigration Service has 3 Bureaus:

1. The Entry and Exit Bureau
2. The Immigration Control Bureau
3. The Files Bureau

The Chief of the Immigration Control Bureau is a sworn-in-officer, qualified as a Judicial Police Officer.

IV. THE COMBAT POLICE SERVICE

ARTICLE 15 — The Combat Police Service commanded by a Chief of Service, is responsible for:

— Support of intelligence activities.

— Conducting police operations to destroy enemy's armed elements (who operate on highways and commit individual acts of terrorism).

— Specific security duties for the VIPs when they are on movement.

— Reinforce and support local police units.

— Military training of its personnel.

ARTICLE 16 — The Combat Police Service has 3 Bureaus:

1. The Reconnaissance Bureau
2. The Operation Bureau
3. The Administrative Bureau

V. THE UNIFORM AND TRAFFIC POLICE SERVICE

ARTICLE 17 — The Uniform and Traffic Police Service, commanded by a Chief of Service, is responsible for:

— Making studies and distribution of Uniform and Traffic Police regulations.

— Making statistics and charts of traffic accidents, recommendations for preventive measures or for appropriate improvements.

ARTICLE 18 — This Service has 2 Bureaus:

1. The Research Bureau
2. The Control Bureau

VI. THE HEADQUARTERS SECURITY BUREAU

ARTICLE 19 — The Headquarters Security Bureau, headed by a Chief of Bureau, is responsible for maintaining security at the Headquarters of the Directorate General of Police. Personnel of this Bureau are grouped in 2 categories:

— The personnel in uniform, in charge of guard duties at vulnerable points at the headquarters.

— Personnel in plainclothes, doing undercover, observing men and things and taking preventive action against any sabotage or infiltration of the enemy in the compound.

SECTION III

Services and Bureaus of the Administrative Block

I. PERSONNEL SERVICE

ARTICLE 20 — The Personnel Service, supervised by a Chief of Service, is responsible for:

— Managing the police personnel throughout the country.

— All social welfare activities for the National Police.

ARTICLE 21 — The Personnel Service has 3 Bureaus:

— The Files and Strength Bureau
— The Personnel Management Bureau
— The Social Welfare and Studies Bureau.

II. THE BUDGET AND ACCOUNTING SERVICE

ARTICLE 22 — The Budget and Accounting Service has a Chief of Service and is responsible for:

— Paying wages and allowances to all police personnel throughout the country, no matter in what unit they serve.

— All expenses made by the Police within the limite of the scheduled budget.

— Planning budget for the Police.

— Procurement, distribution, and administration of sundry materials and office supplies.

— Making files for bid on new constructions.

ARTICLE 23 — The Budget and Accounting Service has 3 Bureaus:

1. The Budget and Liquidation Bureau
2. The Payroll Bureau
3. The Material Bureau

III. THE LOGISTICS SERVICE

ARTICLE 24 — The Logistics Service, headed by a Chief of Service, is responsible for:

— Procuring and distribution of materials, equipment, vehicles, gas and fuel, weapons and ammunition, clothing to various units (except for sundry materials and office supplies which are the responsibilities of the Budget and Accounting Service in Article 22).

— Implementation of new constructions or renovation works sponsored by National or Foreign Aid

Budget.

— Supervise at the General Headquarters operations concerning first aid, ceremonies, physical exercises (callisthenics) and various services.

ARTICLE 25 — The Logistics Service has 3 Bureaus:

1. The Weapon, Transportation and Supply Bureau
2. The Foreign Aid Bureau
3. The General Service Bureau

IV. THE LABORATORY SERVICE

ARTICLE 26 — The Laboratory Service, commanded by a Chief of Service, is responsible for identifying, studying, comparing, analyzing, by scientific methods, all physical evidence, trances and marks, weapons, ammunition and poisons, to assist the responsible authorities establishing the truth in the investigations.

The Laboratory Service shall directly undertake important examination when local police units are unable or have no adequate facilities to operate. It also supervises laboratory elements at regional directorates.

ARTICLE 27 — The Laboratory Service has 3 Bureaus:

1. The Laboratory
2. The Technical Bureau
3. The Files Bureau

V. THE IDENTIFICATION AND RECORDS SERVICE

ARTICLE 28 — The Identification and Records Service has a Chief of Service and is responsible for:

— establishing fingerprint files, identification records and making searches for individual previous records.

— keeping files of National Police records

— making national statistics

— publishing a Criminal Bulletin.

ARTICLE 29 — The Identification and Records Service has 2 Bureaus:

1. The Identification Bureau
2. The Central Records Bureau.

VI. THE LEGAL BUREAU

ARTICLE 30 — The Legal Bureau is headed by a Chief of Bureau and is responsible for:

— Collection of rules and regulations and documents regarding administrative or judicial procedures.

— Making studies of and recommendations for appropriate changes in the administrative legislation relating to the Police.

— Representing the Directorate General with the government attorney and the Court anytime there is a lawsuit involving the Directorate General.

VII. THE TRAINING BUREAU

ARTICLE 31 — The Training Bureau is headed by a Chief of Bureau and is responsible for:

— Preparing and keeping track of training programs and results of training courses at Training Centers, organizing complementary courses on general and technical knowledge at the Directorate General, making studies of and recommendations for more suitable training programs.

— Keeping files and following up progress made by participants in training overseas.

— Preparing, collecting and publishing police training documents, setting up and managing a police library at the Directorate General.

SECTION IV
Services and Bureaus of the Special Police Block

I. THE OPERATIONS SERVICE

ARTICLE 32 — The Operations Service, directed by a Chief of Service, is responsible for:

— Gathering information on political activities.

— Carrying out undercover operations throughout the country, searching for, investigating, keeping track of, and prosecuting elements indulged in subversive activities.

ARTICLE 33 — The Operations Service consists of 4 Bureaus:

1. The Studies Bureau
2. The Active Bureau
3. The Technical Support Bureau
4. The Interrogation Bureau

II. PLAN SERVICE

ARTICLE 34 — The Plan Service, directed by a Chief of Service, is responsible for:

— consolidating all documents of a political nature for study and setting up plans to cope with different situations.

— preparing and filing personnel cards of the enemy's agents and making reports.

ARTICLE 35 — The Plan Service has 4 Bureaus:

1. Bureau of Research
2. Bureau of Reports
3. Bureau of Special Files
4. Bureau of Maps and Statistics.

III. THE ADMINISTRATIVE BUREAU

ARTICLE 36 — The Administrative Bureau, directed by a Chief of Bureau, is responsible for mail, personnel, accounting, materials, general services, headquarters security.

IV. OPERATIONS COORDINATING BUREAU

ARTICLE 37 — The Operations Coordinating Bureau, directed by a Chief of Bureau, is responsible for controlling and coordinating activities of the intelligence nets throughout the country.

SECTION V
Elements under direct control of the Director General and Deputy Director General

ARTICLE 38 — *The Private Secretariat:* directed by a Chief of Bureau, is responsible for checking all correspondence to be signed by the Director General, distributing or conveying the Director General's decisions or instructions to concerned Services and Bureaus and studying or preparing classified documents, programs, operations, trips, receptions and all special activities of the Director General.

ARTICLE 39 — *The Mail Bureau:* directed by a Chief of Bureau, is responsible for receiving and distributing all incoming and outgoing mail of the Directorate General, either routine or classified; for distributing decisions, orders, instructions and circulars of a general nature, assuring permanence at the Directorate General at off-duty hours and on holidays.

ARTICLE 40 — *The Special Bureau:* directed by a Chief of Bureau, is under the Deputy Director General's direct control and responsible for receiving, dispatching and keeping in file top secret and important documents of the Directorate General.

ARTICLE 41 — *The Communications Bureau:* directed by a Chief of Bureau, is responsible for operating, managing the radio system of the Police throughout the country and assuring at the same time the telephone system at the Directorate General.

ARTICLE 42 — *The Central Technical Bureau:* directed by a Chief of Bureau, is responsible for censoring special documents inside as well as outside the country, especially documents from communist countries sent through the Republic of Viet Nam.

ARTICLE 43 — *The Inspector Team:* including 3 to 5 Inspectors, is responsible for representing the Director General or Deputy Director General to inspect different units, either periodically or eventually, and making reports with remarks and proposals to the Director General.

The Inspectors are considered on the same rank toward the Director General and Deputy Director General; however, a high-ranking Inspector shall be appointed as a Dean to manage and direct the Team's Office.

CHAPTER II
SECTION I
REGIONAL AND MUNICIPAL POLICE DIRECTORATES

ARTICLE 44 — The Police Directorate in each region, directed by a Director who is assisted by a Deputy Director, is responsible for controlling, supervising and coordinating the provincial police agencies in the region.

ARTICLE 45 — Each Regional Police Directorate includes 3 Bureaus:

1. *The Police Operations Bureau:* in charge of judicial police, administrative police, immigration control, traffic control, Combat Police and Headquarters security.

2. *The Administrative Bureau:* in charge of personnel, accounting, supply, general services, records, communications, laboratory works and training of personnel.

3. *The Special Police Bureau:* in charge of everything connected with local security conditions.

ARTICLE 46 — The Saigon Municipal Police, headed by a Director who is assisted by a Deputy Director, is responsible for maintaining public order in the municipality (undercover is assured by the Directorate General of Police).

The Police Precincts within the Saigon area, on land as well as on rivers, the Harbor Police, the Tan Son Nhut Airport Police are all directly attached to the Municipal Police

Directorate.

The TAN BINH Police Precinct and the GIA DINH Police Service are now restored to Gia Dinh Province.

ARTICLE 47 — The Municipal Police included 7 Bureaus:

1. *The Private Secretariat:* managed by a Private Secretary, is in charge of the Director's personal affairs and other special affairs.

2. *The Administrative Bureau:* in charge of official correspondence, typewriting, personnel, accounting, records, maps and regulations.

3. *The Judicial Police Bureau:* in charge of all judicial affairs, vice control, — it checks the collection of fines in the precincts and makes statistics — prepares charts on criminal status. The Chief of Judicial Police Bureau has a number of sworn-in officials with judicial powers to assist him.

4. *The Administrative Police Bureau:* responsible for controlling and supervising the precincts in all administrative investigations, checking different kinds of authorizations, developing statistics, charts and necessary recommendations.

5. *The Operations Bureau:* responsible for patrolling, controlling the posts, traffic posts in different precincts; giving first aid, intervening in emergencies or reinforcing friendly forces.

6. *The Bureau of General Services:* responsible for receiving, storing distributing and maintaining materials, equipment, vehicles, weapons, fuels, buildings at the directorate and Precincts, drawings, photography and miscellaneous matters.

7. *The Communications Bureau:* responsible for communications by radio with the precincts, the patrolling cars and the Directorate General, and for the telephone networks of the Municipal Police units.

ARTICLE 48 — *The Traffic Police:* is directly under the Municipal Police Directorate, directed by a sworn-in Chief having judicial powers. It is responsible for action over reports received on traffic accidents, controlling vehicles and taking care of traffic in the municipality.

The Traffic Police Chief is assisted by a Deputy Chief. The Traffic Police has 3 Bureaus:

1. Judicial Bureau
2. Operations Bureau
3. Traffic Control Bureau

ARTICLE 49 — *The Airport and Harbor Police:* under the direct control of the Municipal Police and headed by a sworn-in Chief having judicial powers, is responsible for investigating all violations committed within the limits of the Saigon Harbor and Tan Son Nhut Airport; controlling ship and river transportation, patrolling to protect security and order on the rivers and canals in the municipality.

The Chief of Airport and Harbor Police is assisted by a Deputy Chief. The Airport and Harbor Police include 1 Sea and River Platoon and 3 Bureaus:

1. The Judicial Bureau
2. The Operations Bureau
3. The Administrative Bureau

SECTION II
THE PROVINCIAL, CITY AND MUNICIPAL POLICE

I. THE PROVINCIAL POLICE

ARTICLE 50 — In each province a provincial police having jurisdiction over the province is responsible for maintaining security and order in the province — supervising and controlling the activities of the District Police. The Provincial Police of each province is called after the name of this province.

The Provincial Police is directed by a sworn-in Chief having judicial powers.

ARTICLE 51 — The Provincial Police includes 3 Bureaus:

1. *The Police Operations Bureau:* headed by a sworn-in Police Chief, having judicial powers, is responsible for Judicial Police, Order Police, Administrative Police, Immigration Control, Combat Police and Headquarters security.

2. *The Administrative Bureau:* headed by a Chief of Bureau, is responsible for personnel-management, accounting, supply, general services, communications, laboratory, identification and records.

3. *The Special Police Bureau:* managed by a sworn-in Deputy Police Chief having judicial powers, is responsible for all affairs relating to security and making reports on political violations.

II. CITY POLICE AGENCIES

ARTICLE 52 — In cities (Hue, Da Nang, Dalat), there shall be a City Police independent from the Provincial Police where the city is located.

The City Police has a more restricted organization than a Provincial Police and is headed by a sworn-in Police Chief having judicial powers.

III. THE MUNICIPAL POLICE

ARTICLE 53 — There is a Police precinct in each Municipal Administrative District.

ARTICLE 54 — The Municipal Police Precinct, headed by a Chief of Precinct, includes 3 Bureaus:

1. *The Judicial Police Bureau:* in charge of judicial affairs, fines and economic affairs.

2. *The Administrative Police Bureau:* responsible for administrative investigations, checking family census forms and all kinds of authorizations.

3. *The Operational Bureau:* responsible for appointing and checking guards and patrols, maintaining headquarters security, managing and dispatching vehicles, distribution of gas and fuels, equipment, weapons and assuming miscellaneous services.

ARTICLE 55 — Each Bureau of the Municipal Police Precinct is headed by a Chief of Bureau, except that the Judicial Police Bureau is headed by the Deputy Precinct Chief who has judicial powers and is assisted by a number of sworn-in officials with judicial powers.

ARTICLE 56 — Under normal conditions, Provincial Police Agencies usually contact the Central Police Headquarters through the Regional Directorate; but in case of emergency, they can contact directly the Directorate General while informing the Regional Police Directorate.

IV. DISTRICT POLICE IN PROVINCES AND MUNICIPAL POLICE SECTORS

ARTICLE 57 — Each administrative district has a Police Sector headed by a sworn-in Chief of Sector who has judicial powers. Each sector includes three sections:

— The Police Section maintains order, directs traffic and assures guard duties.

— The Studies Section acts in secrecy and is responsible for pursuing, investigating and interrogating on judicial as well as special police matters.

— The Secretariat is responsible for records, personnel, materials, equipment, correspondence and typewriting.

ARTICLE 58 — In Saigon, the present subposts are charged into Police Sectors responsible for guarding and patrolling in their respective areas.

V. POLICE SUB-SECTORS IN VILLAGES

ARTICLE 59 — In densely populated villages, a Police Sub-Sector may be created, headed by a Chief of Sub-Sector.

SECTION III
TRAINING AND IN SERVICE TRAINING CENTERS

I. THE HIGH COMMAND SCHOOL

ARTICLE 60 — The High Command School, under the Administrative Assistant's control, is responsible for training the personnel from the grades of District Police Chief to Provincial Police Chief; giving refresher courses to personnel of medium level, selecting and training candidates who want to join the Police ranks in medium level ranks.

ARTICLE 61 — The High Command School, under the supervision of a Director, assisted by a Deputy Director, consists of 1 Instructor Staff, 2 Bureaus and 1 Section:

1. *The Instructor Staff* includes all lecturers and instructors directly responsible to the School Director. The senior lecturer shall be appointed Dean of the Staff by the Director and he manages all affairs concerning the lecturers and instructors.

2. *The Administrative Bureau:* in charge of all mail, typewriting, publications, library, personnel, accounting, materials, cooking, ceremonies, headquarters security and miscellaneous services.

3. *The Bureau of Instruction:* in charge of studying and implementing training programs, making training schedules, organizing educational visits and practical training for the trainees, handling training aids, organizing examinations, making statistical charts, keeping trainees' files.

4. *The Supervisory Section:* in charge of supervising daily activities and discipline of the trainees during working hours, off-duty hours and eating time. It collects trainees' problems, takes notes of trainees' behaviour, makes recommendations for reward and punishment. This Section is directly de-

pendent on the Deputy Director of the School.

II. THE POLICE BASIC TRAINING CENTER

ARTICLE 62 — The Police Basic Training Center is under control of the Administrative Assistant (Administrative Block). It is responsible for training subordinate personnel, testing educational level; screening and training new recruits wanting to join the Police ranks at low level.

ARTICLE 63 — The Police Basic Training Center is directed by a Director who is assisted by a Deputy Director. It consists of 2 Bureaus and 1 Section, like the Police High Command School.

CHAPTER III

TITLES, ASSIGNMENTS, GRADES, ALLOWANCES FOR SUPERVISORY POSITIONS IN THE POLICE

ARTICLE 64 — Supervisory positions in the Police include:

1. *At the Central Headquarters:*
   — Director General
   — Deputy Director General
   — Assistant to Director General directing one block of several services
   — Chief of Service, directing one Service
   — Chief of Bureau, directing one Bureau
   — Battalion Commander, Company Commander, Platoon Commander commanding the Combat Police force.

2. *At Regional Directorates and External units:*
   — Director, responsible for a Regional Directorate
   — Director, directing 1 Training Center
   — Chief of Bureau, directing 1 bureau at Regional Directorate
   — Chief of Provincial Police, directing a Provincial Agency
   — Chief of Bureau, directing a bureau in a provincial agency
   — Chief of Police Sector, directing a Sector
   — Chief of Police Sub-Sector, directing a Sub-Sector.

ARTICLE 65 — The position of Inspector is equal to that of Regional Director.

The positions of Private Secretary to the Director General and Chief of the Deputy Director General's Special Secretariat are equal to that of Chief of Bureau at Regional Directorate.

ARTICLE 66 — The positions of Director of the Police High Command School and Basic Training Center are equal to that of Chief of Service. The positions of Deputy Directors of these Centers are equal to that of Deputy Regional Director.

ARTICLE 67 — Except the Director General, Deputy Director General and Regional Director who are appointed by the President, all other positions cited in this decree shall be appointed by arretes of the Secretary of State for Interior.

ARTICLE 68 — Positions recognized by this Decree to have judicial powers must perform the swearing-in procedures at the regional tribunal before assuming responsibilities.

The oath is set as follows:

«I swear to loyally carry out my responsibilities and in all circumstances to comply with the duties imposed by my position».

ARTICLE 69 — With regards to position titles, the police leaders are to hold ranks and grades as follows:

1. Director General and Deputy Director General ....
   .... *Controller General*

2. Assistant Director General
   .... *Controller*

3. Inspector, Regional Director, Director of Training Centers and Chiefs of Service ......
   .... *Commissioner Principal*

4. Deputy Regional Directors, Deputy Directors Training Centers, Chiefs of Provincial Polices, Combat Police Battalion Commander. *Commissioner*

5. Chiefs of Bureaus, Combat Police Company-Commanders
   .... *Redactor Principal*

6. Deputy Chiefs of Provincial Police .... *Redactor*

7. Chiefs of Bureau, Chiefs of District Police, Combat Police Platoon Commanders ......
   .... *Urban Inspector*

8. Chief Police Sub-Sector ....
   Deputy Urban Inspector Principal
   Officials who hold a position title and the rank designated for each position above, will wear their actual grade insignia.

Except for special responsibilities and missions, all Police agents must wear uniforms while on duty.

ARTICLE 70 — The above mentioned positions enjoy a monthly allowance set as follows:

— Director General .... 2,800$
— Deputy Director General . 2,400$
— Assistant to Director General (equal to Director supervising several services) 2,000$
— Inspectors, Regional Directors (equal to Director not having several Services) .... 1,700$
— Director Training Center, Chief of Service .... 1,500$
— Deputy Regional Director, Deputy Director Training Center, Chief Provincial Police Agency .... 1,200$
— Chief Police Agency: Municipal and City; Combat Police Battalion-Commander .... 900$
— Chief of Bureau, Private Secretary at Directorate General, Combat Police Company-Commander, Deputy Chief Provincial Police Agency .... 800$
— Deputy Chief: Municipal and City Police, Private Secretary at Directorate Municipal Police, Chief of Bureau, Chief of Sector, Combat Police Platoon-Commander .... 600$

— Chief of Sub-Sector ..... 300$

ARTICLE 71 — All expenses for personnel, maintenance, equipment, tools and materials of the National Police will be paid by the National Budget (Directorate General of Police).

ARTICLE 72 — During the transitory period, the expenditures for salaries of all the personnel of Municipal Police, City Police and Rural Police who are being integrated into the National Police, as well as expenditures for materials for these 3 organizations, continue to be paid by the local budgets (Municipal and Provincial) until the integration is completed.

ARTICLE 73 — All provisions contrary to this Decree are cancelled.

ARTICLE 74 — The Secretaries of State at the Presidency, for Interior and for Justice, each one in his respective concern, carry out the present Decree.

Saigon June 27, 1962

(s) NGO DINH DIEM

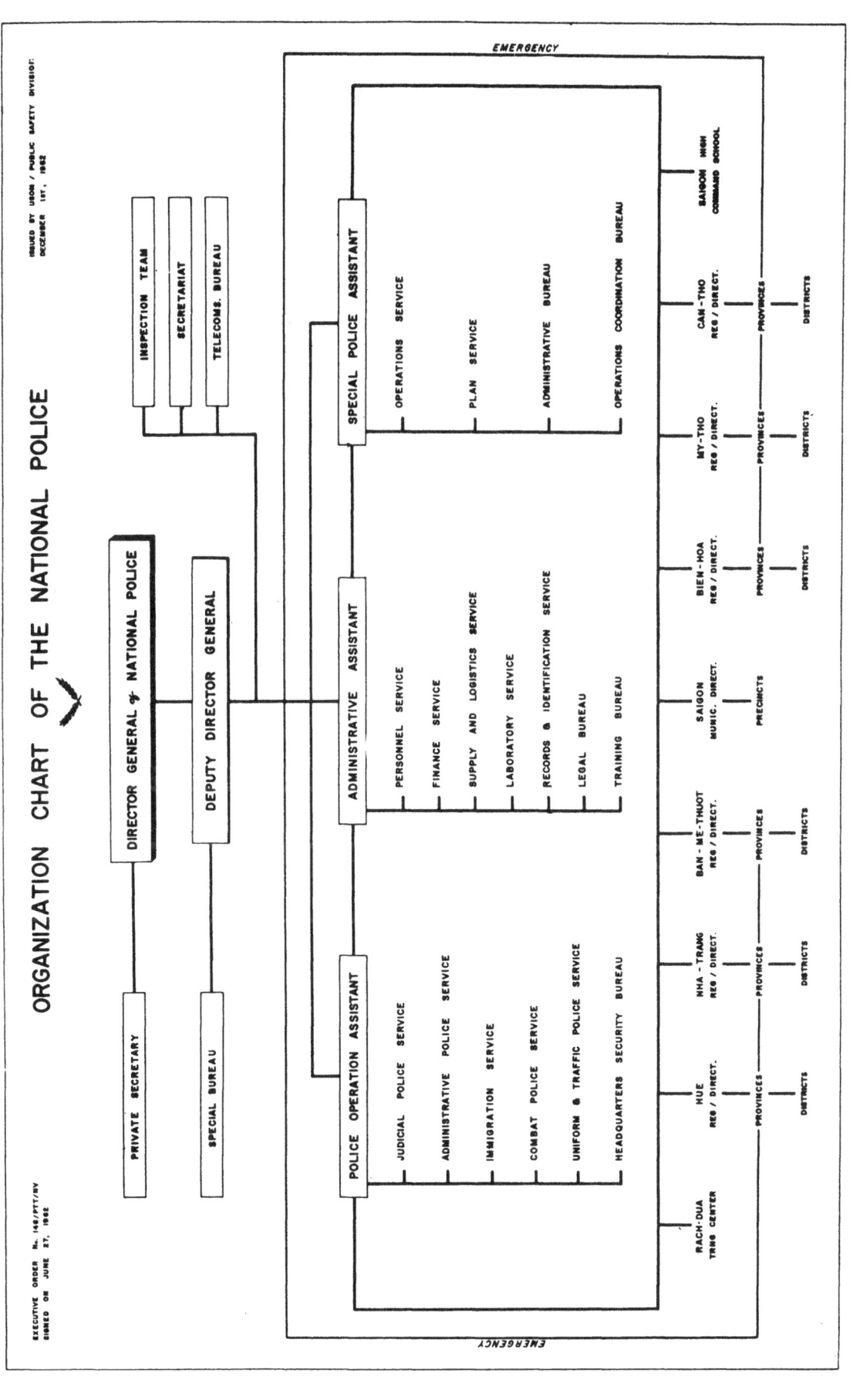

www.ingramcontent.com/pod-product-compliance
Lightning Source LLC
Chambersburg PA
CBHW082119230426
43671CB00015B/2743